Awakening

IN THE
NORTHWEST
TERRITORIES

One man's search
for fulfilment

A Memoir By

ALASTAIR HENRY

Produced by:

FriesenPress

Suite 300 – 852 Fort Street

Victoria, BC, Canada V8W 1H8

www.friesenpress.com

Distributed to the trade by The Ingram Book Company

Cover photo by iStock/RyersonClark

Although the people and events are real, most names have been changed to protect the privacy of the individuals

TABLE OF CONTENTS

Dedicated to...

My children: Darrin, Dean and Nicole

My grandchildren: Caitlin, Kiefer, Madigan,
Andrew, Julia, Beckett and Ashlyn

And to the children of my grandchildren and their children.

I wrote this memoir so that future generations of
my family might better know the man who was
their father, grandfather, great-grandfather, etc.

My hope is that all readers will not only enjoy the story, but
take from it to use in their lives, some of the insights and lessons
that I learned about life which are contained in these pages.

May the wisdom that comes with age and travel
benefit others through enlightenment.

**To live in the world, unconsciously aware of the meaning
of the world, is like wandering around in a great library
without touching the books**
Manly Palmer Hall

CHAPTER 1
Growing up in England

The Dream

I was eleven when I first had the dream, or whatever it was, as I'm not quite sure. It wasn't a nightmare, nor was it scary — it was just exhausting, and caused me to break out into a sweat and wake up. I wouldn't have remembered it had it only occurred the once, but it didn't. It came back many times over the next three or four years, and each time it left me feeling weak and puzzled. And it wasn't as if I could opt out of the dream whenever I wanted to because I couldn't. I was powerless, as if I was on a roller coaster, and I had to hang on to wherever the ride took me.

The dream had me on a sandy path, about six feet wide, and surrounded by flat fields on either side. Sometimes I would be walking or jogging or riding a bike. The first couple of times I had the dream, the fields on my right and left were a brilliant yellow carpet of buttercups, and the sky was bright and sunny. Other times though, the weather was bleak: windy, rainy, and the sky was grey. But no matter the state of weather, the dream always unfolded the same way. Holes kept opening up in the path in front of me, and they looked ominously deep, causing me to jump, side step, or steer and accelerate around them if I was on a bike. And the more I traveled down the path, the more numerous and larger the holes became, and I had to work harder to avoid falling in. The dreams always ended with me waking up lathered in sweat and physically drained.

I thought it odd that I kept having the same dream periodically, and wondered if other people did. When I mentioned it to my friends, Bob and Pete, they thought it was weird, for they couldn't recall an instance of ever having had the same dream twice. The dream became an in joke between us, and they would periodically kid me about it. They were both convinced that it must mean something.

Every autumn the Fair came to Bolton, Lancashire, and stayed for about a week. In the late 1950s and early 1960s, "freak shows" were a Fair staple, and well attended. It seems rather disgusting now that we would queue up for half an hour to see the world's fattest lady, or the hairiest lady, or the world's tallest man, but we did. There were also animal oddities, such as the calf with two heads, and many other one-offs, including a clairvoyant standing outside a small tent with her head wrapped in a bright red and yellow scarf, tied at the back in a knot. The only reason I remember her was because she reminded me of an Apache: an Indian maiden from the cowboys and Indians films I watched at the Ritz Cinema on Fletcher Street in Bolton on Saturday afternoons.

Madame X proclaimed to be able to read people's palms and to tell their futures. She was standing in front of her curtained stall with a large glass orb in one hand, and beckoning to the crowd with the other to step right up, and have your future read. Bob, Pete and I stood in front, and talked about what she might say to us if we went in. And then we got into daring each other. Being the shy, introverted one in the group, I was not keen on talking to a stranger about anything, and I made this clear to my mates, but peer pressure won out, and I felt I had to do it. "Tell her about your dream," Pete said. "See what she says." I felt I could do that because I didn't have to think on the spot and answer who knows what personal questions she might ask, and so I did, with a fake sense of bravado to impress my mates.

As I recall, the inside of her stall was no more than ten feet by ten and consisted of a small, round table draped in a warm, red cloth that hung down to the cement floor; two wooden chairs faced each other; a low hanging red light in a bamboo type shade dangled low above the table; and the magic ball was set in the middle of the table on a bowl type base.

I sat down and she asked to be paid. She spoke with a foreign accent, which I immediately took to be east European — some exotic far-away place that I didn't know much about at the time, such as Bulgaria or Hungary or maybe she was a gypsy: they were rumoured to be magical and mysterious. I told her that I wanted to know the meaning behind a dream I kept having. She smiled, moved closer to the table, put her hands on the magic ball, and nodded. I told her as much about the dream as I could remember. As I spoke, she moved her hands slowly and theatrically over the orb, rotating them gently from right to left and up and down in a mystical fashion. She concentrated deeply for a few seconds, peering into the ball that glowed eerily in the reddish light, and asked, "Is there anyone else in your dream?"

"No. Never." I hadn't noticed that before, and then she asked another question.

"Is the road straight or curved?"

"Straight. It's always straight, and it goes on forever."

"Do you ever stop on the road?"

"No. I can't. I feel that I have to keep going. I don't know why, but it feels as if that isn't an option."

She pulled back away from the table, looked me straight in the eyes, and said with the confidence of a doctor settling on a diagnosis after listening to the symptoms. "The road is your future, your destiny. You will have many obstacles to overcome in life, but you will overcome them through patience, persistence, and plodding! I see a lot of travel in your future, mostly by yourself. You will never settle down in one place for a long time." She looked down at the ball and that was it. I sensed that was all she was going to say and that there was no opportunity to ask questions.

I was in a daze when I parted the curtains and walked out into the bright sunlight. Peter and Bob laughed and said that I looked as if I'd seen a ghost. Peter went in next while Bob pumped me for information about what she did and what she said. I repeated her prophesy and he got all excited thinking about what she might have to say about him. Peter came out and Bob went in. I cannot now recall what they said the gypsy lady told them, but I do remember us concluding, after a little cross discussion, that she must be a fake, because none of us could relate to what she said. At the time, I must have been the least travelled fifteen-year-old boy in Bolton, for I had not yet made it to Manchester, a mere ten miles away.

The two holidays to the Channel Islands to visit relatives didn't count as travel in my mind as us kids felt more like luggage – we had no input as to what, when, where or why regarding the holiday. Children should be seen and not heard was my parents' mantra when we questioned anything. We just tagged along and did what we were told.

As you will discover by the time you finish reading this memoir, her predictions were most prophetic and accurate. I committed her reading to memory because it was the single most exciting thing that had happened to me in my life up until then. And for a long while after, I voluntarily recalled her words and wondered whether clairvoyance was even possible. Do some people really have the gift of seeing into the future, and is our destiny pre-determined, and are we just going through the motions in the erroneous belief that we are in charge?

Later in life, as I reflected on the accuracy of her foretelling, the thought came to mind that perhaps I had been unconsciously manifesting her prophesy all along by factoring in the deeply ingrained message. Did it bubble up from the deep recesses of my psyche whenever I had a decision to make, to influence my consideration and judgement? I didn't know, but it was uncanny how accurate her predictions were.

There is so much we do not yet know about the human mind and about subjects, such as clairvoyance, but maybe one day we will. When I think back to the world I grew up in, it blows my mind how much more we know today than we did then. And when one speculates on what will be discovered and invented in say the next fifty years, given that change is happening at an exponential rate, we cannot begin to imagine what the world will look in 2050, just as my dad couldn't imagine the world we live in today.

It was 1958. My dad said, "Well Ally, I don't think there's anything left to be invented. We've thought of everything." Not only was he in awe of man's inventions – planes, trains and automobiles – he was also terrified of them. He never drove a car, nor flew in a plane. And when they went to the Channel Islands, they always made the same arduous journey: changing trains and stations in Manchester and London, and taking the slow mail boat out of Southampton to Guernsey.

Parents and Siblings

My mum and dad were born in 1908 and 1905 respectively, into large farming families in the Channel Islands. My mum was from Jersey and my dad from Guernsey. My dad enjoyed reminiscing about how much the world had changed since he was a kid, and he wondered about whether the changes would ultimately prove to be good or bad for the ordinary person. By changes, he was referring to the new way people lived their lives: standing in front of machines all day at the cotton mill; sitting down every night after supper to watch TV; buying all sorts of things they couldn't afford on HP (Hire Purchase – so much down with monthly payments; the precursor to credit.)

To my parents, the world was changing too fast, and they had trouble adjusting to it. When they were growing up, farmers tilled fields with horses, peasants picked produce by hand, and people paid for things in cash. As parents, they were old-fashioned minded with strict Victorian values and poor parenting skills.

I don't know much about my parents' early lives except that my mother went "into service" when she was 12, as did most other 12 year-old girls from poor families in Jersey. Going into service meant that she worked long hours six days a week for a rich family: cooking, cleaning and even bottle washing if the family had children. Fortunately for my mother, her employer was good to her or so I understand, which was unusual, and when she got married, they gave her a Royal Doulton biscuit barrel as a wedding present. My mother prized this piece of bone china all her life, and it was one of the few heirlooms she left when she passed away. My sister has it now.

My recollection of my mother was that she was a bitter and angry woman who was disappointed with her lot in life. But she was not always like that my eldest brother said. It was just that life had been hard on her in the ensuing years and this was the result. Mike was born in 1936 and remembered how life was when he was growing up in Guernsey, before they evacuated to Scotland. My parents had been shop-keepers: independent business people who were, at that time, regarded as a class above ordinary folk who had to work for someone else to make a living. They had a sweet (candy) shop and were quite well to do. Mike said that as the only child for the first six years, he was always well dressed and spoiled rotten.

Mike was the second child. The first child was a girl, but she was stillborn, and so the birth of Mike was a blessing that made my parents very happy. The war years changed all that.

The Germans invaded and occupied the islands, and my parents, hearing and fearing rumors that atrocities might happen, decided to evacuate. They heard the news on the radio one morning, packed up whatever they could into suitcases, locked up the house, and went down to the harbour to get a boat to take them to Southampton, and from there the boat train to London. I can't image how terrible it must have been, not knowing where you were going, let alone where you would be sleeping that night. They were directed to board a train to Glasgow, and once there, shepherded into flats on Homelea Road in a grimy district of Cathcart.

Dad must have had some physical ailment, or else he would have been conscripted to fight in the war, but instead, he was given a job as a machinist making heavy artillery guns.

My sister Pat was born at home in 1942, and three days after D Day (June 6, 1944) I arrived.

My parents returned to Guernsey soon after the war ended, only to find a family living in their house claiming squatter rights. We stayed in a hotel at our own expense for a month while we got a lawyer, and had them evicted.

My youngest brother, Kenny, was born in St. Helier, Guernsey in 1946 with a "hole in his heart," and in those days there was no cure: no going in to sew it up. He had no option but to live with this condition until his heart gave out, which turned out to be just twenty-six years later. He knew no differently of course because that was his only reality, and as kids, we siblings didn't fully appreciate the severity of his infirmity – I thought that he only had one lung and that was why he couldn't run as fast as the rest of us – maybe my mother told us that as a more plausible reason for his lack of energy.

I know even less about my father. Someone, I don't remember who, said that he ran away from home to work on merchant ships when he was twelve because his father was violent and abusive. A little later, when he was in his late teens, he had a job in a barber shop. I know this to be true because he sang little ditties when he was shaving, and once, when I asked him where he'd learned the song, he smiled, and said in a barber shop when he was soaping faces.

He had three songs, all very melancholy, that he alternated between, depending on his mood for the day. The one that I liked best and I can still hear him singing it if I close my eyes was this one: *As I was walking through the churchyard in the city / I met a beggar old and grey / With his arms outstretched he asked the folks for pity / And it made me sad to hear him say / Oh I wonder, yes I wonder / If the angels way up yonder / If the angels way up yonder say a prayer for me.*

My dad was a mellow, peaceful and tolerant man, who gave me advice using tried and true proverbs, such as: walk before you run, he who hesitates is lost, and a bird in the hand is worth two in the bush – that sort of thing. He had a Buddhist nature, for he could accept what was non-judgementally, but my mother didn't see him that way. She considered him weak, spineless and a pacifist with no principles.

Isn't it amazing how we can look at situations in different ways when we want to, and through twisting and turning unrelated events, create an illusion that we end up believing in? My mum complained that people walked all over my dad because he didn't stand up to them! This was their one and only disagreement that I recall, but it manifested itself many times over the years.

All of us children usually took my dad's side in a disagreement, which of course made matters worse. It wasn't that he played us to do this; on the contrary, he would go to great lengths to explain my mother's point of view, but my dad's side of the argument always seemed to make more sense.

Mum ruled the roost, for she was the intolerant, stubborn one who never gave in. She could stay mad at you for days, even for up to a week. My dad knew she would never change, and she didn't, and so he resigned himself to the reality of life with her. He just stayed out of her way, kept his mouth shut and on occasion, rolled his eyes with a smile, as much as to say, "that's your mother."

My grandmother on my mother's side was a migrant worker from France, who came to Jersey every harvest season to pick potatoes. She met a young man from Jersey one summer, married him and they had nine children. I don't know what my grandfather did for a living; he died before I was born, and my parents never spoke openly about their past. I only saw my grandmother twice; once when I was about eight, when our family of six went to stay at her little one bedroom bungalow with no running water and no inside toilet that was ironically named Mon Plaisir Cottage in St. Mary's Parish, Jersey, and the second time was when I was eleven. My granny was in her late eighties by then and was a resident of The Little Sisters of the Poor. We visited for about an hour; the most time that the nuns would allow. My memories of those two visits are as sharp and as vivid today as if they had happened just yesterday, not sixty years ago. How can that be?

On my first visit, as Uncle Jack pulled up to Granny Jouan's little cottage in his tiny pickup truck with our family and bags all bundled into the back, my first impression was that granny lived in a gingerbread house. It was so quaint and small compared to our terraced brick house in Lancashire. And as soon as we entered, I was even more convinced it must be a gingerbread house because it smelled of home-made bread and cakes, flowers and other wonderful scents. Bright sunlight flooded through the windows on all four walls lighting up the insides of her little cottage like a magic lantern. I don't remember where we slept, but it obviously wasn't in beds. We must have all been lined up on the floor, but it could not have been horrendous, for I would surely have remembered if it had.

One day we stripped my granny's garden of peas, and she had rows and rows of them. They tasted so good, and maybe because we were hungry, we kept picking, podding and eating them until there were none left for dinner. We dreaded telling Granny, but she just beamed a big smile at us when she found out, obviously pleased that we'd enjoyed the fruits of her labour, but our mother was not impressed. She was livid and scolded us for not being more respectful. Granny didn't speak English – she spoke patois – a type of Jersey French – so all we could do was to look at her and return her big, toothy smile.

On my second visit, I have a picture in my mind of the five of us and Granny (my older brother Mike didn't come on that trip) sitting on white wicker chairs lined up on a pink verandah against the blue wall of the Little Sisters of the Poor home, looking out at the landscape below. The Retirement Center was situated on a hill and overlooked the busy bay of St. Heliers. As my parents and Granny confidentially conversed in patois, Pat, Kenny and myself sun bathed in the chairs while watching the watercraft and traffic come and go down below.

As my father's parents had also died before I was born, I grew up wondering what it would be like to have real grandparents. Many of my friends said that their grandparents were the only ones that understood them and the only ones they could go to when they were troubled. It was a similar situation with aunts, uncles and cousins, for we grew up without access to many of those relatives; they having been scattered across various parts of England when they were evacuated like us.

We returned to Guernsey from Scotland in 1944 and in 1959, when I was five, we moved to Bolton, Lancashire because my mother had a "bad heart." Her doctor recommended that she go to live somewhere flatter because she wouldn't last pushing a pram up and down the high street whenever she left the house. So, we went to live in Bolton, where her sister, my Aunty Irene, lived in a "two up and two down" with her two children and Charlie. We stayed with them temporarily while my mum and dad looked for a house to buy. In the meantime, the housing inspector paid a visit and issued a summons about overcrowding. Someone had tipped off the authorities.

My parents bought a very respectable terraced house in Ainsdale Road, Bolton, but it took most of the wages my dad earned cutting cloth for a furniture manufacturer, as well as the meagre earnings my mum made working part time at a cotton mill making and serving tea.

We were dirt poor by today's standards in that there was never any extra discretionary income, but we didn't feel poor, and besides, most other people were in the same situation. We had a tricycle that would suit a five-year-old, and were told that it was for all of us to play on. It was the only transportation we ever had as kids. We piled on and squabbled about where to hang on.

For the most part, it was just the three of us kids – Kenny, Pat and I – at home growing up, because Mike was conscripted into the army when I was ten. He was based in Preston, about an hour away, with the Kings Own Royal Regiment (Lancaster).

Mum and dad outside their house on Ainsdale Rd

Kenny, Pat and I on the tricycle – 1949

Parental and Religious Conditioning

My parents never wanted to talk about their childhood years, even when we implored them to do so out of curiosity. My sense was that they were ashamed of their humble beginnings and their family, and wanted to keep that part of their lives a secret from us. Oh, how tortured they must have been and for no good reason, but that was the thinking back in those days. And when they did discuss adult topics, such as finances, they reverted to speaking in patois.

There was very little physical contact in our family, such as hugs and kisses, and the word "love" was never mentioned. We sensed we were the most important part of their lives, but their severe Victorian upbringing had conditioned them to regard any show of emotion as a sign of weakness. My mother tried to bring us up the same way that she was brought up, but the world had changed: children were no longer considered chattels and so we rebelled.

Strict discipline was paramount and a bamboo cane, about ten inches long and a quarter inch thick, was the tool my mother used to enforce it. It's strange, but I hadn't realised until now that I can't ever recall my dad ever holding it, let alone using it. It was omnipresent at the meal table, next to my mother's knife and fork, and then moved to the mantle-piece over the coal burning fireplace in the living room between meals. As we only had three rooms on the ground level – the kitchen, a front room that was usually rented out, and a crowded living room where we all spent our leisure hours – the cane was within easy reach should any of us misbehave.

We weren't bad, but we were kids, and kids tease, and siblings wrestle and argue, and that warranted in my mother's eyes some correction. We got a stinging smack across the knuckles or a whack across the bare legs every time we stepped out of what Mum called "the line." Many a time we got into silly moods of laughing and teasing, and if my mum intervened with the cane, we'd run away from her, circle the sofa, and laugh hysterically as she came after us in hot pursuit with her sword.

There was a local bamboo distribution centre in Bolton where my mother bought her canes. Although she went to great pains to hide her inventory, we looked for them and invariably found them. One time in the summer holidays, our friends were flying kites, and that gave us an idea. We took five of her canes, and with string, newspaper, flour paste and a number of rags for the long tail, we made a big five foot kite. Sometime later, when we saw Mum looking for her canes we laughed, but of course we couldn't say why we were laughing, and that made her more upset. We stored the kite in the triangular storage area below the stairs where she kept her stock of canes inside a rolled up carpet. We screamed with laughter as she held up the kite with one hand, and moved stuff around in the cluttered, full cupboard with the other, searching for her canes. The three of us had learned to be tight and we seldom ratted on each other, and so she never got an answer to her perennial question, "Who took the cane?"

Unlike my memories of the two holidays in the Channel Islands, where the images are in bright primary colours of yellows, greens and blues, my photographic memories of growing up in Lancashire are monochrome. Maybe it has to do with the weather, for the sky always seemed overcast when I was a child, or maybe it was sooty Bolton, or maybe it is a manifestation of my emotional memory, which is grey.

My parents were embarrassed because the Catholic primary school and church that we attended referred to us as *children from a mixed marriage*, and that was an almost scandalous situation at the time. My mother was a practising Catholic, but my dad wasn't. He didn't follow any organized religion. The best way to describe his beliefs would be to say that he was a humanist, but back then humanism was not a recognized "religion." If you weren't Catholic then you must be Protestant. We didn't differentiate between a Methodist and a Presbyterian. To us, they were all "proddies," and we were taught that they were not going to heaven because only people baptised in the Catholic Church were going there. When I was growing up, I wasn't aware that there were other religions – everyone seemed to be Christian, except of course for my dad.

The Catholic Church was the only true church. It said so in the Nicene Creed, because it was founded by Saint Peter after Jesus' death. And the Popes – Peter's successors and the leaders of the Catholic Church – were God's only spokespersons on earth. Not accepting the Pope's infallibility and leadership was tantamount to heresy, and so all other sects of Christianity were false. So convinced was I by these teachings, that I didn't doubt for one second that they weren't the truth. I'd been brainwashed and my ego identified with it and said, "*This is me. I know the truth and I don't care what others say.*"

Only Catholics could enter the pearly gates, and this was most troubling because it meant that my dad would be refused entry, and would not be with the rest of the family for all of eternity. Seems ridiculous now, but at ten years of age I really did believe this stuff. I was brought up to believe that God gave some people the gift of faith but not others, and I knew it couldn't have possibly been my Dad's fault because he was such a good human being.

I felt sorry he had not been given the gift, and I felt helpless as well in that there was nothing I could do about it – this was just the way it was. He could have converted to Catholicism and gone through the motions to alleviate the situation, but his principles prevented him. As young as I was, I respected his honesty and appreciated his encouragement that the rest of us should go to church. He thought that was a good thing for us, but not for him.

On Sundays, he got up early and lit a coal fire in the living room hearth so that the room would be warm for us when we all came down for breakfast, and then, while we were at church, he'd prepare a huge Sunday dinner of a beef or pork roast with roast potatoes, cauliflower and cheese sauce and the rest of the trimmings. As we came in the door from church, there was this delicious foodie smell in the house to greet us, and within a half hour, we were tucking into the meal with gusto. It was the highlight of the week for me for many years.

It was not until I was in my twenties that I began to seriously question the religious dogma that I'd been taught. Prior to that, I had always resorted to praying more when I found myself doubting my religion. It was a legacy of being brainwashed as a kid to believe that doubting was a sign that the devil was gaining an upper hand in his bid for my soul, and that only prayer could restore my faith.

We had a set of Sunday clothes; our best set that we wore only for church on Sundays, and as soon as we got home, we changed into our "play clothes." New clothes were first designated as Sunday clothes; previous Sunday clothes became school clothes; and the most worn school clothes became play clothes. A simple system that worked well for poor families.

Thinking back to those times, I have a sense that a lot of the emotional upset and hardship that permeated life in Bolton also had a lot to do with the British class system, and the movement that was taking place within it. Some people were moving up from poor to working class; others from working class to middle income; and others from middle to upper. In Britain in those days, each class had its own particular features: where you lived, who your friends were, how you spoke and dressed, and even where you went for holidays. And as people moved up, buying bigger houses, getting better jobs or wearing more stylish clothes, tongues would wag and say, "Who does he think he is?" It all had to do with small minds and jealousy of course, but at the time, one had to be part of it or else one would be ostracised too.

The same was true if anyone from out of town came to live in Bolton, as Renee did, when her husband, Bert Sproston, was hired by the Bolton Wanderers Football Club as a coach. Renee got a job at the Bolton Gate Company, where I worked, for something to do, as it was obvious, judging by her clothes, her husband's job, their social friends, etc. that she didn't need the job. Her work colleagues seemed to despise her London accent and suggested that she only spoke that way because she felt superior to others. They never accepted her even though she was sweet and kind and went to great lengths to fit in. I can still hear them saying in the mail room, "Who does she think she is? Too good for us I suppose, with her hoity-toity voice and airs."

My parents suffered from this class obsession too because they were not from Bolton; didn't speak like Boltonians; didn't have the same tastes and hobbies as locals; and would always be viewed as outsiders, no matter how many years they lived there.

And the church didn't help my parent's insecurity either. I still vividly recall a visit one Saturday afternoon by our parish priest, as if it happened last week. My mum opened the door, and he marched right in and strode over to stand in front of the fireplace. "Sit down, sit down," he commanded, and proceeded to grill my parents on why we did not go to church the previous Sunday. I was flabbergasted. How did he know we didn't go to church? What right did he have to barge in to our house and speak to my parents like that? He was a thin man, with thin lips and thinning hair, and a stern countenance. He never smiled and to a child, he was frightful. He just had to look at you and your knees shook. I hated and feared him. I could tell that my parents were upset by his visit, but they never mentioned it afterwards, and we never missed going to church after that. Oh the power of self-righteous people clad in cassocks! Of course it was all so dysfunctional, and the psychological intimidation so much a part of growing up in Britain in the fifties and sixties.

Teen Years

I attended St. William of York Primary School, run by an order of Catholic nuns, and when I was ten, sat the "eleven plus" exam, and passed. That meant I was eligible to go to Thornleigh Salesian College, a grammar school run by the Salesian fathers; a Catholic order of priests, founded by St. Don Bosco in Italy way back when. Although I was barely eleven when I started school, I had to catch two buses by myself to cover the hour long journey to get there, cross a major downtown street to change buses, and then walk for fifteen minutes to get to school; a feat that I would never consider asking my grandchildren to do today.

One morning when I was in the second form, I misbehaved, and was taught a painful lesson. My classroom was a couple of doors down from the Science Laboratory, where they pinned and carved up frogs, dissected pig's hearts and the like, and in Chemistry, mixed solutions creating the most disgusting smells you could ever imagine, that wafted down the corridor and into our classroom. The cleaners sprayed the room at night with a powerful chemical to replace the rotting egg smell with a scent of the forest. As we entered the classroom and settled into our desks, I blurted out impulsively, "Who did you have in here last night, Brother?" and looked around to see everyone laughing their heads off. I don't know where it came from because it was so unlike me to say such a thing, but I did.

Brother Peter, a small Irish young man in his early twenties, went as red as a lobster and in a fit of rage, attacked me: grabbing me by the ear he pulled me over the desks, threw me out of the room and sent me to the Head Master. I knocked on the Head Master's door, walked in when commanded to enter, and told him that Brother Peter had sent me. "Bend over," he said, without asking any questions, and proceeded to give me six whacks of the cane that stung like hell. I couldn't sit down for the rest of the day, which obviously pleased the Brother. He kept looking at me with a smirky smile.

Many students had serious split ear problems for the entire duration of their school years, and probably for the rest of their lives, if the truth were to be known. I once got the whack for something I didn't know I had done, and to this day, I still cannot say for sure why. The only thing I can think of, because my three other mates got the whack too that day, was that a prefect had reported us to the headmaster for taking off our school caps one lunch time at a fish and chip shop. We were aware that the school said we should wear our caps at all times during school hours, but we were in our final year, and it made us feel good to exercise a little independence.

Teacher cruelty wasn't just a trait of the Brothers and Priests; it was an insidious and infectious behaviour that most of the lay teachers exhibited too. Our Latin teacher used to swirl around from writing on the blackboard and fire a piece of chalk at whoever he thought was disrupting the class. Many a time his missiles inflicted pain and suffering, but he didn't care. He just laughed.

When my sister Pat was ten, she was appointed by Sister Dolorita, the headmistress of St. William of York Primary School, to spend her recesses waxing and polishing the hardwood floors of her office. She was given cloths to tie under her shoes, and told to skate around the office, first applying the wax, and then, changing cloths, to skate around again to polish, and to do this at every recess. She hated it and complained about it at the dinner table and appealed to my mum to go talk to the Sister because it wasn't fair that everyone else got to play, but she had to work. My mum always supported the church and school, no matter what the situation was. I think Sister Dolorita knew this and that's why she picked on Pat.

Clothes were always purchased two sizes too big to allow for growth over a five-year period. I only had two new school blazers in the five years that I attended college and three pairs of shoes that were resoled over and over. And so it was that my early conditioning was one of making do and for being thankful for what we had. Two great traits that I'm grateful for, but there were other, more important aspects to growing up that were missing from our lives:

the physical demonstration of love between a child and parent and the building up of a child's self-esteem. We know today how essential these practices are in order for a child to grow up well adjusted, but when I was a child, it was almost like the dark ages in our house as far as my parent's parenting skills were concerned.

Upon reflection, the Catholic schools that I attended also reinforced this notion that life was naturally hard, severe and joyless, but that it would all be worth it in the end when we were in heaven. Heaven was the reward for enduring a hard life on Earth, providing of course that you were Catholic, and in a state of grace at the very moment of death. If you weren't, you'd have to go to Purgatory for a while until enough people said the requisite amount of prayers for you. That always puzzled me because I wondered for how long – a week, a year, ten years? And if someone was famous and well liked, and everybody prayed for them, would they, in their ascension to heaven, be able to overtake those who had died before them? I thought it must be like the game of snakes and ladders. With enough prayers, you could zip up the ladder and get ahead of the others.

I also recall feeling sorry and sad for my eldest sister, my parents' first child, who was a stillborn, because she was in Limbo, never having been baptised, and so I would never get to meet her. Oh, the thoughts and imaginings rolling around in a young child's mind.

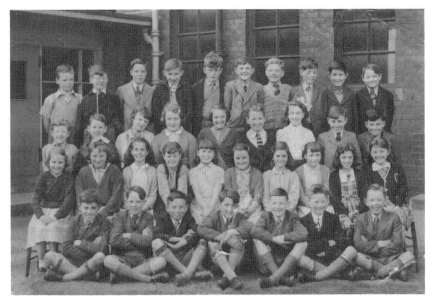

St Williams 1955 – I am second on the left on the bottom row

The Devil and Sins

As I recall my childhood years, I realise now just how dysfunctional life was, both in my home and at school, but of course that was my reality, and so I didn't know at the time that I was not in a healthy mental and emotional environment. The weird attitude to life, primarily instigated by the Church, contributed to a lot of confusion, insecurity and immaturity that was challenging for me, and which took many years to recondition and repair. There are so many aspects that I could write about, but I will mention just a few to demonstrate how the teachings manifested themselves in me as I entered the age of puberty and the beginnings of life as an adult.

One was the position taken by the Church regarding the devil and "unclean" thoughts. The devil was this evil spirit lurking around every corner, and, if I didn't watch out, he'd possess me and make me do bad things. The Church blamed him for everything, even the thoughts caused by hormonal changes, which I knew nothing about because no one told me —sex was a taboo subject in the fifties for parents and educators.

I started masturbating when I was about fifteen or sixteen. Why and where I learned it from, I have no idea. I think it just happened naturally one morning when I awoke. I thought it was grossly weird and wondered if other boys knew about it, but of course there was no discussing a subject like that, even with my closest friends. There was no doubt in my mind that it was the devil making me do it, but I couldn't stop because I didn't want to. I'd sooner enjoy the pleasure of it and walk around a sinful person because being sinful didn't show, and so I could get away with it.

But it did present a big emotional problem for me because there was no way on Earth that I was going to tell the priest that I masturbated three times last week, for which I was truly sorry, and with the help of God's grace, I would promise never to do it again. It was the embarrassment that I feared most. We went to confession every Saturday night so that we would be in a state of grace on Sunday to receive the Holy Communion. I continued to go to confession, but I didn't confess this sin. For a period of time, I can't remember now for how long, but it might have been for about a year, I was mentally depressed and felt heavy with guilt and shame about my secret. I was convinced that what I was doing was unnatural, and must be what the priests called fornication; a term they used often at school but they could never give me a definition of it that made any sense. There were many weeks when, try as I might, when I was at confession, I couldn't think of any sins that I had committed in the last seven days, except of course for the masturbating, and so I would make some up: I misbehaved at home three times, I told three lies at school, and I didn't own up when my mum asked, "Who ate the last of the biscuits, or who took the cane?"

I find it quite incredulous now that for the first thirty years of my life, I had this strange concept of what I was. I didn't realise that I was just another life species on the planet. I accepted that God made me and I let it go at that. From the earliest age that I can remember, the answer to the question, "Who made you," was "God made me," and to the question, "Why did God make you," the answer was, "God made me to love him and to serve him in this life so that I could be happy with him in the next." The catechism answers were deeply programmed into our psyche in primary school, when we had to memorise, through years of daily repetition, the answer to every question. It didn't matter if we didn't understand the words; so long as we could quote the answer verbatim was all that was required. The brainwashing was always there under the radar despite my curiosity and interest in reading about Darwin's evolution theory.

Upon reflection, I think it was the fear of what would happen if I stopped "believing" that prevented me from opening my mind earlier in life to consider other possibilities. There was always the possibility of course that maybe God was like Santa Claus or the Easter Bunny, and that someday it would be revealed that He too was a myth, but in the meantime, I struggled to stay a "believer." And I sometimes wonder that had I not travelled as extensively as I have, and not been exposed to other religions and their adherents, who were just as devout and devoted as Christians in their own way, I might never have evolved spiritually, nor understood the true nature of man in the world.

I barely passed my GCE "O" levels. If it was not for a pass in Religious Education, I would have technically failed, so I was thankful in that regard for having had such a good religious education. If you did not pass in five subjects, then you had failed your GCE, and that was monumental in terms of getting a job, not to mention the embarrassment it would cause, not only to you, but also to your parents, when friends and neighbours enquired if you had "passed," and they would enquire, nothing was more predictable than that in the Bolton of the early sixties. Because if you didn't pass, neighbours would say with a spiteful, pitiful expression on their face, "I'm so sorry," as if they had just been told that you had a terminal illness.

I went back to the College soon after I finished school, when the final marks were out, and asked my form master for a reference letter that I could use in getting a job. He obviously gave it a lot of thought, because his letter contained four paragraphs as I recall, and I do recall it very well, for it is burned in my memory. I burned the letter that very day on the coal fire when my parents were out of the room. The first paragraph stated the usual factual information about my start and finish dates; the second one was about the College and its credentials; the third enunciated my marks; and the last one was his opinion of me. He said that he didn't think I would "go far in life," for I had not learned how to study effectively, had not worked hard enough, and that I had been a big disappointment to him!

Thornleigh 1956 – I'm on the bottom row to the left of Brother Peter

First Job

Humility was a virtue I learned growing up; first from my parents, and then from the nuns, priests and brothers, but overdone, like everything else in life, too much of a good thing can be bad, and for me it was debilitating because it resulted in low self-esteem. I lacked confidence in just about every aspect of life and I felt that I couldn't do anything as well as others. I became introverted and preferred taking a back seat and disappearing so that no one would notice that I was there. I dreaded getting attention, and when I did, I blushed a bright red. My siblings said they could see the process as if my body was being filled with blood: the red would just rise up seemingly from my feet to the top of my head. Knowing that this is what happened when I felt shy just exacerbated the situation, and made me even more insecure.

Today, we would be very concerned as parents and teachers if we saw a child in this state, but it was not so in the fifties and sixties. We'd be scheduling sessions with councillors, and working at building their self-esteem in constructive steps, but back then, my mother just smiled and thought it cute that I was "shy." I haven't heard the word "shy" applied to a human being since it was applied to me. The word seems to have just dropped off the face of earth.

And it seemed to please my mother too that I was quiet and reserved; better that than being a loud mouth and pretending to be someone you weren't. That was the very worst case scenario. There were deep, societal emotions circulating around my town, and negatively labelling people seemed to be enjoyed by everyone as they spread the gossip in the idle chit chat that occupied so much of their lives. Step out of line just a little, and you were in danger of attracting much attention. Being concerned with what the neighbours thought was my mum's main concern. "What will the neighbours think" was her mantra whenever I suggested anything out of the ordinary, or came home a little late, or worse still, bought a pair of "drainpipe pants" because they were all the fashion.

Was it any wonder then that by the time I was sixteen, and leaving college to join the world of work, I was a shy, fearful and insecure lad who was confused about life. I was naïve about everything: sex, girls, money, social interaction, but of course I didn't want anyone to know that.

University was never in the cards for me as I was working class and didn't excel at academics, and besides, there was never any talk of me going to university. My job was to go out and get a job, and to help out my mum and dad financially now that I was old enough to bring home a pay packet. I got a job as a pricing clerk with the Bolton Gate Company and did my job as instructed. My dad's advice regarding work was to keep a low profile; don't cause any trouble; and to build up seniority year after year, thereby minimising the risk of ever being laid off. I gave my pay packets to my mum. She took out what she felt was fair for room and board, and gave me the remainder, which was little, yet it was enough to get by until the next pay day. It helped that I was frugal and tended to only buy what I considered essential.

I developed a persona of confidence to hide my anxieties and fears, and it seemed to fool everyone around me: parents, relatives and friends. They all thought I was adjusting fine and well on my way to making my mark in the world, but I knew otherwise and my inhibitions kept surfacing unexpectedly, making life very uncomfortable.

One Friday night, when I was seventeen, I was out with my mates when we heard a band playing at the St. Helens Road Youth Club. We entered the building and were surprised to learn that the guitar player and drummer were from our school. Tom was the guitarist and Bob was the drummer. I played the trumpet and cornet at school, and when Tom said they were looking for a bass player, I jumped at the chance. By noon the next morning, I had an electric Fenton Weil bass in hand and was all set to become a rock and roller. We called ourselves Paul Venture and the Rebel Beats.

What I hadn't considered in my haste to become a musician was that the group intended to play before live audiences. The first time I went on stage and the curtains opened, I died a thousand deaths. I was an emotional wreck. I kept losing the beat – playing too fast or too slow. I just wanted it to end so that I could get off the stage and away from all of those faces looking up at me. Tom looked over and wondered what the hell was the matter with me because in practices I was coming along fine: keeping the beat, and being tight with the rest of the group. Over time, I gradually gained confidence, but there was always that period of high anxiety, just before going on stage, where I would break out into a cold sweat and my hands would shake uncontrollably.

This was 1962, two years before the Beatles toured the USA for the first time, and an era where rock and roll was vying for a place in the music scene. It was a mixed bag at the time: Lonnie Donegan was belting out "My Old Man's a Dustman" with his skiffle group, Pat Boone was crooning "Love Letters in the Sand," and Lawrence Welk was keeping the big band sound alive. We didn't know at the time of course that British rockers would take the world by storm two years later. We were just a bunch of young guys enjoying ourselves. Tom was the leader and the most mature member of the group. He organised everything from gigs to finances, clothes, music, and eventually to us acquiring a van. Early in 1963, Tom was asked if the group was interested in playing in Hamburg, Germany, as the Beatles would later do. Tom put the proposition to us, but said that he wouldn't be able to go because he had lost his father when he was twelve, and he was now the man of the house. Without Tom we were nothing, and so we declined the offer.

I was so immature and lacking confidence at that time that I never gave Tom any help. My only concern was when and where to show up for the next gig. We had a lot of fun, and played most nights, sometimes into the early morning hours. We all had full time day jobs that we had to maintain, and for the most part we did, except for Pete, our replacement drummer, who lost his job as a mechanic. His boss found him curled up on the back seat of a customer's car fast asleep one too many times.

One early foggy morning, we were travelling down a steep hill in the Pennines after a gig in Burnley when a funny thing happened. I had a poem I wanted to share, but as our cube van had no windows, I opened the back door to get some moonlight to read by. The poem went like this: *Boy meets girl / holds her hand / visions of a promised land.* And then I fell out of the van. I immediately rolled over to the side of the road – survival instinct – and started to run after the van. Meanwhile, the boys in the back of the van made such a racket, banging on the metal sides of the van that Peter, our drummer driver, stopped to investigate the noise. "We lost Ally," they shouted. "He fell out of the van miles ago." Fifteen minutes later we met up: the van ascending the hill, and I descending, as fast as I could. Once safely inside the van, I realised that I was hurting all over. It felt as if every bone in my body was broken, but they weren't, and I was okay to play again a week later.

We were so busy playing most nights that there was not much time for any serious dating. I had a few dates, where I would take a girl for a walk, or go to the movies, but that was about it. My first girlfriend dumped me after the first date because she said I was "too immature." I so wanted to put my arm around her in the movie theatre, but I couldn't. No matter how hard I tried to lift up my arm, it wouldn't move.

Paul Venture and the Rebelbeats – 1962 – I'm on the far right

In May 1963, a young sixteen-year-old girl named Margaret joined the Bolton Gate Company as a stenographer. When she first walked across the floor in the office where I worked, I felt a strange emotion course through my body. It was a wonderful warm and exciting feeling that I had never felt before. It was love and I was smitten. In a matter of weeks I was madly in love. The relationship grew quickly in intensity, as first loves do, and on Sunday after-noons, while sitting around a table at Tognarellis, an ice cream bar in Bolton, we began discussing where we'd like to live, how many children we'd have, and which of our features we'd like our children to inherit. I was infatuated and convinced that this young lady would be the love of my life forever.

And then she dropped the bomb. We'd only been dating for about three months, when one day, with sad eyes and a thin, shaky voice, she told me that she had something very important to say that couldn't wait. She looked me straight in the face and said, "I'm going to Canada with my family."

"What? When?"

"Thirty-six days from now," she replied.

I thought about it for at least thirty-six seconds and said, "Don't worry. I'll come too. I'll go wherever you go."

We waved our goodbyes thirty-six days later: me from the pier of the Liverpool dock, and she from the deck of her ship. I was distraught. I felt as if my heart had been wrenched out of my chest, and all that was left was a skeleton. As she sailed up the Irish Sea for her boat to pick up Canada-bound passengers in Glasgow, I obsessed on the train back to Bolton about how to join her in the shortest possible amount of time.

As soon as I got in the door, I announced to my parents that I was going to Canada. They thought I was mad, as well as foolish; that we were just "ships passing in the night," and that I would change my mind in the near future. But I didn't. As the weeks passed, and my resolve got stronger, my mother began to break down emotionally. She cried a lot and refused to eat at the same dinner table with me.

Margaret and I wrote each other a many paged letter every day so there was always a letter waiting for me when I got home from work, and one for her when she returned from school – she was too young to work in Canada, and so had to go back to school for a final year. Our parents were not supportive and in that they were united. But we were young and in love, and that led to feelings of selfishness and immortality. We were sure we were mature and that we knew better because the world had changed since our parents were young, and they didn't understand just how mature kids were those days!

Without any research or regard for what the possible downsides might be, I quit the group, sold my bass guitar, got a part-time job with my cousin Alf waiting on tables at the Monaco Casino Nightclub in Farnworth, just outside Bolton, and went to Liverpool to get a passport. Four months later, I sailed to Quebec City, Canada on the Empress of England and took the train to London, Ontario to join my beloved. Her parents put me up until I found a job and got a place of my own. Canada was in need of new immigrants in 1963, and part of the cost of my passage was funded by the Canadian government, to be paid back once I had secured employment.

Monaco Casino Nightclub – 1963 – Farewell party
for me – I'm in the middle row in the centre

DEC • 63

Arriving in Canada – 1963 –Al with his two cabin mates

CHAPTER 2
A New Life in Canada

Family and Work

The day after I arrived in London, Ontario, I went to the Unemployment Office and walked out with a job as a Milk Purchases Clerk for Silverwood Dairies, and three weeks later, I had a place of my own in a rooming house with four other boarders.

I decided that I wanted to be called Alastair going forward and not Ally, as I was known in England. Alastair seemed to be so much more a grown up name than Ally, and if people wanted to shorten it, I told them "you can call me Al."

Life was fun and we fell more deeply in love. Margaret left school and got a job as a stenographer with an insurance company. We went to the Treasure Island Gardens in London on many occasions with friends to see the likes of the Rolling Stones, Bobby Vinton, Little Anthony and the Imperials. I learned to drive and bought a decrepit 1957 Plymouth Savoy that looked more like a spaceship with its huge tail wings and chrome accessories. I could see the ground through the rust holes in the body work under my feet, but it served us well for the first two years.

It was normal for couples in those days to get married when they were around twenty years of age. Many "had to get married," for the pill was just coming into vogue, and most young women were not on it, and wearing condoms was not "cool," and not sanctioned by the Catholic Church anyway. It didn't seem to be a big thing when our friends announced that they were expecting a baby, but it was when Margaret told me she was expecting. I was devastated, and the enormity of what that meant sunk me like a ton of bricks. I felt so guilty and sinful, so irresponsible and disappointed with myself. The news stripped me of my persona leaving me feeling weak and exposed. I would just have to buckle down for the next twenty odd years, be a good father and husband, and earn enough money so that I could live up to my obligations.

I immediately enrolled in the Registered Industrial Accounting course, and after work each evening, I tackled another lesson. There were about twenty-five subjects with about fifteen lessons in each as I recall that I had to complete in the five year course in order to get the RIA degree. I was determined to stay the course and get my diploma within the five years.

We married in a small ceremony at Holy Cross Catholic Church; found a small one bedroom apartment that we could afford; and settled down to married life. Darrin was born the following March, and another boy, Dean, came along two years later, followed by a daughter, Nicole, five years afterwards. We had the children baptised in the Catholic Church, sent them to Catholic schools, and took them to mass most Sundays for the first six or seven years of our marriage, and then just periodically after that on special occasions, such as Christmas and Easter. As we wanted to be good parents and ensure our children had good Christian values, we reverted to parenting as we had been taught.

The RIA degree was well recognised and much sought after by employers. I changed jobs every couple of years as I completed more of the program. I wanted more pay, and with it of course came more responsibility. Over time, I progressed from being a clerk to an accountant to a supervisor to a manager, and then to a Vice President of Finance with a large food processing company. And with each new job, we usually moved into a new home and bought a new car. Without being consciously aware of it, we had become the stereotypical corporate yuppie family living in suburbia and keeping up with the Joneses.

Life was very busy, what with all of the overtime and weekends that new jobs entailed, studying after work most nights, coaching the children's soccer teams, and running around to drop off and pick up the children from this and that program. I worked hard, and was extremely successful if you measure success in terms of promotions, job titles and increased income. I overcame my shyness and gained so much confidence that I developed an unhealthy cavalier type ego that I'm sure must have irritated many people. But because I was the VP of Finance, no one was going to tell me what they thought of me, were they?

I now realise just how preoccupied I had become with planning, organizing and orchestrating my work and next career move. For twenty years I had such high expectations for continued progress and advancement that I never thought about an end game; a time when I could say that I had arrived; that I could now sit back and enjoy the fruits of my labour and be happy.

When I was growing up, frugality was considered a major virtue in our house, and I grew up with this trait. Throughout my life thus far, I had always felt a basic urge to recycle, re-use and save, yet here I was buying all sorts of things we didn't need, replacing it for fickle reasons, and discarding perfectly good stuff just because it was out of style, or because we were tired of it. This material-istic drive to have it all and to have it now that so characterized my generation through the sixties to eighties was most noticeable in what we bought our children. I fell into this lifestyle trap and got them every new toy and piece of clothing that was hyped on the commercials. However, my default tendency to make do with everything only applied to me, not to my children, nor to my wife, nor to my home. Most of my personal purchases were at the urging of others. I usually got clothes, such as ties and shirts, for Christmas and birthdays rather than hobby equipment because I guess they thought my wardrobe needed updating.

In 1972, I got a phone call to say that Kenny had died on a beach in Spain. He had gone there on vacation with three of his mates, and while they were in the water, he had a heart attack as he lay sunbathing on the sand. I knew from his correspondence – we had kept in touch through monthly letters ever since I immigrated – that his condition was worsening, but Kenny always understated the facts so as not to worry his family. I went back for his funeral and learned from his friends that he knew he didn't have long to live. The doctor at Guys Hospital had told him to go on vacation and have a good time because time was running out for him. My parents passed away in the eighties, when they were in their mid-seventies.

I can say that I was "happy" for the first fifteen years of the marriage. The birth of the children was joyous and watching them grow and develop into teenagers was gratifying and enjoyable. We did everything together as a family and it was a lot of fun. Every year we went tent camping for a couple of weeks, and took other family excursions to places, such as England to see the relatives, Disney World to see "Mickey," Niagara Falls, etc.

But as I neared forty and began to assess where I was, what I'd done, and where I was going, I got the notion that something important was missing in my life – I didn't have inner peace and contentment: I was always anxious and wanting more, and I didn't know how to change it. It became an obsession. I felt trapped and heavy all the time. Why wasn't what I had enough? How could I not be ecstatically happy when I had everything one could ever wish for: a great career, a beautiful wife, great kids, new house, late model car, etc.? I'd lost my way somewhere, but I didn't know where or when it had happened. I became depressed and miserable and wanted some space to work things out.

We separated on fairly amicable terms. Nicole, who was twelve at the time, went to live with her mother, and Dean lived with me. Darrin was in college in Toronto. The first few years of a separation are very difficult and stressful for everyone involved, particularly the children, but at the time, I was so self-absorbed with my own unhappiness, I was not in the right head space to empathetically assess its impact on the children. I realise this now and feel bad about it, but at the time I couldn't think straight, nor feel any compassion for anyone but myself. The separation and subsequent divorce left me feeling unhinged, and conflicted on a religious level too because Catholics were not supposed to get divorced.

When I started to see other women I felt guilty and uncomfortable in their presence. To remedy this I did something one Saturday morning that permanently helped my situation. I imagined stowing away "my religion" in a backpack, and putting it on the top shelf in the hall closet. I was unsure how I'd fare without it, but I was willing to try, and anyway, if I couldn't cope, I knew where it was, and could retrieve it. I walked out of the apartment ten pounds lighter, an inch taller with a rejuvenated spirit, and never looked back. This one simple act of mental imaging allowed me to shed my religion once and for all, and to go forward with an open heart and mind. Where did this crazy idea of packing up religion into a backpack come from? The only answer that I could conceive of was "The Universe," the place where all creativity and imagination come from. It was profound what a difference that simple change in thought made to the rest of my life.

I had a few relationships over the next ten years; some more serious than others, but all in all, I didn't find the inner satisfaction that I was looking for. Perhaps my dissatisfaction had more to do with my discontentment in the corporate world. Maybe I needed to work for myself.

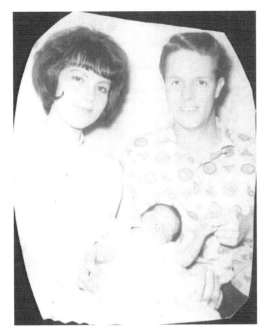

Margaret, Al and Darrin – 1965

My family – 1975

Rural Life

I teamed up with two business partners to export Canadian products to Caribbean countries, and went to the Bahamas to find customers, one of whom was looking for smoked trout. I went to see a man called Andy in Buffalo, New York about buying smoked trout from his fish farm in North Carolina. I got the samples and prices that I was looking for, but more importantly, I came away with the idea of going into the logistics business – that's what Andy had done before he got into fish farming. On Jan 1, 1988, with my youngest son, Dean, we started a freight brokerage company, and on June 1, 1988, I left my VP Finance job to work fulltime in the business. We prospered, and opened an office in Waterloo, Ontario three years later to be closer to the bulk of our clients who were based in Toronto.

I met Sue in Waterloo and we hit it off immediately. After two years of dating, we bought a rural property in Bentinck Township in the heart of Grey County in Ontario. It was an idyllic fifty acre retreat, with a fast flowing river running through it, five ponds, and eighteen acres of hardwood bush. It was to be our retirement home. As I could work from home with just the odd commute to Toronto, the arrangement worked out great. It was a refreshing new lifestyle for me, and I embraced it wholeheartedly.

In conversing with local farmers, we became embarrassingly aware of how little we knew about living in the country. Little things, essential for carefree country living, but of no consequence to us, city folks, were startling revelations. We had bats in the eaves, wasps in the roof, beavers in the ponds, and raccoons and porcupines in the trees, and we had to learn how to manage those wonderful, yet aggravating gifts of nature before they drove us crazy.

I thirsted to learn more, and began accompanying Roy, our seventy-five year old trapper neighbour, on his rounds, helping him to set his beaver and coon traps. I wanted to learn as much about nature from him as I could. He was delighted to have such an ardent student, and appreciated my interest and company. It was obvious that his plan was for me to become his protégé, and to take over his traps when he passed on. We helped another neighbour bring in hay, and assisted yet another with his maple syrup production. In a short period of time, we'd met most of our neighbours for miles around and had developed some good friendships.

For the next ten years the company prospered and evolved from being a non-asset based brokerage business to a full service logistics company, offering transportation, warehousing and distribution services out of a 100,000 square foot facility we leased in Toronto. As we were fine tuning the workings of the distribution center, another opportunity came up to set up a second one, primarily for a single customer. We moved on this quickly and secured another leased facility, but almost immediately there were problems. It turned out that the customer didn't have the business volumes that they purported to have and which we were banking on. The upshot was that we were committed to a second huge leased facility, but didn't have the volume to carry it. Although our sales team scrambled to secure extra business, it was clear that we had a significant problem. The pressures were intense and we were burning through money like there was no tomorrow. After much deliberation and soul searching, we decided that our only option was to enter into a business arrangement with a competitor to take over the company.

What went wrong? In a nutshell, I had been too greedy and too ambitious. We had had a lot of earlier successes that made us feel immortal, and whatever decisions we made, we could usually find a way to work them to our advantage, but not this time. It was a most humbling experience.

Country retreat

And a river ran through it

Early Retirement

And so there I was at fifty-seven years of age, unexpectedly unemployed for the first time in life and unsure whether to look for another job or to take an early retirement. We could afford to if we watched our pennies, but finances weren't our only concern. Were we ready? That was the burning question. I'd always enjoyed working and never considered retiring; in fact, I thought I'd work in one capacity or another right into my eighties. Wasn't retirement what you did when you were too old and too tired to work? Was I now too old and too tired? Had I actually reached that critical point in life? I didn't want to think so, but for sure I was tired; I was drained emotionally and physically from losing the business, but was I ready to spend the rest of my days, just passing time waiting for the grim reaper to visit?

And what about all those years spent in the business world – a lifetime of acquiring and building a bank of knowledge and skills? What was that all for if I didn't continue to use them? Was I going to let them go out of my life, just like that, by default? And if I opted out of the work force now, I was sure that I'd become obsolete overnight and thus lose any chance of ever landing a good paying job again. But to continue working, I'd have to find employment within commuting distance, and if I couldn't, we'd have to sell and move, and that was the last thing we wanted to do. Our amazing property, with its river, woods, ponds and paths was our most treasured possession and it so defined us. As well, the thought of the whole job application process was tiresome so we took the easy way out and retired. The relief was immediate and intense.

We were busy that first summer and enjoyed the change of pace and scenery it afforded. We went to bed early and rose with the dawn, feeling refreshed and ready for another day of hard labour; so different to the dark mornings in the city when I dragged my ass out of bed to race off to work with nothing but a strong cup of coffee in my stomach.

For two months, I laboured on building a wraparound deck out of cedar boards, harvested from our woodlot a few years earlier. We enlarged paths and picnic areas, chopped up fallen and winter damaged trees and burned them in huge bonfires by the river. Rural life was soothing and we were soon completely in tune with the slower rhythm of country life.

A Change in Plans

With the fall and the cooler weather, we spent more time indoors, and in the evenings, relaxed in the living room, in front of the big fireplace, which a previous owner had cleverly built out of round, bleached white stones from the river. Sue and I would discuss our day, the latest local gossip, as well as whatever subject came up.

One evening, Sue was musing philosophically about this and that, comparing life in the city to the country when, right out of the blue, she casually mentioned that she felt something was missing in her life. "Life was too easy – too passive," she said. "It lacked edge. I don't think we were cut out to be country folk," she added, as she continued to sip her Merlot and nibble on a wedge of brie. What an admission! I weighed her words, but it didn't take long to agree. I wasn't a wannabe farmer type either, nor was I ready to pass my days watching life slide by watching sunrises and sunsets while waiting for the inevitable visit from the man with the scythe. Nor was I a corporate guy anymore. I'd shed that persona and moved on, or at least I thought I had. So who was I, and what was I going to do about it? As we couldn't think of anything specific that we wanted to do, we let the subject drop and continued on with our lives as before.

I began to play golf and Sue busied herself with a few new pursuits, but the inner peace and contentment that I intuitively longed for still eluded me. I spent a lot of time thinking deeply about who I was and what I wanted out of life. The introspection was insightful yet scary because the stark realisation was that I didn't know who I was and still had no idea what I wanted out of life.

I wondered about other retirees. Were they happy? How many were as disillusioned as I? How many just stayed with the program because they didn't want to stray beyond their comfort level? I smiled when I thought about how society at large considered retirement to be such a prized state of affairs; the final, successful accomplishment in life and the sooner you did it the better. I chuckled when I thought about how the life insurance ads depicted retirees as ecstatic, successful fifty-five year-olds, leading fabulously fulfilling lives, smiling all over the world, and getting younger by the minute; an image, hammered into our subconscious by plastic and Botox enhanced actors. How many Boomers had bought into this marketing myth and how many were out there right now marking the days off their calendars, with high expectations of a blissful retirement? And how many would ultimately be as disillusioned as I?

The disquieting thoughts of *Is this it? Is this all there is?* surfaced constantly in my mind, but I didn't share them with Sue. I swept them under the bedroom carpet in the spare room where I hoped she wouldn't find them. It was déjà vu time again. Fifteen years after my first aha moment, and here I was, no nearer to finding that elusive inner happiness that I felt was out there. Why was I not ecstatically happy with this idyllic retirement situation? Perhaps what I yearned for didn't exist! Maybe it was unrealistic of me to expect more? Would I never reach a point in life when I felt truly content?

Winter visited us early with its bountiful gifts of white, but it overstayed its welcome by at least a month. We used the opportunity to visit family and friends and our world was perfect. At least that's how it appeared to others. Spring arrived, thrusting her way up through the frosted garden, with gifts of sunny yellow tulips, cold white snowdrops, and hopes of warmer days. We toiled on the land from sun-up to sundown cleaning up the debris left by winter's long visit.

One bright, crisp early morning in April, I was on the deck daydreaming and gazing mindlessly at the last chunks of ice floating down the Rocky Saugeen River. I'd pick out a slab and follow it, watching it bob and swirl in the eddies, and then shrink and break up into smaller pieces, which then got sucked into the main current, swept downstream, and out of sight. And then I'd pick out another slab and follow its journey until it too disappeared. Ice was so fleeting I thought: here one minute, gone the next. Its impermanence struck a chord. And from the deep recesses of my brain bubbled a startling observation. "So too was life!" That was it. That was the epiphany I needed. I could see it all so clearly now: we only have so many days of life and by evening every day we have one day less! My brain went into overdrive, my body temperature soared, and I panicked. I felt feverish. A flurry of thoughts and emotions swirled around in my head, all at the same time; regret for days wasted in not fully realising the importance of this; anxiety for the limited time left; and confusion about what to do about it. These flashes filled up every cavity in my brain, and a sense of urgency consumed me. I went down to the big pond, sat on the snowy bench, and stared at the rippling icy waters: lost in wonderment of fleeting ice and life. I must have been there for over an hour before my mind cleared, and my body sensibilities returned to normal. And then I had another "aha" moment. We must look for a new adventure: a journey of discovery and travel. We needed to find something extraordinary: something with a personal challenge and an edge. I had a sense that if I followed my intuition and forgot about logic and practicalities, I would find the inner fulfilment I craved. There was no time to waste. Life was too precious.

Fleeting ice

CHAPTER 3

Awakening in the Northwest Territories

Dream Job in Canada's North

Changing one's perspective can turn one's beliefs inside out in the wink of an eye. What an about face from a year ago when we were convinced we'd be in our house for life. Now that we'd decided to look for a new adventure, it no longer mattered that we'd have to sell the property and move. Our new mantra was – been there, done that – now let's move on.

We considered options. We wanted something different yet challenging, novel and fun. Maybe working overseas, say in Nepal or Africa, might be the answer, but before we went to that extreme, we wanted to see what there was in Canada. Maybe a little business in Newfoundland might want someone to run things for them, or perhaps an organization in northern British Columbia could use our skills.

Qualified searches on the Internet flushed out many interesting job prospects, usually in the more remote regions of Canada. I applied for positions in the Maritimes and British Columbia, but I didn't get one positive reply. Ageism was alive and well in Canada that was for sure. Some jobs contained elements of what we wanted, but none smacked of being "the perfect job" until Lutsel K'e blipped on the radar.

The Lutsel K'e First Nations Dene band was looking for a General Manager to manage their business affairs. The listing read that Lutsel K'e was a fly-in community, located on a lake in the Northwest Territories. The prospect of living in an isolated community with a bunch of Indians in Canada's far north was bizarre; yet there was a fascinating mystique to it.

The atlas showed Lutsel K'e to be located at the east end of Great Slave Lake, and north of the 60th parallel. I'd never looked that closely at a map of Canada's north before. I thought Edmonton was in the far north, and the only place north of it of any significance, were the oilsands at Fort McMurray, until of course you reached the Arctic, but I'd no idea what lay in between, nor just how big that "in between" was. It was huge.

There was Lake Athabasca and Lesser Slave Lake in northern Alberta, and north of that, Great Slave Lake, and to the north of that, Great Bear Lake, and there at the top of the page, the Beaufort Sea and the Arctic Circle. The map showed only one road north from Peace River, Alberta to Yellowknife, and from there, the only route north was the mighty Mackenzie River. It wound through the western part of the territory and emptied out 2,500 miles later in the Beaufort Sea at Inuvik. Wow, what a strange land!

There wasn't much up there; just a few dots on the map depicting small population centres, as if a geography student had started to pin towns and had got called away. Sure looked different to the map of Ontario: that looked as if the whole class had been working on it, pinning everything, drawing circles all over the place with lots of doodling, all scribbling over each other's work. I read the place names. A few sounded familiar, probably from watching the Weather Channel: Yellowknife and Inuvik rang a bell. Many towns began with "fort": Fort Providence, Fort Resolution, Fort Simpson and Fort Reliance. The mere sound of those names conjured up exciting mental images of pioneers, Indians and missionaries.

My imagination was running rampant with northern possibilities. I was as a child, experiencing the joy of discovery in a new toy. I couldn't stop laughing. That we were even contemplating living in such a hostile, strange land made us feel silly and lighthearted. But more importantly, it made us feel "alive." The more we researched the north; the more intrigued we became. We'd watched the "North of Sixty" TV program a few times, and had always found it interesting in a peculiar sort of way. I thought this must be what it would be like to live in Lutsel K'e. I faxed over a cover letter and resume.

Two days later, a man called to say they were interested in speaking with me. He said Lutsel K'e was a fly-in community of about three hundred Chipewyan Dene people and there were diamond mines in the territory, which favourably impacted the community. One of the General Manager's duties would be to develop joint ventures with businesses to provide the diamond mines with goods and services. He said Lutsel K'e was a dry community. The job content was greatly appealing, but not being able to have a drink was disheartening because we both enjoyed a glass of wine with dinner most nights.

When I inquired about the word "Dene," the caller said that it was the aboriginal name for Indian, and that today to be politically correct, we should use Dene instead of Indian, and Inuit instead of Eskimo. "We pronounce Dene as "Deh nay," Inuit as "In u it," and Lutsel K'e as "Loot Sul Kay," the attentive caller advised, and added that Lutsel K'e used to be called Snowdrift. He said they would like to have a telephone interview with me on Thursday at noon my time. The job had all the elements we were looking for plus many other novel aspects. Maybe we'd learn to speak Chipewyan and become true Canadian bi-linguists!

At the appointed time, Bernard Barnstorm, the Acting General Manager, called. He introduced Vincent Tibbet, the President of the Corporations and Lorraine Basker.

Without any preamble, Bernard said in a polite, whispery voice, "We are going to ask you some questions. Please answer them to the best of your ability."

In a strong, clear, corporate voice, honed over the years to reflect confidence and decisiveness, I replied, "Go ahead, I'm ready."

After a slight pause, Bernard continued. "Question number one is do you have any supervisory experience?"

What? It's all over my resume. I've been managing and supervising for the last thirty years! Hasn't he read my resume? I took a deep breath and politely replied, "Yes, as my resume indicates, I have extensive supervisory experience in many diverse sectors of the economy." I left it at that – concise, to the point – and awaited his response, but there was none. There was no feedback at all. No one asked for more information, nothing, not even a cough.

Vincent joined in the questioning, and asked in a flat, monotone voice, "Question number two is have you ever worked in an aboriginal community?"

"No," I responded without hesitation. This was a deal breaker to be sure and would immediately disqualify me. But once again there was total silence.

Lorraine, obviously reading from a prepared script, asked in a bright, clear, controlled voice with staccato type phrasing, "Kwe—styun—num-ber–three-is-do—you-have-any—accown-tin – ex-per-i-ence?" I felt I was in the middle of a skit on the CBC's *Dead Dog Café* radio program.

"Yes. As my resume indicates, I have extensive accounting experience. I have a Certified Management Accounting degree (The CMA designation superseded the RIA designation in 1985,) and I've held many senior accounting jobs over the years in many diverse industries, and I did my own books when I went into business for myself." I thought that ought to elicit some feedback for sure, but no, once again there was total silence. This silence thing was unnerving and frustrating because I had no idea of how I was doing. And so it went, for about ten more questions. Bernard thanked me for participating and said that he'd be in touch if they were interested further.

This was my first direct contact with the aboriginal world and I was both bemused and intrigued. The simplicity of the interview, the laid back, warm, stress-free tone of their voices, and the unusual manner in which they avoided asking any personal questions was radically different from what I was used to. I expected to be grilled, challenged and questioned. "That's because they weren't serious," Sue suggested. "Sounded like they were just going through the motions as a form of protocol because they've already got somebody." I agreed but I wanted this job. The job content was appealing and we both earnestly wanted to go up there to live with them in their land, and to experience their culture.

Two days later, Mr. Barnstorm called and asked for a photo. "No problem, I'll fax one over right away," I said, not knowing if I even had one that would be suitable. Now why on earth would they want a photo? Was it important how I looked? Things were sure different up North! After supper, I pulled out the photo albums and bundles of more recent holiday snaps that hadn't made it into albums yet to see if I could find one that would serve the purpose. I soon became engrossed in a pleasurable journey of revisiting the past, and went far beyond looking for a recent photo. It was all there: photos of the family when the children were small, and of holidays and special events, as well as more recent photos of the grandchildren. After two hours, I hadn't found one head shot that would be remotely suitable.

A flash from the past zapped my brain. Maybe I still had a few professional photos from a project I did about six years ago. A brief search found them in an archive box. There were three 4" x 5" black and white glossy prints. How serendipitous! I'd changed a lot. Gone was the mop of permed, dark brown, curly hair. It was now shorter, straighter and lighter, so light some would say it was silver. I didn't wear glasses back then, and I was pleasantly surprised at how trim my face was. Bernard hadn't specifically asked for "a recent photo" I rationalized as I made my way to the fax machine to send over a picture of a much younger man looking for a job in Lutsel K'e. I anxiously awaited his response.

A much younger man looking for a job in Lutsel K'e

It came quickly, the next morning in fact. Bernard called and offered me the job. He recited the terms of the offer, and said that the job came with a house, and the only cost I would be responsible for would be utilities, and all I needed to bring was a pillow, bedding and some towels. He said that a new three bedroom

General Manager's house was being built, but it wasn't ready yet, in the meantime, I'd have to live with a guy called Lester. "Would that be OK?" and added, "when can you start?"

I had many questions about the organization, community, climate, Lester and so on. As he spoke, I scribbled, making copious notes to share with Sue. There was so much to ask. One question led to another, and an hour and a half flew by before I realized I should end the conversation so as not to appear too eager and demanding. I thanked him for his patience and requested that he fax over the job description, the company's latest audited financial statements, and the job offer in writing. He agreed. As I read over my notes, converting words into images, I became enthralled: enthralled with the Dene, with their culture, and with their land, as well as with the whole northern business scene. Three days later I received the faxed job offer and the job description, which was generic and could apply to any administrative position in any company, except that it mentioned creating jobs for the Métis people, which was odd, because Bernard hadn't said anything about the Métis! He said the Lutsel K'e community was Chipewyan!

I called Bernard and asked him when he was going to send the statements. He apologized and said he didn't have them; they were still with the auditors. Well, that piece of news was reassuring – at least they had auditors, because I was wondering what shape the books were in, after hearing so many horror stories from the media about the financial mismanagement of some northern aboriginal bands. He said he'd do his best to get them to me by Friday, but reassured me that the companies were profitable. He proceeded to throw out big numbers, like millions of dollars, and rambled on in a lengthy soliloquy about something that I couldn't relate to, and ended his speech with, "And so you see Al, there's a lot happening up here for you to look after." To be polite I concurred, but inwardly I wondered if he knew what he was talking about!

The end of the week came, but the financials didn't. Sue and I discussed our circumstances, and we agreed that I would accept the job regardless. Our reasoning was simple. If it didn't work out, I'd just pack up and come home. As it was, I intended to go there for three months, and if that worked out, Sue would sell the house and join me. There was little downside risk because we were both going primarily for the adventure. Our curiosity had been piqued, and we just had to go see this place called Lutsel K'e. I gave Bernard a July second start date.

The next day, the fax from Lutsel K'e arrived, documenting the travel details: Air Canada from Toronto to Edmonton, Canadian North to Yellowknife and Air Tindi to Lutsel K'e. There was a room reserved for me at the Chateau Nova in Yellowknife for the first of July.

With only eight days to go, I frantically surfed the web to find out as much as I could about what I was getting into. For starters, there was this huge, cultural divide between my "white" and their "aboriginal" world to contend with. I was vaguely familiar with the Indian Reserves in Ontario, but Lutsel K'e was purportedly different so Bernard said – more of a hamlet, a little town. I thought *yeah, right – you mean more like "North of Sixty."* Going to live on an Indian Reserve wasn't appealing, but going to live with an aboriginal people with ancestral beliefs and lifestyles, in a remote encampment, north of the 60th parallel, was as exotic to us as going to Africa.

By now we were bewitched by the little bit of Dene history we'd extracted from the web. The opportunity to experience Canada's far north appealed to us greatly, though strange, because we usually preferred to go to hotter climes. Bernard said they only got about sixteen inches of snow a year due to the aridity at that latitude. Once Great Slave freezes over, the air was as dry as a desert. So much for speculating on how much they must get based on the many tons of "white stuff" that I shoveled off our driveway last year!

And then there were the Northern Lights, the Barren Lands, the caribou herds of up to four hundred thousand strong, and the long summer days, and long winter nights to experience. Maybe I'd canoe the Mackenzie and visit some outlying settlements, or go white water rafting on the Nahanni River. Ignoring the outline in the job description, and relying on what Bernard said about new business opportunities with the mines, I felt for sure that I was the right man for the job, and that I'd be able to do good things for them. My gut was telling me that it was my destiny to go to Lutsel K'e. By this time, my children were fully supportive of my decision and tickled pink that their dad was setting off on a Great White North adventure. Although I would miss them dearly, I knew that it would not be forever – maybe a few years, but I would be in touch regularly by phone and internet.

Second Thoughts

The Toronto/Edmonton flight passed without incident. Though not consciously thinking about direction, I sensed we were travelling west. Going west just felt different to going east, and I wondered if other people experienced that sensation. I had the same feeling on the Edmonton/Yellowknife leg, but the South/North movement was more palpable. As our aircraft jetted towards the land of the midnight sun, I closed my eyes and savoured the magic Boeing 737 carpet ride. I was leaving a world of comfort and familiarity for a land of mystery and uncertainty, and that was exciting because it had an "edge" to it.

Seventy-five minutes later, the big plane began its descent. I peered through the window at the great body of water below, and tried to imagine what Lutsel K'e looked like. As the plane manoeuvred into its final landing approach, I thought more about the future. Would I be safe? Or would my epitaph read, "He went to Lutsel K'e." What would happen if I were to be struck down with some serious illness or accident so far from home? Would the Dene accept me, a white guy with an English accent, or would my voice trigger negative memories about colonization and residential schools? And what would happen if I had latent racial feelings? I read somewhere about that happening and it wasn't pretty. These were not new questions, for they had all been asked and answered many times before, but now, their significance was imminent and concerning. I vacillated between confidence and fear. It seemed such a huge undertaking, far weightier than when I went over the final details with Sue at the kitchen table.

There down below, perched on a jut of rock, and surrounded by water and more rock, sat Yellowknife, the thriving, rich capital city of the Northwest Territories, and the first sign of man's existence on the planet in over an hour. Yet it consisted of just a few buildings and roads, all tightly contained on a rocky promontory.

The plane landed, I disembarked and headed for the one entrance door in the terminal. A massive, stuffed white polar bear with paws at least a foot across, menacingly towered over the sole baggage carousel as we waited for our luggage. I expected a larger terminal, but then only eighteen thousand people live in Yellowknife. Nick, the Chateau Nova Hotel shuttle bus driver, was there waiting to greet me and the three other passengers destined for the Nova hotel. He took our luggage and led us to his toasty warm vehicle, parked conveniently outside the front doors, in what for the north was a balmy minus two degrees night air. As my sleepy companions huddled in their parkas and dozed, I sat bolt upright, determined to see all.

I checked in at the Chateau Nova and called Sue. She was pleased and relieved to hear that I had arrived safely in Yellowknife and was anxiously awaiting my next call about my first impressions of Lutsel K'e.

Over Great Slave Lake to Lutsel K'e

It was a perfect day for flying over the Lake. The sun was high and bright and the sky a deep blue. As I alighted from the taxi at the Yellowknife Airport, motes of dust floated gravity-free up into the bone-chilling air; sparkling and swirling in a mystical spiral dance in the taxi's hot exhaust. I paused just before entering the terminal to suck in deep breaths of pristine northern air, filling my lungs to capacity, sharpening my senses a hundredfold. Yellowknife was literally the end of the road. Everything beyond was only accessible by air.

Small regional carriers acted as taxis providing commuter services to communities and mines. Aircraft ranged in size from the two-seater Cherokees to the mid-sized nine-seat Caravans to the larger De Havilland Twin Otters that held up to seventeen people. There were larger aircraft, such as the Dash 7s and 8s and Buffalo Freighter planes, but these were mainly used by the mines for cargo.

A prefabricated, metal-clad arched building, about forty feet by twenty, served as the Air Tindi passenger terminal. It consisted of just one room with a door at each end and twenty feet of benches down the middle. One door exited onto the street, the other onto the airport apron and the waiting plane. The ticket agent office, baggage and cargo staging area were located along one wall. I picked up my ticket at the office, chose a spot in the middle of the benches and sat down. I felt foreign and "white," a tourist in Mongolia or some such strange place.

The two women who sat opposite me could well have been sisters, for their facial features were similar, and they had the same long, silky black hair, flowing down to the middle of their backs. They appeared to be in their early twenties. Their eyes fascinated me: so inky black and penetrating – blacker even than Spanish eyes – and their brown skin appeared soft and healthy. They reminded me of Pocahontas and the other Indian maidens I'd seen in old cowboy and Indian movies that I'd watched as a kid. The young ladies wore well-fitting, trendy clothes and their mannerisms were sophisticated, which to be truthful, surprised me greatly because I expected them to be "rougher." I caught myself thinking these stereotypes and was disappointed. Was I that out of date and igno-rant? The young women busied themselves in animated chatter and laughter and didn't seem to notice me, which was fine, for I was keeping a low profile.

A tall, lean fellow helped himself to a cup of coffee at the counter. When he turned around, I examined his face and studied his mannerisms. His high cheekbones and chiselled jaw gave him a gaunt look, something like a Jack Palance or a Kirk Douglas. His shiny, straight, coal black hair was combed back into a tight pony tail and tied with what looked like an elastic band – nothing fancy. An extra ten inches of hair spilled over his slight shoulders and tumbled down his vest. It was obvious that he too took much care over his appearance. Images of Geronimo came to mind. Another stereotype I know, but my mind was desperately seeking to make a connection. He sauntered past in tight, straight-cut jeans with a bowlegged sort of cowboy gait. His large, silver belt buckle was like a searchlight; something a coal miner might strap on in the dark. The measured clicking of his rigid, cowboy boots on the linoleum floor reflected self-confidence and ease. In fact, all the Dene passengers exuded that same sense of calm that I picked up on in my phone interview for the job.

Another passenger entered: an elderly lady in a green floral head scarf, a blue nylon parka and wearing soft faded brown moccasins. She carried a shopping bag that nearly touched the floor. Diminutive in size and slightly hunchbacked, she smiled at me with warm, wrinkled eyes as she took a seat next to me, adding to my sense of ease. "Good afternoon," I cordially greeted her. She expanded her smile and silently nodded her head in acknowledgement.

I was enjoying these new experiences and thirsted for more. Everything up until that point had been preparatory, but when I entered the Air Tindi building, I knew that that was it, there was no turning back now, the same sort of feeling I got when I passed the point of no return on a roller coaster ride. I was locked in with no option but to hang in there, confront my fear and go for it.

A pleasant young lady opened the door to the airport apron and announced that we were ready for boarding. I took my time, ensuring I was the last to leave, out of courtesy perhaps, for I was a stranger in their midst, or perhaps more truthfully out of uncertainty, for I felt out of my depth in that strange land. We handed her our tickets and strolled out into the sunshine to the aircraft fifty feet away. There were only four other passengers that morning on the Caravan, so there were four empty seats to choose from. I opted for the front window one on the right so that I could get a good view of the lake to take some pictures to send back to family and friends.

The pilot ran through the safety briefing, passed around earplugs, announced it would be a good flight and that we'd be in Lutsel K'e in about forty-five minutes. Cramped in such a small plane with "foreigners," and seated only a few feet away from the pilot, co-pilot, cockpit gauges and controls, was strange and intimate. There were no heavy duty safety precautions up there. Adrenaline coursed through my veins. Everything that was happening was new and exciting.

The novelty of sitting so close to the pilots, looking over their shoulders and following their every move was riveting. I watched intently through the cockpit window, as the young, well-scrubbed aviators went through their pre-flight routines, taxied out to the runway and throttled us up into the blue yonder. We banked to the right, climbed to about five thousand feet I'd guess, and circled over Yellowknife until the aircraft pointed due east. With Yellowknife behind us, all there was to see were rocks and puddles. I looked intently at the flat, white and pink land mass below and concentrated my gaze. Other features began to emerge: faint, wispy thin black and yellow lines of spruce and birch appeared and meandered crazily across the landscape; small lakes, creeks and ponds briefly came into view and then magically disappeared into the white sunlight. The land was alien, still and barren. Was I still in Canada?

In the distance on my right, I spied the southern shore of the lake. A half hour later, we banked to the right and flew over the waters in a south-easterly direction; over the North Channel; past Christie Bay and the stunningly picturesque Red Cliff Island; and on past innumerable islands of all shapes and sizes. And there straight ahead, at the tip of a peninsula, lay Lutsel Ké: the shining jewel on the East Arm of Great Slave Lake.

The quiet cabin stirred to life, friendly chatter erupted, and seats strained as passengers squirmed to look out windows. Bags and papers rustled as passengers prepared for the landing, and the crew's voices crackled into radio communication with ground control. We flew over the hamlet to the airstrip at the end of town, which was laid out on the southern and western shores of the peninsula. A large hill extended the full length of the hamlet in a west to east direction. Bernard said the General Manager's house was being built at the top of the hill but I couldn't see any sign of construction. I wasn't concerned, merely puzzled. The plane flew past the airstrip, turned around and came back to land. I had arrived in Lutsel K'e.

Lutsel K'e – the shining jewel

First Impressions – Lutsel K'e

Bernard Barnstorm stood out from the crowd for many reasons. He was the tallest. At about six foot four, he towered over the Dene, who were waiting to greet the arriving passengers. He wore bright clothing: a red shirt, black lightweight baggy pants drawn tight at the ankles and stuffed into a pair of high cut white running shoes. But his most attention getting feature was the black patch over his right eye. I chuckled when I first saw him through the plane window as we taxied to the hut that served as the airport terminal. When he greeted me with a "Hi, I'm Bernard Barnstorm – you must be Alastair Henry" salutation when I stepped off the plane, I didn't know what to say. He grabbed my backpack and led me across the apron to the terminal. "Did you have a good flight and what's the weather like in Ontario?" he enquired, engaging in the usual small talk strangers use to break the ice, while we waited for the airport truck to bring out the bags. When the truck arrived, he grabbed my two suitcases and threw them into the back of a 2001 Ford F150 pickup.

On the way into town, he spoke slowly and softly, triggering my memory of our conversation of just a month ago. I studied him, while he focused his attention on the pot-holed road, and tried to marry up the mental image that I had of him with this gentle giant of a pirate. He seemed so odd yet so uncommonly friendly.

As we bumped along the one lane, gravel road into town, he told me a little of his past. "Lived here for over thirty years now. Born on a farm in Saskatchewan, I first came north to teach, got into trapping, did that for twelve years, got married and then did whatever jobs in town needed to be done." His open honesty about his life, and the ease with which he spoke to me, a total stranger, was refreshing and disarming. I felt relaxed and carefree, as if I was on vacation. He proudly continued. "Tackled most administrative jobs over the years: Band Manager, Housing Manager, Co-op Store Manager, and now I'm the Development Corporation General Manager. At least I was until a few minutes ago when you arrived," he said with a chuckle. We laughed.

"How come you don't look like your photo?" He reached over and pulled out of the glove compartment a copy of the photo that I'd faxed him. I smiled quietly but inwardly I was roaring with laughter.

"It was taken a few years ago but it was the only one I had at the time." He got the joke and laughed, giving me the impression that he wasn't going to make an issue of it. I was relieved. Further down the road, he pointed out the Forestry Base, which was owned and operated by the Corporation and the Lutsel K'e Housing warehouse. The road bent to the left around a hill, straightened out and ran along the lake shore road into town. Bernard said that it was seven kilometres from the airport to town; the bay had just cleared of ice last week; and the big barge from Yellowknife would be in on Thursday.

"With my six boxes of my personal effects?"

"Let's hope so," he replied with a smile, and continued with the guided tour, pointing out the important buildings as we drove into the heart of the downtown: the RCMP detachment, health clinic, primary school, Department of Public Works garage, community hall, church and mission hall, Band and Council Chambers, seniors centre, Coop store, as well as the Administration Office Complex, where I would work. Most buildings were prefabricated, brought in by barge over the last thirty years and assembled by visiting contractors in the summer months, he advised.

We drove to a large log house – a teacher's residence – one of four homes on a cul-de-sac lane. As the teachers were away for the summer, I was to stay there with a fellow named Lester until my house was built, or until the teachers returned. Bernard gave me a house key, moved my bags from the truck to the porch, and wished me, "Good luck settling in. Take your time and come down to the office when you're ready. Bring your lap top."

When I'm ready? He's gotta be kidding! Does he think I'm gonna start work today? No way Jose! I need time to unpack and adjust – maybe a day or two, certainly not the half hour he implied! And what about the General Manager's house? When will that be ready?

He didn't say anything about that. *Ah well, I'll see it soon enough*, I thought, struggling to digest all that was happening.

The log house was a two storey affair with spacious rooms. It had a homey, family type feeling to it. The living room cum kitchen sprawled across the main floor. Two small adjoining rooms housed the 1,000 gallon water and sewage tanks. My bedroom, at the top of the stairs, contained a single bed with a firm mattress, a three-drawer dresser, four dusty open shelves about ten inches deep on one wall, and a large window overlooking a stand of scraggly spruce on the other.

It didn't take long to unpack. I found a spot for my clothes and personal items and put the bedding on the bed. I was ready for work. Just like that. There was nothing else for me to do. And it took less than half an hour!

I headed off to work and within minutes, was sweating profusely. Had I known the climate would be so benign, I would've worn lighter clothes. I was grossly overdressed in a bulky northern parka with a wolf trim hood, a pair of Kodiak boots guaranteed to be good for fifty degrees below, an oversized pair of snowmobile gloves and a back pack containing a 17-inch HP Presario laptop computer. Though sweaty and uncomfortable physically, I nevertheless found the tranquillity of the place to be soothing. Other than the rumble of the water truck struggling uphill and the raucous arguing between ravenous ravens, wandering the community in gangs looking for something to eat, there was little noise.

I felt vulnerable and unsure of myself as I neared the Administration Office Complex. I was conscious of my whiteness and, try as I might, I couldn't shake off the thought that many in the community would see me as just another white guy from the south coming north to rip them off. That's what I had read. I knew I wasn't, but the thought that some would say that bothered me. Sure I was being overly sensitive and paranoid. I realized that, but it didn't help me overcome my unease. I stopped for a moment to take a deep breath and run through some affirmations. I resolved to be strong; to keep an open mind; to be tolerant and patient no matter what; to give of my best at all times; and to try to make a difference before I left the community. I would prove to them that I was different. Preoccupied in thought, I stumbled on the rocky path, twisted my ankle and limped the rest of the way to work.

Bernard was waiting for me in the General Manager's office. He gave me a set of keys for the front door and for the General Manager's office and introduced me to Sunrise, my Administrative Assistant. She greeted me with a big smile and a handshake full of enthusiasm. This was important because we would be just a two-person office and I'd need a lot of help from her to get up to speed in the days ahead. She had the same classic Dene features as the young ladies I saw in the terminal: high cheek bones with deeply set eye sockets where jet black eyes twinkled out at the world; plump red lips and strong white teeth that gave her a beautiful and beguiling smile; skin so soft-looking and dark, and her hair was shiny black and flowed down over the sides of her face and shoulders to the middle of her back.

Bernard said, with the air of a schoolmaster who was still in charge, that office hours were from nine to noon and from one to five and any overtime was to be taken as lieu time.

I asked him what the corporations did. "Well, we own real estate in the community, such as this building, and we lease out offices to various parties, such as the Band and the government, and the senior's centre is ours too; we charge the government for that. And then there's the Forestry Base that we passed coming in. We get government contracts every summer to run fire crews out of there in the summer. It's more of a fire prevention program than the fire hall you'd be familiar with." He rattled off the services from memory, as I'm sure he'd done many times before. "Another one of our companies provides manpower for ice flooding contracts in the winter and we build homes in the community as well, such as the General Manager's home we're working on. We also have a wood shop, where we make surveyor stakes for mining companies, and we do whatever small projects come our way," he proudly informed.

Didn't sound too complicated, which pleased me, because it meant I should have time to work on developing new businesses and to making a difference. That's what I really wanted to do.

The Administration Complex was a one floor wooden structure with individual offices located around the sides. In the centre was a large boardroom with a cathedral ceiling. Small upper windows ran along the outside walls. A hallway ran around the outside perimeter of the boardroom giving access to each office.

My office was in a corner of the building. It was about twenty feet by twelve and had a large picture window overlooking the bay. That was great. People in Toronto would give their eyeteeth to work in such a fantastic business setting.

Sunrise worked in an adjoining, smaller office, dominated by a big desk. She sat amid cabinetry and high shelving on all sides, full of books and papers, which made her space look small, dark and disorganized.

The Corporation owned two pickup trucks: one was used as the Forestry vehicle by the fire crew and the other was for my personal use, but it wasn't working. Although the trucks were barely a year old and had less than 5,000 kilometres on their odometers, they were in rough shape. The fire pickup had a cracked windshield, many large dents in the body panels, as well as loose windshield weather stripping, which flapped annoyingly when we drove in from the airport. The rear view mirror was also missing.

I acknowledged that the roads were bad and probably accounted for the cracked windshield and loose fittings, but it didn't seem to account for the serious damage to the body panels. I wondered about that, and images of fights and scuffles with bodies being thrown through the air at the truck came to mind. The old van, parked in the office driveway, was brought in on the barge the year before to be the town taxi, Bernard informed, but they hadn't got it working yet.

Right at five o'clock, Sunrise and Bernard got up from their chairs, said goodnight, and went home. This surprised me because we were in the middle of reviewing the fire crew project and hadn't finished up on a final note. Their inappropriateness and inconsiderate behaviour riled me. I made a mental note to speak to Sunrise about it the next day.

I dragged my ankle, now the size of a baseball, up the hill to the log house. The sun was still high in the sky and hot. It felt like noon, not five. At that latitude in July, the sun didn't set until two o'clock in the morning and then rose again two hours later. From the hill road, I could see all of the downtown area laid out at the bottom of the hill. It looked to me to be more of a model village set out on a table top than a real town. I looked across the bay to the other shore, and panning around in a 360 degree sweep, noticed the surrounding waters and islands. The view was spectacular.

Most homes were larger and more modern than I expected and none had basements because the land there was pure rock. Some homes sat on pilings drilled into the rock, some on beds of crushed stone while others were perched on jacks. Many had sheds that Bernard called warehouses, where townsfolk kept their fishing and trapping gear, and many also had separate smoke houses or tipis, for drying and smoking fish and wild meat. The tipis were simple constructions fashioned conically out of spruce poles and draped with canoe canvas or blue tarpaulin, with a hole at the top to vent the smoke. Many in the community had built saunas onto their homes.

Clumps of fireweed – a spiky, bright purple flower about four feet tall – grew in open areas on exposed rock and crushed stone, adding a needed splash of colour to the dull, dust covered landscape. Patches of wild raspberries and blueberries, not yet in season, provided the greenery. A network of well-defined paths ran this way and that, snaking past homes and open areas, providing residents with shortcuts to work, neighbour's homes and the store. Big dogs lazed in front of their dog houses on their bellies with paws outstretched and eyes closed. Smaller dogs raced around playing tag, pretending not to notice the encroaching mob of ravens coming for their food.

The Administration office

Downtown Lutsel K'e and the barge

Hay River barge

I arrived home, lathered in sweat, out of breath and in pain. A young man's voice shouted out, "Hi, I'm in the kitchen." Lester was stirring noodles and sauce for supper and offered to share his meal when he learned I hadn't bought groceries yet. The clean-cut, young man with short cropped, brown curly hair and an angelic face, that seemed so out of place in a community such as Lutsel K'e, commented with a friendly smile, "Bernard should have told you to get groceries before you went to the office."

Over supper, he brought me up to speed. "I'm from Boston, Massachusetts and I'm here working on a fish project with the Wildlife, Lands & Environment office. I'm measuring the size and condition of the fish in Stark Lake because the locals have noticed some aberrations in the fish in the last few years, and that's why we're doing the study. Some say it's because of radioactivity from the abandoned uranium mine, but it's too early to tell. We need more samples to prove it's an abnormality and even if it was, it could be caused by other things that we don't yet know about. Interesting work though, and the opportunity to be up here is awesome."

He set his fork down and took a large drink of water before continuing. "You have to watch how much water you use and you have to keep an eye on the level in the water tank, because it's a pain to have to prime the pump, which you have to do if you run out of water." He continued as I tucked into his noodles with gusto. "Water in Lutsel K'e is pumped from the lake and delivered to each house by a truck every two days. The water goes through some type of rudimentary filtration process, to remove fish and other solids." We laughed. "But don't worry. I've been drinking the water from the tap since I got here and I've never been sick."

He stopped eating to take another large swallow of water. "And every home has a sewage tank, which is pumped out every five days into a truck, which goes out of town to discharge its load into a lagoon. If the sewage tank is full, the water stops, so there are two reasons why you might not have water."

"Lester please. I'm eating." I pleaded with his sensibilities.

He smiled and changed the subject. "Every home has a wood stove as a backup in case of sustained power outages, which frequently occur. The electric power in the community is diesel generated by a small power plant located at the tip of the bay."

Lester commented on my exuberance and said that he was glad to have me for a roommate. I marvelled at this young man, so far from home and doing such important and interesting research and yet so young. I washed and dried the dishes in appreciation for the food, the information and the good company.

Although I tried to give Lester my full attention at supper, I was preoccupied about calling Sue to tell her about my first day. "The phone isn't working," he said when I asked. Man was I pissed. "There's only one public phone in Lutsel K'e at the Co-op store, and you can only use it between ten and noon and one and six in the afternoon," he added.

"That's so ridiculous," I muttered, immediately realizing that this was the first negative comment I'd made since arriving. I made a mental note to be more careful. As I wasn't comfortable asking a neighbour to use their phone, I decided to call Sue from work in the morning.

I retired early and lay there in my bed smiling, mulling over the day's events. I thought of family back home, fast asleep in their beds, for I was two hours behind them. They'd all wonder why I didn't call. The daylight of the night and the flimsiness of the curtains prevented me from having a sound sleep, as did the itching on my neck and scalp from the black fly bites. Lester suggested I pick up some cardboard from the Co-op and put it in the windows to shut out the light.

I called Sue in the morning from work. She laughed when I told her about the phone situation and what I'd learned over the last twenty-four hours. She said she couldn't wait to experience the adventure for herself, but in the meantime, she was keeping herself busy looking after the property and visiting with friends and family.

I spent the day with Bernard; watching what he did, and listening to what he said, but most of it was confusing. He just seemed to react to whatever came up. I understood what the Fire Crew Project was all about, but I didn't know what my role in it was on a day-to-day basis. He spoke of other projects, but none were on the go at the moment. I couldn't pin him down as to what he did every day. "How's the General Manager's House coming along?" I asked.

He smiled, thought about his answer for a moment and said, "Let's go up and see, shall we?" Harry, the Fire Crew Leader, brought over the Forestry truck. I dropped him off at the Forestry Base and drove up the hill with Bernard to see the house. It consisted of an outward frame of steel I-beams welded onto pilings, one foot above ground level. I stared at the structure in disbelief. "This is it? I thought you said it was nearly finished?"

"Not going as fast as I'd like," he replied, slightly embarrassed but not overly so. A work crew of five hung around the site but it wasn't clear what they were doing. They appeared to be taking a break; waiting for someone or something. Bernard introduced me to Bob, the Crew Boss, who in reality was a truck driver from Newfoundland. He was visiting his daughter, who was married to a Dene living in the community, and his two grandchildren for the summer. Bob had a Burl Ives build, beard and voice and the weathered face of a seafarer. His easy manner was so likeable that I took to him immediately. We walked around the five empty twenty foot shipping containers lying on the side of the road. All contents had been removed and were scattered everywhere. He identified the larger items and attempted to tidy up the site by piling and straightening the smaller cartons and packages, as we strolled through the debris!

As the General Manager, I was now responsible for the completion of this house! What a scary thought that was! I had absolutely no construction experience. The closest I had ever come was to pick out paint colours and choose carpets with a house builder! I gazed at the bare bones construction and the only thought that came to mind was to get the hell out of there – just pack up and fly out on the next plane. I felt I'd been had. Bob interrupted my musing and admitted, with a wry smile, that he'd never built a house before either, but he assured me that he had done many large home renovations. As if that qualified him to build my house! "Only reason I'm doing this," he said with smiling eyes and a broad grin, "was because the community asked me. I'm just helping out and anyway, how could I turn down the opportunity to make some big bucks on my vacation!"

How indeed, I thought. "You've gotta be kidding," I said.

"No," he replied and we spontaneously burst out laughing.

The prospect of a Newfie trucker and a ragtag crew of five building a $300,000 home was too much. Bernard joined in the laughing. Why was he laughing? From relief now that the construction job was mine? I felt "more had." Or did he too find the whole situation ludicrous? I asked to see the blueprints. I'd never actually looked at a blueprint, never had cause to, but somehow the question just popped into my mind as being the right question to ask. "We've looked for them but we can't find them. The previous General Manager must have taken them with him when he left, but we can't find him either," Bernard replied for Bob.

"How are you building the house then, if you don't have blueprints?" I asked.

Bob smiled and said, "We're figuring it out as we go along. What else can we do?"

"I'll get them one way or another" I said assuredly, and then realized that by saying this, I'd sent a message that I was on board, whereas in truth, I was unsure about everything. I didn't even know if I would still be there twenty-four hours from then. I needed time to think and to speak to Sue about what to do.

The monstrous Hay River barge, which plied the mighty Mackenzie River in the two summer months, supplying coastal communities from Fort Providence to Inuvik, with goods too bulky, too heavy and too hazardous to be flown as air cargo, floated into Lutsel K'e that night, and when I went down to the dock in the morning, the hoses connecting the gargantuan drums of heating oil and gasoline to the community's storage tanks were hooked up, and the two day pumping job had begun. The dock area was a busy place. Onlookers – children, elders and the unemployed – were all there to watch the two front-end loaders pull the contents off the barge. There were bundles, pallets and packages of housing materials for the four new homes that were going to be built plus housing material for the warehouse, supplies ordered by community members, and four lifts of two by four wood, ordered by Bernard for the stake operation. In addition there was a brand new, black Ford Explorer van for the Health Centre, three new ATV's and two used pickups for community members, as well as my six boxes of personal effects. A quick call to the Forestry Base brought Harry and the truck. He loaded the boxes on the truck, drove me home and insisted on carrying the boxes into the back room.

Back at work, I asked Bernard about job objectives. He smiled and said he didn't have any – he was just helping out until the new General Manager was on board. I asked again about the audited statements. "You'll have to see the auditors for that," he replied. "I know nothing about them." My feeling of "being had" was intensifying by the hour. What to do? I decided to stay at least until the weekend, and in the meantime, to learn as much about the whole situation as I could, and then discuss it with Sue and make a decision by Sunday night. As a financial guy, I needed to see numbers to make sense of things, and so I plunged into the process of preparing my own financial budgets. Sunrise pulled together the necessary documents and I worked away until five to six.

By the time I got to the Co-op they were locking the door and they wouldn't stay open for another two minutes to allow me to buy groceries. What's with this place? Why does everybody make everything so goddamn difficult? I marched home greatly pissed and angry. Everything seemed to be confirming my feeling that I shouldn't be there. I was not a good fit.

The Co-op store was the only commercial business in Lutsel K'e. There was nothing else – no donut shop, pizza place, not even a coffee shop. Nor were there any trades people – no electricians, plumbers or mechanics, except for Larry, who worked for the Department of Public Works fixing the band's trucks and equipment. However, as I was to later learn, he refused to service other vehicles in the community.

I don't know what the teachers did with their dishes, but there were so few in the house. Surely they hadn't taken them out on their school break! I found a small margarine tub which I began to safeguard with my life, for it was my only food bowl for breakfast and lunch. Lester had two plastic plates and a metal one that we used for suppers. The one small saucepan had to perform culinary magic. Kitchen utensils were also limited – no spatula or masher or anything of that sort. Bernard never said for me to bring dishes or kitchen utensils – he said just bring a pillow, bedding and towels. Lester hadn't bothered to upgrade the kitchen stock because he was on a student's budget and was leaving in a few months. I wasn't going to buy anything because I didn't know if I was going to stay, and besides, once the house was built, the Corporation would buy all I needed. It was terribly inconvenient though, not having the simplest of tools in the kitchen to strain spaghetti or flip a burger, and greatly disheartening to me personally, because I was passionate about cooking Indian dishes, and intended to while away the evening hours concocting kormas and masalas. Indian dishes were my comfort food. I'd been preparing them every couple of weeks ever since I was in my early twenties. I'd go a few weeks and then I'd have what I could only call withdrawal symptoms for a rich curry. It had been that way ever since I first went into an Indian restaurant on my lunch hour with a work mate when I was eighteen. I'd never tasted such sumptuous food and I was hooked. My mother used only salt and pepper in her cooking. Ah well, one more thing to look forward to if I were to stay and get my own house.

There were seven Directors on the Board. A Board meeting, scheduled for one o'clock, was cancelled because only two people showed up and at least four were needed for a quorum. Bernard rescheduled the meeting to coincide with the BBQ at the river in the evening in my honour. Wow, I felt special and thought that the people that truly mattered, the Directors, must surely appreciate my coming to Lutsel K'e. Perhaps I'd been too hasty, too judgemental. Perhaps I hadn't adequately prepared myself for the culture shock. It was obvious that if I stayed, I'd have to get used to their ways and learn to be more patient and understanding.

Bernard picked me up at six o'clock in the Forestry truck and drove out of town turning onto a pot-holed trail, which led to the river and the BBQ spot. The river ran between Stark Lake and Great Slave Lake. It was a great location for a picnic, so scenic.

A few people were fishing for grayling and lake trout in the fast flowing river. In the centre of the grassy area was a large, concrete BBQ, big enough for two sets of oversized grills which provided the focal point for the event. The fire was roaring when we arrived.

Bernard introduced me to Vince Tibbet, the President of the corporation, the person that I would be reporting to at work and one of the people that interviewed me. He was as I had imagined – smart, polished and business like. It was obvious that he was a key person in the community and well respected. I also met Mickey, another Director, but the other five Directors couldn't make it! So much for thinking that I was special. Vince was nonchalant about the whole thing saying two Directors were out of town and he didn't know where the others were. He too noticed that I didn't look anything like my photo. Did all the Dene have amazing photographic memories? How could he possibly remember what I looked like? Maybe he had a copy of my photo in his jacket pocket and had just glanced at it before saying hello?

"I've changed my hairstyle and I now wear glasses," I abruptly replied, not caring how he took my answer. He laughed as Bernard did, easing the edge off my tension. For some reason, the thought crossed my mind that I had gone there primarily for the adventure, so why was I looking at everything so seriously? Sure, it was a different world with a different type of humour, but it was interesting and was I not curious about learning more? Why not just take a deep breath, go with the flow and enjoy the journey, no matter what the outcome. It was of course against my basic nature to do this because I had always worked in a highly organised environment, ensuring everything was thought out ahead of time so that progress could be made smoothly and efficiently. Once again my mindset instantly shifted from negative to positive. Another simple change in thought having such a big impact on my mood.

Bernard introduced me to about twenty other people, some of whom were fire crew, but who they were and what they did, I don't remember for I wasn't concentrating. I was in a daze and going with the flow, smiling, shaking hands, lost in wonderment at all of the excitement.

Bernard unwrapped a large box containing thirty, half-inch thick, New York strip loin steaks, which immediately attracted everyone's attention. A dozen hands appeared and dove into the carton to grab a pound of flesh. Bernard pulled one out for me, put it on the grill and grabbed the big fork, because with a fire that strong, it wouldn't take long for the steak to be a medium rare, which was the way I said I preferred it. He handed me the fork and I flipped the meat. Some observant diner noticed and jeered, "He likes his rare." And with that, the whole crowd chimed in with a loud "oooooh."

From that point on, they watched me like a hawk, no doubt beginning to form an opinion about the new guy. I felt awkward and out of place and wondered if that aspect would ever change because I would always be the "white guy" in their eyes. As I removed my steak and put it on my plate next to the baked potato and coleslaw, the throng laughed and kidded that it was still raw. I welcomed their light-heartedness and poked fun at their well-done steaks. They were burning. Five minutes later, when the once delicious steaks were now charred black, they put them on their plates and boasted about how great they were. Done to perfection. I laughed and they laughed with me.

For the balance of the week, I worked on the budgets until ten in the evening and by the weekend, I'd gained a much clearer picture of the whole situation. As the numbers came together, so did my understanding of why I was there. It truly was going to be a wild ride, full of challenges and personal growth, but the opportunities were definitely there to develop some new businesses.

Sunrise lacked basic bookkeeping knowledge. She seemed to just guess an account number, assign a project code, and if the computer accepted it, she moved on to the next one and did the same thing. She was defensive and didn't want me to have access to the accounting program, which was only loaded on her computer. She shooed me away with "I'll do it," or I'll print it – just tell me what you want." Rather than upset her and get off to a bad start, I began fixing the coding errors in the evenings when I went in to the office to work on budgets. She did however seem to want to learn more, and I sensed that she was beginning to work more diligently now that I was on board.

Two directors seemed receptive to my suggestion that they become more involved in the decision-making process and in improving the Corporation's communication with the Band, which they said was a problem with the previous General Manager. They said he made a lot of decisions but didn't tell anyone what he was doing. He feathered his own nest they said, and they didn't believe the results of a forensic audit, conducted after he left, that didn't find anything out of order. This much ingrained belief concerning the white guy ripping off the Dene would continue to underpin many of my conversations with the Directors. The statement or innuendo always made me bristle and I implored them, in a tactful way, to keep an open mind for I came to help.

Pictures of our home and grounds helped. They solicited a lot of interest and questions. Sunrise found it inconceivable that I had chosen to be there while my partner was living in a big, beautiful home and grounds in Ontario. I explained that Sue was coming soon and that we had decided to start a new chapter in our lives in Canada's north. I think it was the idea that we had options about where and how we wanted to live, and that we had selected this option out of many, that most confounded her.

Granny and Mrs. Smith, two lady Elders, who took it upon themselves to speak to me on behalf of the community at every opportunity, said they wanted a new hotel, a coffee shop and a pool hall for teenagers. The men Elders told me they wanted lots of new jobs for the unemployed men in town. *You mean the ones who don't want to work!* I mouthed under my breath. I tensed when I saw Granny and Mrs. Smith coming towards me, for I knew the inevitable rant that would follow. They all wanted me to wave a magic wand and make it happen overnight. I smiled through gritted teeth and told them I was aware of their needs but it would take time. Lots of it.

Although I was in my own office, people from the community wandered in, poured themselves a cup of coffee from my pot, took a seat and just started talking. No one asked, "Are you busy? Do you have a minute? Is now a good time to see you?" Instead, they asked, "Have you got a smoke? Could you loan me twenty bucks? Do you have a job? I need some money." And to add insult to injury, some spat in my wastebasket! I was livid but I didn't know how to respond. Being new, I wasn't comfortable nor confident enough to call them on it. I just took a deep breath and sucked it up.

We'll see what happens, I thought, but I wasn't hopeful that I would be there for too much longer. There seemed to be too many hurdles to overcome. Maybe it wasn't a good fit after all? No one listened. Everyone wanted something –they were so needy. It was as if people only saw me as a "hired hand," someone to borrow money from and to do their bidding. I expected this to some degree but I expected it to be more subtle.

Three young men came to see me about starting up their own businesses. The community was ripe for entrepreneurs of every sort but no one wanted to put the effort into making it happen. "To get funding you need to have a business plan with forecasts of sales and expenses. I can help with that but you have to do the work," I said, giving them a one sheet summary of basic information to read. No one returned.

Saturday finally arrived and with it the chance to buy groceries. The windowless, prefabricated, metal-clad building that served as the Co-op store was about a hundred feet by sixty and had one customer service entrance. A long counter with two old fashioned tills ran along the front wall and behind the clerks, shelves displayed cigarettes, chewing tobacco, chocolate bars and smaller grocery items. The shelves on the back wall carried hardware and larger items; everything from light bulbs to sleeping bags. A bank of upright freezers down the right hand wall stocked dairy items and frozen prepared foods. In the centre, five chest type freezers stocked frozen meats. Grocery aisles filled the rest of the store. It was not a big store compared with stores in the south, and considering it was the only store in town and had to provide everything a community of three hundred and fifty people needed, from babies to elders. Nothing in the store was priced. You shopped and crossed your fingers that you had enough money when you checked out. Prices were typically twice as much as Yellowknife, which were twice as much as Ontario.

It was a busy place. The four shopping carts were already in use, so I filled my arms with as many boxes and cartons as I could hold and hung on to whatever I could grip with my hands and fingers. At one point we waited for what seemed to be an eternity, but it was probably only a couple of minutes, for a lady to return to the store. She didn't have enough money and went outside to borrow off someone. When she returned, no one seemed the least perturbed. All waited patiently, except for me. I was boiling over with anger from impatience and heat from my clothing. Though we were all dressed in northern parkas and snowmobile suits, I seemed to be the only one with perspiration beading on my brow.

The second the counter was clear, I let the contents of my arms, hands and fingers spill onto the aluminum tray, and took a delicious breath of relief! The young female teller fingered the prices into the cash register at great speed with great dexterity while simultaneously holding a conversation with the teller in the next lane. I marvelled at the skilful multitasking, but decided to withhold final judgement pending checking the cash register tape.

"Hi. I'm Lars. Been here seventeen years," said the tall, white guy immediately behind me. He knew who I was and said he worked for the Lutsel K'e Housing Authority; that people called him Charlie Brown but he didn't know why; and would I like to go fishing tomorrow?

"Love to," I replied.

"See if Lester wants to come too," he added. I paid the teller and grabbed my bags. "Be down at the dock at two," he called out as I left the store.

I returned home in a buoyant mood and gave the good news to my room-mate. "Great," said Lester, "Charlie Brown is a good guy.

The two of you will get along fine and we'll have a fun day out on the lake," he said as he helped put away my groceries.

Big Black Giants

Lester and I went down to the dock at two o'clock. I'd bought a fishing license from Vince the day before for ten dollars, so I was legal to fish in the Northwest Territories.

Lars' boat was ideal for a day out on the big lake. It was an eighteen-foot aluminum Lund, powered by a 60 hp outboard and decked out with a well-appointed cabin up front for the pilot, and two comfortable bucket seats for Lester and myself in the mid-section. Lars had built the cabin out of materials harvested from the community landfill, but looking at how well the pieces fit, you'd never have guessed its humble beginnings.

We headed for Red Cliff Island. I felt greatly relieved as we pulled away from the shore, away from the chaos and confusion that I wasn't yet used to. I pictured my concerns as a package that I left on the dock, all neatly wrapped. I secretly wished someone might pick it up while I was out on the lake. My travelling companions knew well, from their own experiences, how stressful culture shock can be in the early days for newcomers to the north.

"How's the house coming along," Lars teased, knowing full well the circumstances, as did everyone else.

"Have you seen it?" I replied.

"What's there to see? Lars laughed and Lester joined in.

"Exactly. Looks like it's gonna be quite a while before we move in. I'll have to rent a tipi for Sue when she gets here. Anybody got one to rent?" The joking continued unabated for the next ten minutes or so. The bonding put us in a giddy light-hearted mood and set the scene for a pleasurable afternoon. As we approached the first group of islands, Lars turned down the throttle so we could fish. When he handed me a heavy-duty rod and a mega-sized lure with three upturned hooks, I took one look and said, "There`s tuna in the lake?"

Lars said he wouldn't fish. He'd mind the boat and show me how to catch the big ones. "See. You hold the line with your thumb like this," he instructed as he pushed my thumb over the line on the rod. "You swish the rod back over your shoulder like this, and then you whip it forward, lifting your thumb at the last moment to release the line like this." I'd never fished before so it took a little getting used to, but I got the hang of it after a few tries and within ten minutes, had a good-sized fish on the line. "Keep the line taut as you reel it in, and then slacken it if the fish runs." The fish did run, right under the boat. Lars suggested I hold the line firm and wait for the fish to come back out, which it did. I enjoyed playing with the fish, letting out the line and winding it in, until such time as I decided that this was it. I was going to reel it in all the way. Lester waited with a big net. The fish was enormous, at least to my eyes; over a foot long with a huge mouth and large gills. "Well done. You've got a lake trout – about twelve pounds," Lars guessed. Lester shoved his fingers behind the gills of the slippery, slimy beast, to show me how to get a good hold on it and said, "You have to do it with determination or else the fish will wiggle out of your hands. You can't be afraid of it."

I was apprehensive and unsuccessful at first but I persisted. I yanked the trout out of the net with a hefty pull and plopped it into the pail. It was really no big deal but to me it was. I was as pleased as a toddler riding a bicycle for the first time. Lester landed a fish and I got another, about ten pounds, Lars guessed.

"All the fish in this lake are big. People come from all over the world on fishing trips that cost $3,000 US for three days of fishing," Lars said. "The record for a trout out of here is fifty-five pounds, but many are in the twenty and thirty pound range, and we might be lucky enough to snag one at that weight before the end of the day. Wouldn't that be something for you to write home about."

"And I have a camera to prove it if we did," I said.

Big, black giants inhabited those waters and they weren't fish. They rose up two thousand feet from the bottom of the lake and continued straight up, past the surface of the water, for another thousand feet, to look down imposingly on all who passed by. The sight of those Precambrian giants was awesome, the pristine beauty of the place breathtaking, and the tranquillity sublime. Those gargantuan monsters had been sitting in those icy waters, patiently waiting, since the last ice age. Lars had purposely taken this scenic route because he was as proud of the land as the Dene. He motored past with great reverence. Other islands were made of black granite, some were light coloured and appeared to be composed of shale, while others had stratified multi-coloured sections. Many islands had rock falls on their beaches and a few had pure white sands, as inviting as any tropical paradise.

The deep, aqua blue water glistened with the reflection of the sun and millions of tiny, diamonds blinked on the ripples of the gently lapping waves. I stared at the twinkling stars, felt the warmth of the sun, and was mesmerized. It was wondrous and hypnotic. The view calmed my mind and stopped all thinking. My heart felt as if it was beating at half speed. Everything was in slow motion

– the waves, the bobbing of the boat and the sparkling diamonds in the water. The stillness was weird and wonderful and it would take a long time before I understood the phenomenon.

After a few minutes, our captain pushed the throttle forward and headed the boat for his favourite spot. We puttered lazily past silent islands and slipped in and out of picturesque bays. My mind drifted and I began to think of the Dene and their land; of a people who had lived in those parts for thousands of years; of a people who had never been interested in living anywhere else nor ever would. This wasn't just water and rock. This was father sky and mother earth that the Dene spoke so reverently about. My spiritual awakening had begun. And that land, which was so light, warm and comfortable that afternoon, would soon mutate into a brutal, frozen landscape for the next eight months, with dark days and searing cold temperatures that instantly froze any exposed flesh.

I thought more about the Dene and how different their views on life were from mine. I had no real ties to any land in particular, having left Britain at a young age for Canada, and having moved from one place to another many times over the years. I'd always enjoyed travelling and exploring, and the thought of not wanting to do that made me smile and brought to mind what my dad used to say about people who didn't venture far from home. He called them, "Stick in the muds." Maybe I'd share that with Vince one day.

Around three o'clock, we headed to an island with a gravel beach. Lester jumped out, pulled the bow up onto shore and secured the boat by tying a rope to a large rock. I climbed out, in no particular hurry, for I was still at peace with the world and myself. Lars found three long, flat rocks and positioned them to form the three sides of a fire pit, while Lester and I hunted for driftwood. There was lots to choose from and all as dry as bleached bones. Lars lit a match and coaxed the dried spruce twigs into life. They burst into flame and within a minute, the fire was ready to cook fish and boil water. Lars put on the grill and kettle.

Down at the water's edge, Lester had gutted a fish and was loosening the unwanted bits of intestines with his fingers, when I arrived. He swished the fish in the water to remove the bits and bobs, cut off the head and put it in a brown paper bag to take back to an Elder in town who enjoyed boiled fish heads. Eagles and other wildlife would clean up the entrails within minutes of our leaving, Lester explained, when I balked at our not cleaning up the mess. He began filleting one side of the fish on a large flat rock. He filleted both sides at home he said, but the fish cooked better on an open fire, if you only filleted one side.

Lester placed the first of three fillets on the grill next to the hot dog buns and bread. A quick flip to cook the other side and one meal was ready. Lars took over the cooking while Lester went down to the beach to get water. "Here, drink this – there's no purer water in the world," Lester urged as he pushed the metal cup up to my lips and waited for my reaction. I took a mouthful, swished it around my teeth and gums and spat it out. I sipped and savoured the next mouthful. It was cool and refreshing. "I believe you," I said.

What a perfect way to spend a northern Sunday afternoon: lying on our backs on warm soft gravel, hands locked behind heads, eyes glazed over watching eagles soar and plummet in the bright blue sky, while listening to the water gently lap the beach. After a little while, we packed up and motored back to town. I reluctantly picked up my package on the dock and went home.

Later that night, two of Lester's friends, François Jonas and Marty Pettigrew, dropped by the house for a visit. Marty took one of my fish and showed me how to fillet it. He gripped the fish with his left thumb and index finger, and using the side of his left hand, applied pressure to keep it stationery. With the fillet knife in his right hand, he tickled a piece of skin loose from the bone and began to cut the meat from the skin by angling his knife down, applying pressure towards the skin surface, cutting cleanly all the way to the end, all the time pulling up on the skin of the fish with his left thumb and forefinger. At the end, he made a diagonal cut across the body to release the fillet. Turning the fillet over and using the same method as before, he removed the skin from the other side. One last straight cut across the top and bottom of the fillet and there was a tantalizingly, perfect looking fillet. "That's fantastic," I said, picking up the consummate meal and turning it over for further inspection.

"That'll be twenty bucks. Ten for me and ten for François," Marty said.

"What?" I exclaimed. "For what?"

"For traditional knowledge, man. You have to pay for traditional knowledge," Marty responded with a deadpan face.

I was lost for words. For the want of something to say I muttered, "You must be joking."

"No, man. You have to pay for traditional knowledge. You owe us twenty bucks." I seethed. I hated being put on the spot like that. It wasn't the money so much as the principle of the thing. I'd been had again and I didn't like it. I was being taken advantage of because I was a naïve newbie. The lesson was worth something I guessed, but not twenty bucks. I defiantly said "no way, man" and left the room for five minutes. For the rest of the evening, I felt like a cheapskate and wondered if Lester thought that too, but I'd have to wait until Marty and François left to find out. Though I spoke and laughed and feigned friendliness, I was ill at ease and wanted them to leave. A couple of times, I considered pulling two tens out of my pocket, but I was worried about how that might be perceived. If they were pulling my leg, then I was sure they'd have me down for a sucker and I couldn't afford to have that reputation for I was the General Manager. I kept my hand in my pocket.

Boating on Great Slave lake

Al and his fish

Terror in Northern Waters

On the weekend I spoke with Sue at length about the whole situation and shared my doubt that the house would be completed within three months. She was okay with it despite her eagerness to join me, so we agreed to play it by ear and see how things developed over the next few months. One week was not enough to determine whether it would be a good or bad move for us long term. As long as Sue was okay with it, I was willing to stay the course and learn more.

On the Monday, Vince invited me to attend the Spiritual Gathering, which was being held the following week. For hundreds of years, maybe thousands, the Chipewyan Dene had celebrated their heritage in July with a Spiritual Gathering at Fort Reliance, on the eastern shore of Great Slave Lake. To be invited to such an auspicious event was a great honour. I thanked Vince sincerely for the invite and was pleased that Sue and I had made the decision on the weekend to stay, because this serendipitous invite confirmed my gut feel that there was a lot of adventure waiting in the wings for us in Lutsel K'e.

I could have travelled in the Health Centre's chartered float plane, but Miki, the "nurse in charge" at the Health Centre, and I, decided to go instead with Harry Petersen, an Elder, in his boat. Miki didn't like small planes and I wanted a closer look at the land. We also hoped Harry would point out places of interest along the way and reminisce about when he hunted and trapped in those parts when he was a young man. Harry was big and bulky and as strong as an ox, despite his seventy plus years, but he did have a heart condition that Miki said was under control, so long as he took his medication.

Miki was from the Philippines and came to Canada when she was a young lady to study nursing. She had spent most of her adult life being of service to the Inuit and the Dene in remote locations all over Canada's north. I admired her courage and enjoyed her happy disposition. She always brightened up a room when she walked in. She was petite, about five foot two, and weighed maybe a hundred and ten pounds, but what she lacked in body weight, she more than compensated for in guts. The north was not for the fainthearted, particularly if you were only one of two medically trained people in a fly-in community. Many times Miki had to be surgeon and doctor while waiting for the medi-vac plane to arrive.

We would have to take the long way to Fort Reliance, because Harry's boat, a 16-foot aluminum Lund with a 40 hp motor, was too heavy to be portaged. It would be an eight-hour journey instead of five. Miki and I bought the gas and oil for the round trip.

After milling around the dock for over an hour, Harry stepped into the boat, and with an expert eye, strategically selected a piece of luggage. "That one. Gimme that one," he barked in a deep, gruff voice at Miki, pointing a thick finger at a large package on the dock. Miki grimaced. From the dock, we watched Harry place boxes of groceries and square luggage items under the bow and stuff the spaces in between with garbage bags of blankets and pillows. He continued to load the boat with items that shouldn't get wet, moving from the bow to the mid-section, and then placed a huge blue tarp over the load, tucking in the edges to secure it. The old man moved to the back of the boat to load the tents, camping gear and the rest of the luggage that was packed in waterproof bags, as well as two extra cans of gas. He worked his way from the back to the middle, leaving this section un-tarped. In the middle of the boat was a wooden bench for Miki and I. We would have to sit up straight, rest our feet on the tarp and hold onto the bench and sides for stability. On the right, in front of the bench, was a white, plastic kitchen chair for Harry, and in front of him, his customized throttle and control set up. Harry was proud of his boat.

Looking at the heavily laden boat, barely bobbing above the water line, Miki was concerned. She paced up and down the dock. One had to know Miki to appreciate her dilemma. As a nurse, she was safety minded and cautious, but as an adventurer, she was intrepid and resolute. She loved to trek in remote regions of South America whenever she could get away. Harry reassured us that everything was fine. "Are you not concerned?" she asked, looking me straight in the eye.

I pondered her question for a few moments and replied, "Harry is an Elder. He's lived and survived on this land all his life, so I trust him, but you have to feel comfortable and make up your own mind."

With that, she hopped into the boat, plopped down on the bench, wrapped a thick blanket around her shoulders, and with arms folded in a defiant posture, stared straight ahead and commanded, "C'mon then – let's go."

The sky was clear; just a few puffy white clouds billowed overhead when Harry pressed the starter button bringing the engine to life, and pushed the throttle to ease us away from the dock. The lake was calm with little wind but the air was icy cold. I tried folding my arms for added warmth but my bulky life vest prevented me from doing that. Instead I hunkered down into my parka and snuggled into the fleecy layers wrapped around my neck. Our hopes for a guided tour commentary by Harry were immediately dashed – the incessant droning of the outboard motor made all conversation impossible.

We first went northwest to get around Utsingi Point, and then turned east into the North Channel to get to McLeod Bay and on to Fort Resolution. As soon as our little craft turned east, we encountered a frigid headwind. The skin on my cheeks and forehead tightened and the sub-zero wind penetrated my gloves, numbing my knuckles. I pulled a sleeve over my right hand glove to keep in the warmth and tried to do the same with the left, but my coat was too tight. I snuggled closer to Miki for warmth as Harry manoeuvred the boat through channels and shoals. Three hours into the journey, the wind increased in intensity. Our boat began to shake in the churning water and sprays of iced water flew at us when the bow crashed through the big waves. I couldn't see a thing out of my spotted glasses yet I didn't dare release my grip on the side rail to clear them.

Around hour four, we pulled over to the shore of an island for a pit stop. We built a fire, made tea and ate sandwiches. Harry disappeared over a small hill for about ten minutes while Miki and I chatted about the experience and our concerns about the rough waters. Harry reappeared, hurriedly announcing that we had to go fast because the wind was picking up and the waves would get bigger. He rushed past us, jumped into the boat and fired up the engine. We doused the fire, packed the basket and hastily followed. As soon as I had one leg in the boat, Harry let out the throttle and we roared away from shore.

After a few minutes, the engine spluttered and died. We were out of gas. Our boat bobbed erratically in the heavy waves. We gripped the rails. Harry grunted at me, "Pull the plug."

"What?"

"Pull the goddamn plug," he growled.

"What plug?" I yelled back, rattled by his language and tone of voice.

The old salt shook his head. He stormed off his chair, scrambled over the bags to the back of the boat and "pulled the plug" by putting the plug in! He then condescendingly explained, as if I were a five year old, that you pull the plug out when the boat's moving and you put it in when the boat stops. The look on his face said it all. He thought I was useless. I felt useless.

He disconnected the fuel line, switched over to a new gas can and reconnected. We took off at full throttle; a thoroughbred horse exploding out of the starting gate. It all happened so fast. I was ejected backwards onto the camping gear and looking directly up at Harry, who was pinned against the back of the boat. Miki managed to stay seated, gripping the side rails with both hands, as our boat leaned and roared around in a right handed arc. Harry yelled a barrage of instructions at Miki, but they didn't reach her. He resorted to swearing, but his curses froze in the arctic wind and drowned in the wake. Icy torrents smashed over the bow as we crashed through one wave after another. I tried to move sideways, towards the centre of the boat to stabilize it, but I couldn't. Harry, pinned down by centrifugal force, continued to swear at Miki, whose death grip on the side rails was the only thing keeping her in the boat. If she'd only turn around, we might be able to get her to pull back on the throttle, but the little nurse was frozen in a state of shock. Her tiny body bumped up in the air with every wave.

The boat began to make tighter circles and the right hand side began to scoop up water. We were in danger of sinking or capsizing. I was shaking uncontrollably with fear. Our boat, like Harry, was old. I was sure it was going to fall apart any second or slide into the water on the next dip. I prepared myself for the inevitable.

What was I doing there goddamn it? I shouldn't be there. I didn't belong in that godforsaken place. I couldn't see us getting out alive. We needed a miracle.

Harry squirmed around to face the bow. He lowered his weight like a cat stalking prey, tried to crawl forward to grab the bags in front, but they came away in his big hands when he grabbed them. His moving rocked the boat more. My first reaction was to yell at him to stop, to be still, but I knew he was the only one that could save us. Again, Harry tried grabbing the bags. His breathing was laboured, his face flushed – he looked just one beat away from a heart attack. My mind willed him to make progress, but he couldn't get a firm grip. The bags, securely nested when we set off, were now floating. I felt Harry's every move, every inch of progress and every setback. With one last mad lunge in a frantic frenzy, he scampered over the bags, reached past Miki and pulled back the throttle. The boat slowed abruptly and gushed to a stop. We had our miracle.

No one spoke for the balance of the journey. Wet, cold and miserable, I stared straight ahead and longed for the trip to end. The northern version of dusk was descending when we reached shore, three hours later. I jumped into the cold, shallow water with the securing rope, waded to the sandy beach and tied the rope around a rock. I turned around to go back for Miki but she was right behind me, followed by Harry with his arms full of luggage. He put down the boxes, bent down to the earth and motioned for us to join him. He placed some tobacco under a stone. "Now you have good visit," he said, and returned to the boat for the rest of the cargo, as if nothing had happened. I was speechless.

It had been one of the most hair-raising times of my life and I was still shaking. I then realised how fraught with danger the north was, and how men like Harry had learned to live in it. It was no big deal to him. I admired his calmness and his simple acceptance of the dangers in living in that environment.

The Spiritual Gathering

Great Slave Lake washes up onto a half mile stretch of sandy beach at Fort Reliance. Between the waters and the Boreal Forest of spruce and birch is a grassy area, where the Dene pitch their tents for the Spiritual Gathering. It is an idyllic setting for those people of the land. Fort Reliance is a sacred place and The Lady of the Falls, the most sacred of sites, is just an overnight hike away. Elders swear by the miraculous, therapeutic powers of the river waters there and take bottles of it back to their communities to give to the sick and dying. From the air, the Falls looks like a woman lying on her back. The river splits into two at the base, giving the impression of a right and left leg. I immediately thought "Lourdes of the North" when they described it to me, and I smiled at the similarity and how the Dene had assimilated the teachings of the early Christian mission-aries into their culture.

Campers began to arrive on Friday by boat as we did and by chartered float plane from Fort Resolution and Yellowknife throughout the weekend. By Sunday morning, most people had set up camp and settled in.

The Fort McPherson Tent Company, a successful business venture of the Fort McPherson band, located on the Beaufort Sea, made most of the thick canvas bush tents used at The Gathering. The tents were sixteen feet long by ten feet wide and were erected using spruce poles, cut down at the site. A long pole went through the tent loops across the top and sat in the Y of the tripods at each end. The tripod consisted of three spruce poles, roped together. They tied ten foot ropes to the three flaps on each side of the tent, pulled them taut and fastened them to pegs hammered into the ground. On larger tents, they ran poles through the side flaps.

Each tent had a wood burning bush stove, located near the door, on a bed of sand. The stove was about three feet high by two feet wide and two feet deep. It was made of metal, had a door at the front to load the wood, and a flat top, upon which you could place pots to boil water. A tin chimney piece, about eight inches in diameter and connected to the back of the stove, extended upwards for about two feet, bent at a 45 degree angle, and went through a hole in the side of the tent to the outside. The chimney then bent up again at a 45 degree angle and extended upwards past the top of the tent.

Each tent also had an "Indian carpet," created by laying spruce boughs face down and then weaving them together. The carpet gave the tent a homey feeling and filled the air with an aromatic bouquet. It filtered out the dirt and sand providing a warm, soft surface for bare feet. An amazing utilitarian feature, but I wondered about safety – fumes from the fire when sleeping and the possibility of the carpet catching fire from sparks. It looked like an accident waiting to happen but Vince assured me it was normal fare for the north.

I didn't have a northern tent nor a bush stove nor an Indian carpet. I had a two person nylon pup tent, a sleeping bag from Lars and some blankets from the nursing station. The days were mild but the nights were cold. Miki and I had brought our food because we wouldn't be fishing or hunting. We dug a two foot hole in the sandy soil and lowered our coolers into it. The permafrost would keep the food as cold as a freezer at home. Band members went into the bush every day to cut trees to provide us with wood, and to a spring for water.

For most of the morning I wandered around, visiting people with familiar faces. At two o'clock, the community assembled around a large bonfire. Chief Charlie opened the proceedings by speaking of the spiritual significance of the area, and of the sign he received from the Lady of the Falls as he arrived on Friday afternoon. He said the sky to the East was blood red and two puffs of white smoke appeared and went skyward, straight as an arrow. He said that was a sign that the Lady was pleased and it meant that we would have a good gathering. Other speeches followed, mostly in Chipewyan with the odd one in English. They told of visions and of people in the community who had been healed by the waters of the Falls, and they offered thanks to the Creator for giving them this special place. They called upon an elder to say a prayer to officially open the event, and to light the fire. It would continue to burn for the next seven days; the duration of the Gathering.

All able-bodied souls, young and old, lined up in single file and walked slowly around the fire in a clockwise direction. They stopped at a point facing east, said a prayer, and made an offering before taking up a position around the fire. Some Dene were quite demonstrative and held an outstretched arm with a clenched fist at shoulder height while they prayed. Others turned and faced first south, then west and north, stopping at each compass point to recite a prayer. Some offered tobacco, pieces of dried meat or fish or sweetgrass. When all had done their duty, I moved up behind the last person and paid my respects. I listened intently to the crackling of the fire, breathed in the crisp air filled with smoky smells, and savoured the solemnity of the occasion. As I walked around the fire, I experienced a strange sensation. I felt lighter in body weight as if I was floating; as if my legs were moving but they weren't really doing the walking, just as one swings their legs on a swing.

Drummers from the Dettah community in Yellowknife began to beat their drums. The assembled responded, swaying and stepping in time with a sort of shuffling, and forming a conga line that snaked around the fire. As they passed, many nodded politely at me and smiled. I deeply appreciated their friendship. At one point in life, when I was younger, less travelled and thought I knew it all, I would have scoffed at this ritual but now I didn't. Not only was I respectful of their traditions, but their spirituality was beginning to resonate with me. I sensed their connectedness to the land and to all life on it, and their conception of the Creator was beginning to make more sense to me than the existence of a personal God.

Over the next seven days, the Gathering held many events and much visitation was conducted because most people were inter-related by birth or marriage.

Andy and Rosa, friends of Miki, invited Miki and I to go berry picking with them. They had been married for over thirty years and were an exemplary example of a stable, happily married couple. They tended to mind their own business, keep a low profile and smile a lot. Andy was an avid reader and Rosa liked to hunt rabbit and ptarmigan early in the morning before anyone was up. All acknowledged her prowess with a shotgun.

We set off around noon. Andy drove the boat, Rosa brought the picnic basket, Miki provided sandwiches, and I supplied the soft drinks. Although it was less than ten minutes away, just past the beach and around a bend in the river, the berry patch was a totally different world. It was a low lying flat plain, about an acre in size, bordered by stunted spruce trees and full of diverse vegetation. It had a unique natural beauty and goodness. Andy stayed on the boat to read a book.

Rosa gave us a brief orientation of the land. She pointed out the different vegetation and commented on some of their uses to the Dene. She said the blueberry was the predominant berry bush in this patch and that it was at the peak of its season at the moment. She proceeded to identify the cranberry, which was a month away from being ripe; the Labrador tea, which people used for herbal brews; and the spongy sphagnum moss, which Dene mothers used as diapers not too many years ago. Twiggy honeysuckles, rubbery willows, greedy dogwoods and low sprawling junipers with purplish-blue berries vied for space on the land with the blueberries and cranberries. Underfoot, we trod on muskeg and dry, crunchy lichens.

The tour over with, we spread out, and with a focused mindset, got down to the task we had come to do. Picking one berry after another, intently focusing on a six-inch area, and moving the feet a couple of inches at a time, was hypnotic and pleasurable. It was as if time stood still. I don't know how long we were there, maybe an hour, maybe three, before Rosa called out from across the land that it was time to eat.

Miki and I each had about three quarters of a pail, but Rosa had two full ones, which was odd, because I didn't stop picking for more than a few seconds at a time. How did she do it? She must have found the mother lode bush that I was looking for! Andy was pleased to see our satisfied faces and most pleased when he saw Rosa's two full pails.

We spread a blanket on the grass next to the boat and sat down to feast on Rosa's dried caribou and fish, cold bannock and shortbread biscuits, and Miki's ham and cheese sandwiches. Diet Cola and Sprite replenished our body fluids. No one spoke much. We ate quietly, enjoying the serenity and spirituality of the place, as if we were in church. About five o'clock, we returned to the campground and parted company. The berry picking was another special memory to be cherished forever.

After supper, I walked up the beach and noticed a crowd of about fifty people gathering at the water's edge, looking out to sea. I looked but I couldn't see anything. More people continued to arrive. There was a palpable, mysterious excitement in the air. "What's happening?" I enquired of twelve-year-old Caitlin, one of Geraldine's brood, as she raced towards me.

"The canoes are coming," she blurted out, and carried on running, without missing a step, to excitedly join the growing mass of humanity on the beach.

"Canoes, what canoes?" I peered out across the water and scanned the horizon from east to west. There, about a half mile out, or maybe a quarter for it was hard to tell, was the focus of their attention. One, two, three, four distinct black specks were now visible on the light blue water. Well I never! I stood transfixed and watched the specks take on the more discernible shapes of canoes. The throng on the beach were hollering and frantically waving their arms in the air; some used towels as flags; some brandished guns while others just waved their empty hands, stretching their fingers as far and wide as they could to increase their visibility. So absorbed was I in the progress of the canoes, that I didn't notice George Petersen appear by my side until he spoke.

"One of em's my grandson ya know," George said, with a smile that only a grandparent could produce, pointing a thick finger in the general direction of the canoes.

"Where are they coming from?"

"Artillery Lake. There are ten of 'em. Three are youth leaders. They left last Tuesday. Been paddling four days. Gonna meet up with their families for The Gathering."

The throng now numbered at least a hundred merry souls; half in the water up to their waists; some clinging onto babes in arms and hugging towels close to their bodies to keep dry.

Ten athletes in birch bark canoes, frenetically racing to the finish line on a glass-surfaced lake, was what it was all about. Paddling in perfect unison, worthy of an Olympic Gold Medal in synchronized paddling – if there ever was to be such an event – the proud warriors thrust their crafts forward with each stroke, breaking the mirrored surface cleanly, leaving shattered ripples in the wake. What a sight! Although it was 10pm, the sun was still high in the clear, blue sky, which up there, accounted for about ninety-five per cent of the panoramic view. Despite it being "north of sixty," the air temperature was untypically warm enough that only a light jacket was needed.

I gazed in a north-easterly direction, past the canoes towards the opposite shore, and marvelled at the beauty and simplicity of it all. A smooth, slightly undulating ribbon of black boldly outlined the contour of the land against the light sky. A perfect coal-black mirror image reflected in the pancake flat, silvery water. The dazzling white midnight sun spilled sparkling diamonds into the water every second. It was a Kodak picture-perfect moment.

I strolled up to within fifty feet of the gathering and sat down, content to be on the periphery. The sense of personal intimacy of the impending reunion was intense. I was humbled and most thankful to be there to share in this personal celebration. This was not a re-enactment of Dene in canoes for my entertainment. This was for real and it was serious family stuff. I thought of family back home, fast asleep in their beds and completely oblivious to what was happening out there on the beach. And mused about everything else that was happening all over the world, at that very moment, the knowledge of which escapes all except for those present. I found the thought profound but had no idea what it meant, if indeed there was something deeper to consider, and anyway, I didn't have time to think about it because the action was out there on the water.

With each stroke, the young oarsmen leaned forward and pulled harder on their paddles, adrenalized by the thought of the finish line. With each stroke, the eager onlookers grew more animated and vocal; some fired guns into the air as welcoming salvos, making the brave children shout and jump, and the younger, more timid ones, to seek refuge in their mothers' arms. With each stroke, the boats closed in on shore, bringing them ever closer to their reunion with family. Guns continued to blast into the air, seemingly at will, bringing to mind images of Palestinians in the streets, celebrating some victory or other. The jubilant crowd screamed, urging the athletes to paddle faster and faster. The crew heard and responded, and increased the rate at which they dipped their paddles.

When the canoes were within thirty feet of shore, the oarsmen pulled in their oars and let their crafts continue under their own momentum. The boats slowed to a stop and the young men, with strong, but tired limbs, plunged into the water to hasten their reunion. The pack of people left on the sand went wild and moved as one down to the water's edge. Children ran, splashing into the water, fighting off each other to grab the paddles, the holy grails of the Dene gathering. The sailors were welcomed as exuberantly as if they were astronauts returning from a distant planet. There was great hugging and laughing. The pride and happiness in the air was thick and intense. I was deeply moved.

Personal recollections of being reunited with loved ones surfaced from the archives in my heart and appeared in my mind, evoking warm loving feelings. Many times the Dene had surprised me by happenings such as this. In the south, this event would have been sponsored by commercial interests and promoted as an annual significant cultural event, with ever increasing crowds, bussed in from far and wide. There would be safety barriers, fast food stands and vendors selling T-shirts and other memorabilia. And of course, the media would be there capturing images for their nightly news programs. But that's not the way it is with the Dene. They are low key. They don't see events as money making schemes the way we capitalists do. It was refreshing to be amongst them.

The next evening, I went to the pavilion to watch the drum dancing. There was a good crowd in attendance, particularly of Elders. The band brought in five drummers from the Yellowknife Detah band to assist in the festivities, because drumming was essential for events such as this. They drum for the opening and closing ceremonies, for the dancing, as well as for other special events, such as the hand games.

One drummer started beating his drum with two sharp hits, the first one louder than the second, then paused a couple of seconds before hitting the drum again, in a consistent one note beat. One by one, the other drummers joined in. They soon began beating the drums harder and louder and then one drummer started to sing, which was really a chant in the Chipewyan language. The chant was composed of sounds, not words. Melodies were simple, repetitive and lasted for at least ten minutes. One by one, the party-goers got up from their chairs on the edge of the pavilion, sauntered onto the dance floor and started to walk around in a clockwise circle, in a conga chain. They moved their feet with slow, hesitating shuffles, swaying slightly from side to side, feeling the beat vibrate through their bodies. Some joined in the chanting, but most were like me; content to just shuffle, sway and enjoy the moment. People left the dance floor intermittently while others joined in. There was no formal beginning or ending to the dances. I reveled in the dancing and in the socializing with various family groups, who stopped by the pavilion on their evening walk, and took time out to come over and visit with me.

The next evening I went back to the pavilion to see how the Dene hand games were played. The Dettah drummers were up on stage again and about fourteen volunteers, all men, were getting ready to play. I will describe what I think I saw but I'm sure there are nuances to the game, which I missed, and for that, I offer my apologies to the Dene.

The contestants split into two teams of seven per side and sat on the floor opposite each other, at a distance of about four feet. A few, large blankets were spread between them, covering their legs up to their waist. A drummer banged his drum with the traditional two beats to start and the game began. As the other drummers joined in and began to chant, team A put their hands under the blanket and began to sway, contort their bodies and ruffle the blankets with their hidden hands. After a couple of minutes, they brought out clenched fists from under the blanket and crossed their arms. Only one fist contained a stone. An appointed member of team B studied team A and pointed to the left hand. The three players on team A with a stone in their left hand had lost and had to sit out the balance of the game. Wooden sticks were used as counters. Team B gave four sticks to team A for the four remaining players who had a stone in their right hand. The game restarted but with only four players on Team A. The swaying, contorting and ruffling continued as the drummers beat louder and faster while the crowd cheered for their friends. Clenched hands once again appeared above the blanket. The drumming stopped and a hush fell over the assembly. Arms went up into a tight cross-armed configuration, and with serious countenances to confuse the enemy, they waited for the guess. A member from team B deliberated for a few seconds, looked at his opponents for a tell-tale clue, and then announced his guess, at which point, the audience oohed and aahed depending on who they were rooting for, and the trophy sticks were once again given out. Once Team B had correctly guessed all of Team A, the game switched sides, and Team B had to hide the stones. The winning team was the group holding the largest amount of sticks after a predetermined number of games had been played.

As I watched their happy faces and listened to their hearty laughs, I smiled thinking of how simple yet powerful this game was to the Dene, and how much they still enjoyed this pastime, which their forefathers had played for centuries, maybe even for thousands of years.

The Sweat

"Hey Al. Wanna go to the Sweat?"

The voice was deep and raspy. I opened my eyes and squinted at the flap on the tent wall.

"Hey Al, you awake? Wanna go to the Sweat?"

"Who's there?" I snapped, struggling to shed my sleeping bag.

"It's me, Taylor. We're having a Sweat tonight – wanna go? You'll enjoy it.

"Sure. Love to. Thanks for the invite."

"It's at eight. See you there then."

I zipped up my sleeping bag and went back to sleep.

When I awoke, I felt elated that I had been invited to attend the Sweat, a deeply spiritual ritual of the Dene people, and was moved that Taylor, the youngest member on the corporation's Board of Directors, had gone out of his way to personally hand deliver his invite.

After lunch, I went down the beach to find the location of the Sweat. On my way, I noted the three score plus of tents littering the grassy common; the battery of fifty or more small boats bobbing at the water's edge; and the industrious, light-hearted Dene happily doing their camping chores. I listened to the drone of boat motors; the high-pitched whine of chainsaws; the laughs and screams of children playing; and the chants and whoops that intermittently filled the air. I inhaled deeply when strange aromas of wild meat and fish wafted my way. It was a sensory feast.

A half hour later, I came upon a tall, sinewy young man clasping two large stones to his breast. I stopped to watch him stagger over a small bank to a grassy common and go towards a huge pile of wood about a hundred feet away. The woodpile was at least ten feet high by twenty feet across. I followed. The man carefully put down the rocks in an opening in the wood pile, adding to the ones that were already there. He returned to the beach many times for more rocks. Taylor arrived and asked if I had met Eddie, the Spiritual healer's son.

"No, not yet," I replied.

After Eddie had deposited the last rocks, he closed off the opening with logs and brush and lit the bonfire. It blazed into life within a minute, crackling and spluttering. Fire raced through the underbrush kindling, hot embers torpedoed skyward at shotgun speed and soon the intense heat forced us back at least five paces. The exploding dry wood cracked and banged, eliciting oohs and aahs, and rekindled for me exciting childhood memories of Guy Fawkes Nights in Lancashire, England. Eddie said, "The forty rocks will cook for the next six hours," when Taylor introduced me to him. I stared into the flames and basked in the welcome heat for over an hour before moving on to further explore the campsite and to visit people I knew.

Vince and his wife, Patti, fed me a jar of Labrador tea and gave me some dried meat to chew on when I stopped by their campsite. Other Dene that I recognized waved as I strolled by and signalled for me to come over to their camp. But I just smiled and waved back. I was still too new and uptight to sit comfortably with them and their extended families. I felt I had nothing in common to talk to them about and was uncomfortable speaking about my world when asked. This was their Gathering after all; their highlight of the year, and I didn't want to detract from it by talking about me.

Many children hung around the temporary nursing station, which had been set up for The Gathering, because Miki was a good babysitter. She liked to entertain the children by playing CDs and getting them to dance in circles, simulating the dances of their parents. She also made sushi and sticky rice, and once the word was out, kids from all over the camp flocked to the nursing station to sample the unusual food.

At a picnic table, I spread out the UNO game cards and within minutes it was standing room only. Children magically appeared from all corners of the campground. At least twenty kids, ranging in age from five to fifteen, huddled and pushed for space around the table. I shuffled the deck and asked who knew how to play. No one did, but the children caught on fast and were a lot of fun. I enjoyed their silly antics and humour. We played intensively for about half an hour, before boredom set in and other interests became more attractive. The crowd dwindled away leaving only the Madison brothers, Jimmy and Johnny, at the table. I rewarded their passion for the game by giving them the cards. They ran off as happy as prospectors finding gold.

Around six o'clock I hurried down the beach to hang around the Sweat to ensure I wasn't bumped by some late invitee. I tried making light conversation with the other "sweaters" to pass the time, but it was hard work – no one wanted to talk. In the Dene culture, one gets around to talking specifics later; just being in the silent company of someone was perfectly acceptable.

The Sweat lodge was an odd looking structure – half a decorated Easter egg came to mind. The frame, about five feet high and fifteen feet across, was fashioned from bent willow branches. Spruce boughs, carpets, blankets and other light-defying materials were layered on top, ensuring it was as black as pitch inside. The single entrance faced east towards the offering table and bonfire. Inside, a circle of small stones divided the space into two halves; an outer ring for people and a centre area for the heat source. A lush carpet of spruce boughs provided a cushioned seat for the congregation.

Around seven o'clock, Eddie scooped up a hot rock from the bonfire with his shovel, walked around the offering table and entered the Sweat. Full of reverence and care, he gently let the stone jiggle off his shovel onto the open ground. The dutiful, lean Spiritual Healer's son returned to the fire for another rock and repeated this procedure ten times. We were now ready to begin the Sweat. We stripped down to our shorts and left our clothes on the rocky beach with our towels. It was Dene tradition to walk clockwise at spiritual events; to the left of the offering table when entering the Sweat, and around the opposite side of the table after exiting.

I was the fourth of twelve to enter and immediately sat down on the spruce carpet and crossed my legs, one over the other. It was tight: bodies and legs touched as we jostled to get comfortable before the entrance flap was lowered. Lazarus, the revered guest spiritual healer from Saddle Lake, northern Alberta, was the last to enter. His presence was palpable. He had an intense high energy field about his person that I felt as soon as he entered. It was spooky and slightly unsettling. I felt like an apostle at the Last Supper. Once the flap was lowered, it was as black as a coal mine. The veined rocks glowed an eerie deep red, conjuring up images of dinosaur eggs, alive and threatening to hatch any second.

As my eyes adjusted to the dim glow, I began to make out shadowy figures bathed in warm surreal light. I felt joyous anticipation and excitement. The silence intensified my senses. Someone sprinkled sweetgrass and tobacco on the rocks, which hissed, sparkled and filled the air with a heady aroma. Someone splashed water, which instantly morphed into intense, steamy heat. Spiritual leader BJ, whose voice I recognized, began to speak about the Dene and their traditions. He spoke about the Creator and the land and the caribou and gave thanks by chanting and shaking a small leather pouch filled with stones fastened to a stick. I couldn't see the rattle but I knew what it was. Others joined in the chant and there was a refrain, which was repeated many times. I joined in with my best impression of a Dene chant and began to get into the mood.

Lazarus spoke at length about his people, their struggles and their future. He detailed the mystical healing powers of the Lady of the Falls and listed the names of people in the Lutsel K'e community who had been miraculously healed by the holy waters in times gone by. More chanting and singing followed. When the heat became unbearable, someone opened the flap and we all scrambled out eagerly and orderly. We were vaporizing; steam rushed from our bodies straight up into the night sky. No one said a word. I felt at peace and introspective, my mind in a strange, meditative state. Round one had tampered with the spiritual aspect of our being.

Eddie shovelled ten more, much hotter rocks and added them to the pile. We lined up in the same order and in silence, shuffled along behind one another until it was our turn to crawl into the oven for round two. More sweetgrass and tobacco were sprinkled on the rocks, saturating the air with organic vapours and mysterious powers. People began to speak about their lives, about their problems and challenges; many centering on their victory over drugs and alcohol. The speaking was purely voluntary. Long periods of silence occurred between speakers.

I reflected on my own life: Sue, the children, grandchildren, brother and sister in England, friends, and even the people in Lutsel

K'e, whom I'd known for less than a month. Recollections came easy, fast and unprovoked. Clear, vivid mental images of times past magically appeared. I had entered a strange world; a pleasant, non-threatening natural world of sensory exploration. I found it easy to switch between reminiscing and listening to others when they began to speak, as if I had pause and play buttons. Given the hyper-focused state of my sensitivities; listening and concentrating on the speaker's words came easily. The Sweat soon became a sauna with the constant addition of water to the hot rocks. The temperature soared by at least twenty degrees within five seconds. When the heat became intolerable, someone opened the flap and we scrambled out, a little faster this time. This round had tampered with our emotional states as well as intensifying the spirituality aspect of round one.

Some went into the lake to refresh themselves; others sat swaying, humming and chanting to themselves; whilst others stretched out on the ground and closed their eyes. I sat quietly by myself and thought about what was happening. It was surprisingly comfortable sitting half naked in the chilly night air, periodically looking up at the bright night sky while contemplating life, as steam lifted off my body and drifted up into the heavens. My mind was calm and content. No one spoke. I was in the moment and it was blissful.

The apprentice sorcerer added ten more, even redder rocks, and we returned for round three. As soon as the gathering had settled and the flap lowered, the revered holy man announced that this round was to give thanks to the Creator. The great spiritual healer proceeded to speak at length about the Creator giving the aboriginal people a special land to live on, clean water to drink, clean air to breathe, and fish, caribou and other animals to eat, and of how they, the Dene, had been entrusted by the Creator to be the custodians of the land.

My appreciation for the Dene way of life and their beliefs was deepening and I was beginning to more clearly sense the spiritual connectivity they had with the Universe and the land. It was a most peculiar feeling; similar to the relief I used to feel when I got home from work after working in the city all day and replaced my work clothes with just a pair of shorts and a T-shirt. I felt lighter and less encumbered. Lazarus asked us to thank the Creator for the good things He had given us. We verbally expressed our gratitude in unison. Some prayed in Chipewyan, some in Dogrib and other Dene languages and some in English. Some sang praises while others chanted. I felt inclined from old habits to recite the Lord's Prayer, but I resisted, and instead spoke to the Universe about the beauty and wonder of the natural world.

Our gratitude increased in volume and intensity. We chanted with more confidence and purpose now, as if the Dene drummers were there, beating out incantations on their caribou skins, inciting us to pray harder and louder. I was sure there were no illicit drugs involved, but I was as spacey and as weird as I think a person would be after tripping out on LSD. The whole proceedings were bizarre yet astonishingly enjoyable. I relished the strange tongues and talk about Mother Earth and Father Sky, the exotic aromas choking the searing air, and the experience of sharing intimacy with total strangers, whose sweaty semi-nude bodies occasionally, but inadvertently, touched mine. I felt spiritually bonded to my brothers. Once again, the heat drove us out.

Eddie added ten more rocks as we took a breather. We returned for the final round as before but this time with our towels. Lazarus lamented the struggles his people had endured over the years; how the government had taken their land; how the white man's church had taken their children and put them into residential schools for ten months a year; how they were punished for speaking their native languages; how they were told sweetgrass and the drum and their songs and dances were evil and of the pressures put on them to abandon their traditional ways. Lazarus finished his heartfelt discourse by describing how the mothers and fathers had lost their traditional parenting skills.

His oration snapped me out of my reverie and plunged me into a deep paranoid state. My heart beat faster, my breathing quickened and sweat flowed and beaded my brow. Did I not represent these people he was talking about: the colonizers, the white men from the south that came to take over their trap lines and poisoned their families, and the English who tried to remake their children into little Englishmen? Was that why Taylor had invited me? I looked around expecting them to be staring at me, but it was too dark to see their faces. I willed the strangers on my left and right to look at me, if only for a fleeting second. That would prove I was right.

Okay, maybe they were too polite to turn their heads, but I knew what they were thinking. I wanted to disappear, to escape the personal assault, but I just sat there, nervously waiting for the consequences. Why did I feel guilty anyway? Had I not gone there to help, not hurt? Why did I take his remarks so personally? Guilt by association was the only logic I could muster.

My neighbour to the right nudged me with his elbow. He got my instant attention. "Bear grease," he whispered, handing me a tin. A peace offering maybe! The goo was warm and thick like bacon fat. I scooped up a blob and rubbed it into my ankles and worked

another blob into my knees and elbows. The massaging was soothing. My body relaxed and my up-tightness began to melt away. I
dug out another wad, passed the tin to my neighbour on the left,
and continued to rub the exotic paste into the rest of my limbs.
I sensed the fat deeply penetrating my ligaments, lubricating my
tendons and oiling my tissues. My eyelids gently slipped down over
my eyes, and sleep crept up into my body seeking to occupy, but I
stopped it. I needed to stay awake, to be alert and on guard.

I massaged my neck vigorously, kneaded my shoulders with
strong penetrating jabs, and rubbed my oily hands onto my chest
and arms with as much physical exertion as I could summon. My
body was now as pliant as Play-Doh. Sweaty steam droplets dripped
from my eye brows onto the spruce boughs and my head floated
around in some other dimension. I felt great. I thanked the bear
for his gift. Someone splashed more water onto the rocks, making
them angrily spit, hiss and crackle. The air became a sweat bath.
Perspiration dripped off my body continuously like a dripping tap.
Even though the physical pain was excruciating, people still added
more water to the rocks. The air was alive with fire. I could taste
it, smell it and feel it. I was persevering but with much difficulty.
I couldn't think of anything but of how hot it was. How much
longer before someone had the sense to make a move to get out?
The covering of my pores with bear grease had contributed to the
increased level of pain I was experiencing. The feeling of relax-
ation that I had, just a few short minutes ago, disappeared and was
replaced by intense discomfort.

The heat was too much. I couldn't stay focused on what was
being said. My concentration had evaporated with my body fluids.
The only sensation I had was that of the excruciating physical pain

racking my body. I held the towel to my lips to filter and cool the burning but I couldn't do anything about the searing air singeing my ear lobes, kneecaps, ankles and knuckles. Even my chin felt aflame. There was some talking or chanting going on, but so preoccupied was I with trying to breathe that my mind drifted in and out of consciousness. My whole objective was to simply endure and stay awake. Someone finally made a move and raised the flap. Blinding white daylight and frigid northern air rushed in, instantly morphing the steam into dense vapours that rushed out and up into the crystal night sky. We held our breath and scrambled to the exit, as if escaping a burning building. I felt proud and pleased that I had endured.

As I walked home, dazed as a zombie, I felt like a warrior of sorts. I sensed that something spiritual had happened and that I'd never be the same again, but I didn't know specifically in what way. It was just an intuitive feeling that I had changed. I crashed into my sleeping bag, slept until ten the next morning and awoke, feeling refreshed and ten years younger.

A few days later I returned to the community with Miki in the Health Services plane. We checked up on Harry and he arrived safe and sound, as did all of the other campers.

Drying caribou

Living Out of a Suitcase

"Hi Guys, Gerry here. Sorry for the short notice, but you gotta move out by the end of the day. The teachers are coming in tomorrow. I only found out last night. Sorry." That was the shocker on the answering machine from the school principal that we woke up to. Life was always full of surprises in Lutsel K'e and mostly they were of the unpleasant variety. We had been led to believe that the teachers were coming back the following week. I told Vince when I got to work what Gerry had said and asked him where I would live. He smiled and said, "You'll have to find a place!" I assumed the

Corporation would find a place for its General Manager, but really, the Corporation didn't exist; it was just Sunrise and I.

And the General Manager's house, Bob advised, was still at least six weeks away from being ready. Sunrise thought she could find me a room with somebody in the community but I was uncomfortable with that idea. I was still too new for that kind of arrangement. I went home and discussed the situation with Lester. He'd worked out a deal with Norton Brokengoose to house sit his home until Christmas, because Norton was going out of town for the balance of the year. It was perfect timing for Lester, because his contract was up at the end of the year, and he was going home to Boston for Christmas. He suggested I call Lars to see if he could help. "Yeah. I've got a room you can have. How about four hundred a month?" Lars said when I called.

"No problem. Can I bring my stuff over now?"

"Sure."

I packed up what little I had and moved in. It was great to only have a few boxes to move and no furnishings to struggle with. Lars' house was at the end of a lane below the big hill on the north shore; about a ten-minute walk to my work. He'd built the house himself, as he had the cabin structure on his boat, from surplus housing materials he'd found at the landfill. It looked like a regular home from the outside and from the inside too, if one took a cursory glance, but there were serious deficiencies. For starters, there was no inside toilet. A shower yes, but no john. We used the "honey bucket" in the small wooden shed located just outside the front door, which consisted of a toilet seat on a can over a garbage bag. The hut was not heated nor was it lit. You did your business in the cold and in the dark. There were other deficiencies too. The little

Danby bar fridge was scarcely big enough to hold Lars' meagre rations, let alone mine. So once again, I had to postpone all ideas about cooking Indian until another day.

"I don't have a bed for you," Lars said as we moved into the bedroom. It was a nice room. No bed, dresser, drapes or pictures; indeed there was nothing. But it was a nice, clean room as far as rooms go and it had a little window that let in the light. I stacked my three boxes of personal effects up against one wall, set down two boxes of groceries at the other end, piled my clothes neatly on the floor, laid a sleeping bag on a half inch blue foamie in the centre of the room, and placed my pyjamas inside to keep warm. As I left the room, an inner voice whispered in my ear, "This is not good Al." "Sure it is," I countered, convincing myself that it would be just like camping in the south in the fall.

Sometime during the night, I woke up shivering and added my parka to the pile of clothes on top of me. When I awoke I was frozen and stiff. It was an effort to stand up straight and get going. "What have you got for insulation," I asked Lars at breakfast.

"Batts, but probably not enough." He smiled apologetically. "It's the permafrost. It makes the floors cold you know." I knew only too well. He was up off the floor on a bed! I should have got a room in someone's home after that first night, but I didn't because I felt I needed my own space and privacy; my own type of environment to relax in when I came home in the evenings. I vowed to tough it out and to put pressure on Bob to complete at least one room in the General Manager's house so that I could move in. From that night on, I layered all of the blankets I possessed under the sleeping bag, donned thick, woollen work socks, long underwear, fleeced sweat pants and wore a sweater to bed. It seemed to do the trick, but I was also losing weight and that aggravated the hardship.

I was eating only because I knew I had to, and not from any great appetite or desire to rustle up something. My usual fare for supper was beans on toast or a can of Spaghetti-Os. Kitchen facilities were limited. Lars only had a coffee pot, toaster, two-burner stove, microwave, two saucepans that were in their prime twenty years ago, and two plastic plates. He mostly cooked on the outside BBQ, but unlike him, I wasn't motivated enough to barbecue in minus ten degree weather. He ate differently too. He chewed on dried meat and fish mostly, and I never saw him put together a proper meal with his pans and stove. Even when he barbecued, he just tore off pieces of meat and ate them while standing and talking. "Don't you want potatoes or peas with that?" I suggested. He smiled and shook his head. I think that's what happens when you've been in the north for seventeen years!

On the fourth day, Lars said, "I don't know how to tell you this Al, but you've been peeing in the honey bucket and it makes the bag too heavy to carry down the lane. You'll have to go in the bushes from now on – same as me."

"What? Good God! What a pain in the ass it was to get up in the middle of the night, put on every piece of clothing I owned, and now he wants me to stumble around in the bushes on the hill in the dark to take a leak. "That's insane," I replied. I knew, from previous conversations, that he was sensitive to the culture shock I was experiencing, and I could tell by the pained look on his face, when he made his request, that he felt bad for having to ask. As I didn't want to touch, let alone lug, the "poo" bag anywhere, I willingly agreed to his request. I cut back on the amount of fluids I drank during the day and stopped drinking totally after supper to minimize nightly visits to the bush. But even so, there were times when I had to go.

It was horrible. Most nights were now in the minus twenty and thirty range. As soon as I opened the door, the cold blasted me in the face and penetrated my clothing. It was a race to see how quickly I could do my business versus how quickly the cold could bring down my body temperature, and the cold always won. And then I couldn't go back to sleep for a long time – not until my body temperature warmed up to normal and I stopped shaking. What did help, however, was my imagining that my sleeping bag was a warm bed, the hard floor a firm mattress, the fleecy clothing around my chin, flannel sheets and the heavy load of clothing on top of me, a thick duvet. I was continuing to learn about the power of the mind and trying to use it to my advantage.

Once again, my ability to adjust to circumstances when needed amazed me. I had been in the community just five weeks and to my mind, I was taking everything in my stride and to be honest, I was proud of roughing it, of being a pioneer of sort. I was surprised and pleased with my resourcefulness and resilience, but my patience with Bob was ebbing fast by the day. In July, he said he'd be sure to have the house ready for me before he left the community in mid-September. This was important because we both knew there was no one else in the community who could take over. And based on that situation, I was approving vast amounts of overtime for him and his work crew.

"Now," he said with a smile, "It looks like it might be October before it's finished!" Was he purposely dragging his feet to piss me off? He always seemed sincere when he apologized for the delays and slow progress, but sometimes I wondered whether he was just yanking my chain. Was there no one I could trust?

I began visiting the work site at least once a day in the hope that my presence would speed things up, but it didn't. Bob always had a plausible excuse why this and that wasn't completed as requested: he was waiting for a part to come in from Yellowknife, or one of his crew was sick, or he didn't have the right tools. All I could do was to accept his alibis and cross my fingers that there would be more progress tomorrow. Next month, the night temperature could drop to forty five below. I was unsure of my breaking point but sensed it wasn't far away.

The next Saturday, Lars went to Yellowknife on a week-long training course. I tried to light the wood fire in the same way that he did, but all that happened was a lot of smoke billowed into the room. Lester looked up the chimney, but couldn't figure out what the problem was. I called Lars. He wasn't helpful. He said he'd look at it when he returned. So, I forgot about having a fire and resigned myself to watching TV wrapped in a parka and going to bed early. Sleep was a great panacea. I now wonder why I didn't sleep in his bed, but at the time, the thought did not occur to me. To me, his room was private and off limits. I was only a boarder and my strict, conservative English upbringing ensured that the thought of violating his privacy by sleeping in his bed would never cross my mind.

On Wednesday, I visited Miki because my cold was getting worse. She gave me a physical and her diagnosis. I had pneumonia. She loaded me up with pills and strongly suggested I stay at the nursing station until I completely recovered. When I hesitated, she insisted that I not sleep at Lars' house again because I'd surely die if I did. The hospital bed was heavenly. I dozed in and out of consciousness for the rest of the day and had the most wonderful dreams, but of what I cannot now recall. I just know they were blissful.

I felt a little better when I woke up on Thursday, and on Friday, staggered off to work, even though I was still sick. Why did I go? I don't know. Strong work ethic I suppose. I returned to the nursing station two hours later, went back to bed, and slept for most of the weekend. I did venture out Saturday morning though to get a little fresh air and a few things from the store. As I walked back to the nursing station, I sensed that something was different. People whom I hadn't yet met smiled knowingly at me when I passed. It was the oddest feeling. On the way home I met Alex, the youngest member of the Fire Crew.

"How's the nurse? You taking good care of her I hear." I laughed, shrugged it off and carried on walking. But then I met Max, another of the Fire Crew. I was just about to disappear into the nursing station when he caught up with me at the door. "Keeping the nurse happy, I hear?" he smirked, and asked such personal questions I wouldn't repeat to anyone. "Fuck off," I said, and with that I disappeared into the nursing station. Not only was I physically sick, but now I was emotionally upset too. I just wanted to get the hell out of there. Why stay? What sort of masochist was I? I didn't tell Miki what Alex and Max had said, but she no doubt would have been teased by her contacts too.

Though still groggy and weak from the pills and illness, I decided on Monday to go to work, if only to quell the rumours. Around ten, I stepped outside onto the office porch for a cigarette. That's when I met Joe. He was on the front porch of his house, which was located directly across the street. He called out and beckoned me over. Joe was from Sault Ste Marie in Ontario and was Julie's partner. Julie was from the Moose Cree First Nation band in Moose Factory in northern Ontario and had just assumed the role of the Senior Administrative Officer for the Lutsel Ké Dene band. They were both in their mid-forties, had met a year ago on the internet, and you could see by their gleaming smiles that they were still in the honeymoon stage of their relationship, and were having the same great adventure in Lutsel K'e as I was.

Joe was about five foot eleven, slim, but with a noticeable paunch around his midriff, which probably added at least ten pounds to his body weight. His rough, full brown beard, which glinted orange in the sunlight, gave him the look of a lumberjack. Julie was maybe five foot four, compactly built but not overweight. They had been in the community for three weeks. Not long, but long enough to be in on the gossip. Joe smiled knowingly when I introduced myself as the Development Corporation's General Manager. He knew exactly who I was and had heard the rumours too.

I gave him some background information on myself, told him that Sue would be coming soon, and that I was in an embarrassing predicament because I had nowhere to sleep other than at the nursing station. He offered me their extra bedroom for the same $400 and invited me to eat with them if I shared the grocery bills. He would do the cooking. I offered to share the culinary duties but he said no; they liked to eat right at five when Julie came home, and besides, it gave him something to do in the afternoons. I then asked if he cooked curries. "Oh God no, we don't eat spicy foods." I couldn't believe it. My longing for a spicy curry was getting so out of hand that I was even considering flying into Yellowknife just to eat at the Thai restaurant.

I called Sunrise and told her that I was taking the rest of the day off to get better. I brought my things over from Lars' house, put my personal effects in the back room, clothes in the bedroom and what was left of my groceries on the kitchen shelves. Unlike my bedroom at Lars', this room had a single bed, three-drawer dresser, clothes closet and a window with heavy drapes.

After a little chat with Joe, I took my leave and went to my room because my eyelids kept dropping, and I couldn't stay focused on what he was saying. I slipped beneath the warm, inviting flannel sheets, pulled the thick comforter up around my neck, and snuggled into the oversized white fluffy pillow, just as I had imagined when I lived at Lars' house. Wishes do come true. Sometimes.

Joe apparently called me for supper at five and checked on me throughout the evening, but I didn't wake until seven the next morning. Joe and Julie's house was warm and comfortable, and because it was across the street from work, I got to stay in bed until eight thirty every morning. I could shower, eat breakfast, leave the house at eight fifty eight and be at work at eight fifty nine, two minutes before anyone else. What a great situation. I used to have to get up at six thirty in the south to get to work for eight thirty.

With Miki's magic pills and Joe's stick-to-the-ribs down-home cooking, I recovered quickly. In fact it was obvious I was recovering well because I was putting on weight. We ate a roast every night, accompanied by delicious thick gravy, buttered mashed potatoes and creamed corn or peas.

Managing Difficulties

Managing the Firefighting contract for the last eight weeks had been the most challenging aspect of my job so far. I was greatly relieved that it was over and the Fire Crews had disbanded for the year. What I thought was going to be straightforward turned out to be exceedingly stressful. The entire brigade, from Supervisor to Crew Boss to Crew, behaved immaturely and irresponsibly, as far as I was concerned, because not one of them could make it to payday without an advance. How pathetic was that? Alex was the first to ask, three days into the contract. He said he had some bills to pay that couldn't wait. I felt sorry for him, but was mindful that if I gave him an advance I would be opening the floodgates. Then Mathew and Albert came to see me on the fourth day, desperately pleading for cash – even suggesting that I lend them money personally, secured by what they had earned. I consistently said no to every request.

Sunrise sided with them and couldn't see why I had a problem. Working a few days and then getting paid for it seemed to be the "norm" in Lutsel K'e. They continued to pressure me with every excuse in the book, but as far as I was concerned, the seemingly financial chaos in their lives was self-inflicted. I thought that by now, these grown men would have learned how to budget their financial affairs and to even put a little away for a rainy day. I wanted to help them become financially responsible so I took a firm stand and even used the opportunity to lecture them on money management.

I called a special Board meeting in week two of the contract to get the directors approval on a new policy of no payroll advances, unless the money was needed for medical purposes, or if the employee was travelling on a payday. One would think that should have fixed the problem, but it didn't. It made things a little easier, because I could now say that my job was to enforce company policy, and if I didn't, I could lose my job. But the reality in the north was different from the reality I was used to in the south. The northern reality went something like this: Employees have a right to their earnings regardless of when payday is! In other words, I was expected to pay for this and that for them, out of their earnings, because I owed them the money and they didn't have a bank account or a credit card to handle the transaction. This included calling vendors, ordering goods and arranging payment on their behalf.

I mulled over this logic and to my surprise, found their reasoning to be sound. They were right. Just because it was more convenient and cost effective for us, the company, to pay wages once every two weeks, that didn't justify us in denying them access to what they had legitimately earned if they were in need of the money. I reversed my position on the issue and began to agreeably comply with all of their requests, but it was taxing. When Tundra, the Fire Crew radio operator, mother of three little ones and the fiery spokesperson for the Fire Crew, called me the day before she was leaving for the Spiritual Gathering at Fort Reliance to ask that I call the Yellowknife Co-Op store, order her a tent, two sleeping bags and a stove, and to make arrangements to have them flown in on the afternoon plane, I stopped what I was doing and happily made the arrangements.

Assisting the community by helping them out of difficult personal situations was apparently a required but unwritten expectation of the General Manager. I knew they appreciated my efforts but most people didn't know how to express it. Very few said, "Thanks for helping Al," and that was okay. I was becoming more comfortable in handling oddball requests and even began looking forward to being of assistance wherever and whenever I could. To my amazement, I was enjoying being of service. In retrospect, I appreciated that they had challenged me to think through the inappropriateness of a policy that had clearly benefited the company to their detriment.

But I still had a problem with their behaviour. The Fire contract was only eight weeks long, yet, for eleven positions, I had to hire a total of twenty-one people over a two-month period. As one crew of five ended their weekly shift, they'd fly to Yellowknife to party at the "Strange Range" – the Gold Range hotel, for two days. Some would invariably not make it back for their next rotation, resulting in my having to find qualified replacements for them the morning of the shift as our contract with the federal government required that we provide a full complement of qualified employees at all times. I had to drive around town asking men on the street if they had been trained as "firefighters," and if they had, did they want a job for the day.

I have to be honest and tell you that when this happened on the first shift rotation, I was livid and wasted no time in writing stern warning letters to the individuals saying that they'd be fired if it happened again. But this didn't stop the occurrence from happening on every shift rotation, because going to Yellowknife with money in your pocket to party was a tradition. The Fire Crew looked forward to it greatly. That's why many of them worked in the first place. I followed through on a few warning letters and officially fired a few individuals, only to rehire them a couple of weeks later, because I needed them. There were only so many trained firefighters in the community to choose from.

In August, we exported one crew for two weeks to fight the fires in Saskatchewan. They were sent home two days early by the government by helicopter. There were problems on their first day; the crew complained that their food was not as good, and their showers not as hot as those provided to crews from other parts of Canada. They said this was because management didn't like the Chipewyan Dene down there! I think there was much more to the situation than a simple case of paranoia, but that was how it was officially reported to me. The straw that broke the camel's back and resulted in their premature termination was when they refused to fight a fire in the rain. They said they were trained not to fight a fire in the rain! Regardless of the facts, they obviously had a difficult time taking direction and had a different opinion on what constituted employer/employee relationships.

On payday, they appeared in my office en masse wanting to know why they were two days short in their pay. "You don't get paid for those two days because you didn't work them. We didn't get paid, so we can't pay you," I replied. They left my office disgruntled. Jake, the most senior and experienced firefighter, who acted as the Fire Crew Supervisor for most of the season, got drunk and hounded me relentlessly the next day. Even though the community was officially dry, alcohol was available on the black market; some people brought it in on their sleds from Yellowknife and sold it to supplement their income.

"Where's ma pay. You owe me two days," he demanded from the visitor's chair he occupied in my office. He came in around nine, shortly after I had started work, slumped himself in the chair and went to sleep. Every once in a while, he'd wake up and drawl, "When you gonna pay me?" I politely repeated my reasoning the first few times he asked, but he didn't hear because he had dozed off again. Every fifteen minutes or so for the first couple of hours, I asked him to leave but he just sat there. I made phone calls and worked away on the computer, but no matter what I did, he showed no signs of stirring let alone departing the office.

Around eleven thirty, I got up and told him that I was leaving and asked him to make sure he closed the office door when he left. This got his attention, but he wasn't done with me. He followed me to the Co-op, mumbling the same refrain as he quickened his step to stay up with my brisk walk, and then he followed me around the store, aisle by aisle. He waited for me at the checkout, as the teller rang through my purchase, and trundled behind me as I returned to the office. I stopped at the front door to the office and told him that he was not going to be allowed to enter. I stayed there with him until he got the message and went home.

A few times I thought about calling the RCMP to come get him and put him in the drunk tank, but I decided to tough it out, and I'm pleased that I did. It proved to him and to the others, who were witnesses to the goings on, that I would not be intimidated by such behaviour. The surprising outcome was that from that day forward, he was always most respectful, regardless of whether he saw me in Lutsel K'e or on a street in Yellowknife. I smiled to myself and was pleased with the intuitive way that I had handled the situation. I had just relaxed and gone with the flow, and that was a major change in behaviour for me.

On September 7th, Bob advised that he would have all of the rooms finished, except for painting, by the end of the month. I called Sue and gave her the good news. We knew this didn't mean the house would be ready to move into at month's end, but it was a watershed mark. We decided that it was time to list our property for sale, and to think seriously about when she would come out.

I flew out the next day to go to Quality Furniture in Yellowknife to buy the furnishings for the house. I met Neil, a bright, young salesperson, who came north two years ago from Halifax, Nova Scotia, for a change of scenery. He loved it up there and vowed he'd stay for the rest of his life. After a half hour of browsing, I told Neil I was ready to order. He walked through the store with me, aisle-by-aisle, item by item, writing down code numbers and colours, as I pointed them out. Within an hour, I had the three bedroom house fully furnished with the large items: beds, dressers, lamps, pictures, coffee and end tables, TV, entertainment unit, sofa, love seat, dining room table and chairs. Not only did Neil offer to arrange for the goods to be shipped to Lutsel Ké on the next barge with Joe Mercedes, the barge operator, but he also offered to package the smaller purchases I intended to make and put those on the barge too. He even drove me to and from Wal–Mart, and waited in his car for over an hour while I went on the shopping spree. Now that is what I call supreme customer service.

On September 22nd, Joe Mercedes shunted his barge into Lutsel K'e for the last time in the season. Joe helped me load the furnishings onto the back of the pickup truck and take them up and into the house. It took five trips. We placed all of the goods in the centre of rooms and covered them with plastic so Bob could finish painting.

Also on the last barge, were two lifts of two by four lumber for the surveyor stake operation. Production would continue through the winter months, but unlike previous production runs, this time it would be at a healthy profit because the crew had agreed to work on a piecework basis versus being paid hourly rates. We used the bonus plan on the last three weeks of production and surprisingly, employees made around seven dollars more per hour than their regular rate, and the company made a profit. Ecstatic with their new earnings, the crew questioned me on how it was possible for the corporation to pay them more. All I could surmise was that in the past, a lot of wages were paid for hours never worked.

So why was I still there? Everyone asked that – the cops, nurses, teachers and even some of the community! They told me that they wouldn't have stayed. They policed, they nursed, they taught, they had real jobs. Julie and I worked with the community on a daily basis, on a very personal level. As Julie was aboriginal, it was easier for her in some respects, but I was "a white guy from the South." All I could say was that I came north for an adventure; for an opportunity to contribute and build something and for personal growth. And I felt that I was actually achieving all of those things. Sure, some situations were traumatic and emotionally distressing, but all in all, I was thoroughly enjoying myself. And most importantly, I believed that I was making a difference: to the community, to the employees, and to the well-being of the Corporation. I just needed more time to make more things happen.

I must share with you though, that at times, I did get depressed and wondered if I was okay in the head. I questioned whether I was martyr or masochist, because every day I perceived the insanity to be getting worse. Yet I would go home, have a good sleep, and return to work, more determined than ever to make progress. It was the strangest situation one could ever imagine. I had this feeling that it was my destiny to be there, and I was trying to live life more intuitively now. I wanted to stay the course, but sometimes I felt that it was more than I could handle. I had a sense too that I was changing on a personal level, but I couldn't quite define how. I sensed I was becoming more fluid, more tolerant and less rigid in my thinking, and that change pleased me. It felt good.

Construction by Trial and Error

I pushed Bob hard to get as much of the house finished as he could before he left the community at the end of the month, but daily setbacks slowed his progress. He came to the office every morning with a list of materials to buy because he couldn't find them. All materials to build the house, down to the last nail, had been sent to the site in the shipping containers, which Bob had emptied, and spread the contents out on the side of the driveway, to verify that everything had been received, as well as to be able to find what he needed, but there was no way to secure the site from theft. Items disappeared daily and many materials, such as the drywall, deteriorated in the elements. I wasn't surprised that items, such as the decking lumber, the bath, shower fittings and toilets had disappeared, but when Bob couldn't find the three mammoth picture windows for the front of the house, I was gobsmacked. In the matter of a few months, the community had obviously upgraded their homes as well as their cabins out on the land in a big way. No one said anything of course.

Procuring materials on credit was another problem because the company had a poor credit history. Only one hardware supplier in Yellowknife gave us credit and only because I promised to pay them in thirty days. If he didn't have the part, I bought it from another supplier with my personal Visa card and got reimbursed later.

Another problem was the electrical and plumbing work. I contacted every plumbing and electrical company in the Yellowknife Yellow Pages and put the word out on the street that we were desperately in need of these trades-people, but to no avail. They were all too busy or unwilling to come to Lutsel K'e.

The company Directors held me responsible for the delay and for the escalating costs, but I had no recourse but to continue buying what Bob said he needed and to continue paying the time sheets he turned in.

Joe, Julie's husband, now worked at the site full time Glen, a plasterer from the East coast, was in the community working on the four homes that were being built for the band, and was moonlighting for us in the evenings; taping, mudding and painting whatever walls Bob could finish. When Glen showed me a pair of foot high, metal stilts that he said he put on to plaster ceilings, I told him that I'd have to see him to believe him. He was a mountain of a man: six foot four at least and over two hundred and fifty pounds I'd guess. I couldn't see the metal contraption holding up a person so big but it did. Joe said he looked like an elephant on ice skates.

Glen on stilts

G.M. House – driveway

The construction was a disaster. The house was designed to sit on a square of I-beams mounted on pilings, because the land was rocky and uneven. But the pilings did not line up in a straight line, necessitating the welding of brackets to the pilings to catch the I-beams. With that problem solved, there was another challenge: the I-beams under the back half of the house, the side that looked out towards the road, were shorter than the I-beams under the front half, which overlooked the lake. To compensate, Bob built two "pony" walls out of two by fours, about eighteen inches high. The back half of the house sat on these "pony" walls, but it was not a good solution. The house swayed slightly from left to right when you walked through from front to back, and as I would later learn, shake violently when the clothes dryer tumbled through its cycles!

Bob had done the best he could under the circumstances and there was no one to blame but myself. He didn't profess to be a house builder, nor did he have the blueprints to work from. I couldn't locate the previous General Manager nor the name of the architect, and I only found a copy of the blueprints in August, in the old Hudson's Bay warehouse that the company used for storage of surplus materials.

Another serious problem was the unnecessary cutting of the preformed panels, which significantly increased the overall cost of the house. The house was designed to be constructed by gluing together foam panels, which were pre-cut to size. The panels had the appropriate cut-outs for the windows and doors. It should have been a simple procedure to glue A to B, B to C and so on. When the first couple of pieces didn't fit, someone took a chain saw and made them fit, and from that point on, need I say more?

I will. The result was that the roof didn't have any eaves, so "ladders" had to be built and added to the roof, as best they could, but they weren't straight. The fascia had to be cut in many places to compensate and then nailed to the eave to make it fit. The inside walls weren't built to specification so the custom fabricated kitchen cupboards didn't fit. Joe changed the configuration of which cupboard went where to maximize cupboard space, but that resulted in having two cupboards left over and some vacant kitchen wall space.

The master bedroom should have had a cathedral ceiling to work with the fresh air unit that was to be mounted in the attic crawl space, to provide the home with fresh air. The unit was designed to draw in fresh air, when the kitchen and bathroom exhaust fans were activated, warm it up and circulate it through the bedroom and the kitchen. This was critical because of the airtight properties of that type of glued panel structure. Bob had built the master bedroom with a normal dropped ceiling, rendering the air freshener unit useless. It sat in the attic, waiting to be discovered by some future tenant.

The walls in the house weren't straight either, as could clearly be seen when looking down the hallway from the entrance to the other side. If an outside contractor had built the home, I'd still be in court suing for incompetence. One thing was for sure and that was the home had lots of character; lots of humorous peculiarities to point out to guests and lots to laugh about, particularly when it was windy and the house swayed as you poured cups of coffee and handed out cake to guests. Bob left the community at the end of the month and Joe replaced him. Joe had five guys working for him; two steady and the three casuals.

Finally in October, I got an electrician from Yellowknife to come to Lutsel Ké to complete the wiring. I showed him the fresh air unit and asked what we could do about it. He smiled and said, "Leave the front door open for half an hour every day!" I also secured the services of a plumber to work on the house over the Christmas holidays.

In retrospect, I realized that I didn't get involved enough or try harder in the early days of the project. And the reason for this was because I had no experience in building a house nor did I have the confidence to manage a project such as this. I didn't know what to do, so I put my trust in Bob, and delegated the responsibility for completing the house to him.

I told Sue that the house would be ready for us to move into after the Christmas holidays, and brought her up to speed on what events had taken place, what I was doing and some of my thoughts and feelings about what I had learned. She listened but she couldn't relate to much of it. Lutsel K'e was such a different world than the one she lived in. All she said was, "Are you sure you want to stay?"

"Sure I do. Where else would I go? What else would I do?"

"Just checking," she replied.

"You'll like it once you're here," I reassured her. "Just takes a little adjustment at first to get used to the way things are, but I know you can do it," I replied.

Over the last few months, I had sensed in our phone calls that we were growing apart, and the more I told her about the place, the less interested she seemed in coming. I was going home for Christmas and hoped that our house would sell by then so that we could come out together and make a fresh start in the New Year.

No Man's Land

Snow machines began to make an appearance, their summer mantles were being removed and their engines revved back to life. One could sense the excitement in the air with the approach of winter. This was the Dene's most revered season; the time of year for the taking of fresh caribou, which more than anything defined the Dene of the Northwest Territories. Until they settled in communities such as Lutsel K'e, as recently as fifty years ago, the Chipewyan Dene were a nomadic people, following the caribou, totally reliant on them for their survival. They followed the 400,000 strong Beverly herd as it migrated north to the Barren Lands in the spring for calving, and then south to the shelter of the Boreal Forest in the fall. Sometimes the caribou cluttered the Lutsel K'e airstrip preventing aircraft from landing on their first approach.

Even today, the Dene of Lutsel K'e still get most of their protein directly from the land, principally from the caribou and fish; both fresh and dried; their carbohydrates from the bannock (the Dene bread) and vitamin C from the berries they pick in the fall. But their lifestyles have changed dramatically in the last fifty years, resulting in many problems. They can't go back to the way life was. They must move forward and complete the transition, as best they can.

The treaties they signed with the Government of Canada gave them free health care, education, social services and subsidized housing, but those rights necessitated that they settle in communities rather than roaming the land, and the price they've paid has been the change in their lifestyle. It seemed to me, that in many ways, they were floundering in a no man's land. They were trying to live in the "white man's world," because the government had pushed them to do so, and because they were attracted by the materialism of the south – the cars, boats, snowmobiles and ATVs – but I sensed that their ingrained traditional value systems created conflicts for them when they tried to function in this new environment. As the "white business man," I represented that new environment, and so it was no surprise that I would encounter conflicting philosophies as I went about my business.

I'd now been there four months. I'd settled in and was beginning to be viewed as a quasi-resident, with a resulting decrease in pressure and stress. They knew me and I knew them. I got along well with everybody, and always attracted a friendly nod of the head and a shy smile from the wizened faces of the Elders, as they went about their business.

Unlike the younger generation of Dene, the Elders were generally spry. They walked fast and at a steady pace. They took long, deliberate strides, keeping up a consistent speed, regardless of terrain, their upper bodies and heads bobbing forward with each stride, like the caribou they hunted. It was the most unusual gait that I had ever seen. I was beginning to better understand their way of thinking and had gained a deeper appreciation of the differences between our cultures. The Spiritual Gathering was where I first noticed how at ease and happy they were when they were on the land, compared with how uptight and stressed they were when they were in an office. They were a gentle people, just looking to be happy, as we all are, in our own way, who generally avoided confrontation and complication and wanted to be free to come and go.

One of their philosophies, which I was reminded of time and time again, and which I thought was responsible for much of their difficulty, was their "live today, don't worry about tomorrow" credo. For thousands of years they'd been independent thinkers; living in a simple world and daily reliant upon the land, the weather and the seasons. Their life's rhythm had been anything but a Monday to Friday, nine to five routine. When they arose in the morning, they "felt" the day and then decided what to do. This was basic to their nature. Worry didn't seem to be a part of their daily mindset, as it was mine. By contrast, it was easier for me to get up and be punctual for work, having been conditioned in a society that worked a regular Monday to Friday.

Their reluctance to plan ahead created major chaos for them and for their employers, in work related settings. What I initially viewed as unreliability, I now considered to be more to do with them not wanting to make a commitment today for tomorrow. When I pushed for a commitment they would give me one, and I think that at the time, they honestly intended to keep it, but when tomorrow came they felt differently about the day and what they wanted to do. I witnessed that with both work and family commitments; a brother agreeing to babysit tomorrow for his sister, but then declining in the morning, because it was a sunny day and he wanted to work on his snow machine, and his sister accepting this logic as being "normal and reasonable" behaviour. Some men, who tried working at the mines on a two-week in, two-week out basis, had simply quit and said it was not for them. Others hung in there, because the money was good, but for many, this structured lifestyle and bloated pay cheque resulted in many personal and family problems.

I thought long and hard about our cultural and philosophical differences and the process made me realise just how far we, in mainstream society, had strayed from the natural world in fashioning our way of life, compared to that of the traditional Dene, who live and breathe in unison with the rhythms of life. We get a taste of the freedom and peace that they enjoy when we get out of the city to go camping in a rural setting, or go to a beach for a walk on the sand and a swim in the water; our body energies resonate differently when we are in nature. I found I could now empathise with them on a deeper level on how difficult and stressful it must be when they try to live the way we do.

Another major difference was their approach to money. To them, money was for spending; you earned it, you spent it, and you had the best time money could buy with it. And when it was gone, you started over and got some more. No one was concerned about RRSP's, or what they'd live off if in their old age. They'd live off the land and their children. They didn't worry about whether they would have enough money for their old age. Most people in the community didn't even have a bank account, or a credit card.

Matt, the Dene who gave me the fish filleting demonstration, said to me one day, "The difference between you and me is that you live off your pay cheque. I live off the land!" That got me thinking about money and I realized what Matt was saying. I thought about how different our societies were. Mine had evolved and still revolved around money; his had evolved and still revolved around nature. Perhaps the ideal society would be a blend of the two? Man invented money. It wasn't a natural phenomenon.

No other life species on the planet depended on money for its survival and enjoyment of life, yet in our society, money has become larger than life, and every strata of our society, from individuals to corporations to governments, spend most of their waking hours obsessing on how to get more if it. How insane and dysfunctional was that? Money does have a purpose of course, but it seemed to me that it had gone way past the point of what it was designed for. I could now see why Matt and the other Dene placed other aspects of life, such as being free to live in the moment, as more important than money. I sensed my values were changing and I was pleased with the enlightenment that was occurring. I kept thinking about the meaning of life, and had a sense that there was a lot more yet to learn from being in the north.

The band, unlike private "for profit" businesses, with which I was familiar, received funding for this and that and the objective was to use it all up. That fiscal philosophy transcended the Band's activities and was ever present in the minds of the Directors and the community. Consequently, there was a mindset that all monies were for spending, including the profits of the corporation. There was a feverish attraction to finding more money and once found, a feverish desire to spend it. On the other hand, with my financial background, I was at the other end of the spectrum. I was trying to retain profits and to make the companies as profitable as they could be, by spending as little as possible, which of course created a stressful difference of opinion.

Another aspect, which initially led to much frustration, were misunderstandings caused by differences in our worldviews. Things weren't as simple in the business world as the Dene thought. The band Manager and I couldn't just write cheques for this and that. There were policies and procedures to follow and we had to run things by our bosses and get approvals. The community seemed to think that, because we had access to the company's bank account and were cheque signatories, we could write a cheque for them, usually in the form of a donation for some trip they wanted to take.

Waistlines in the community were beginning to bulge and their once strong, lean bodies, as depicted in old photographs, were now seen only on a few, and not surprisingly, on those who continued to hunt and fish in traditional ways. Obesity and diabetes were increasing at an alarming rate in the community, particularly in the younger generation, due to their new sedentary lifestyles as a result of television and video games, and new foods such as chips and soft drinks. That was sad to see.

I realized just how much I was changing in the four short months that I had been there, when I met an interesting character at the nursing station. Miki and a visiting nurse had invited Marc and me for supper. Marc was a twenty something, tall, lean Frenchman from Paris, who was living with the seventy-some year-old Eddie Brokengoose and his wife, in their one room cabin out on the land, about five miles from the community. Marc said he had wanted to live on the Barren lands ever since he was a child growing up in Paris. He wanted to learn how to be self-sufficient and that's why he was apprenticing with Eddie. He only came into town once every three months for staples, and that's why I'd never seen him before.

Many times thereafter, I thought about Marc and his different approach and expectation of life compared to mine. He challenged me to think deeply about life and how you lived it. There was no doubt that I secretly admired his outlook and even his lifestyle, but it was too extreme for me at my age and stage of life. Four months earlier, I would have categorically dismissed him as a crazy, misguided young man, but now I understood his passion for the natural world and why he wanted to live simply; on the land with an aboriginal Elder; someone untainted by the modern world.

Business Development Officer

I attended a few Band meetings at the community hall and they were always interesting. For one thing they never started on time. If it was a seven o'clock meeting, I'd set out at about seven forty-five knowing full well that I'd still be one of the first ones to arrive. Quite a few times the meetings were cancelled and deferred to another night because the turnout was too low to constitute a duly called meeting. In the Dene culture, it was impolite to interrupt someone when they were speaking, so the Elders rambled on for thirty minutes or more at a time. No one interrupted or put pressure on them to finish.

When the Dene wanted to voice an opinion they couched their statement by using "they." I cannot recall anyone ever saying,

"I think this and I think that." It was always, "They say this and they say that," giving the impression that it was a collective opinion. Every time I heard this, I got an urge to go to a microphone and say, "Excuse me, but specifically, who are the 'they' you are referring to?" This reluctance to take responsibility manifested itself in many ways daily throughout the community. "They" wanted jobs but they also wanted to be free to come and go. "They" wanted businesses; a coffee shop, a pool hall, a pizza place, yet no one wanted to run them. "They" wanted me to create these businesses and be the operator. You'd think that after forty years the community would have spawned a number of successful entrepreneurs, considering they'd be selling into a captive market with no competitors! Rainbow's Bed and Breakfast was the only private enterprise, but then, she mainly provided that service for out of town guests.

I puzzled over that phenomenon and concluded that it was the result of three things: first, no one wanted the responsibility; second, they knew they'd have problems collecting money because everyone was family and they'd expect things for free; and third, their life would be more difficult if they were successful. The community would expect them to donate goods and services and to give and loan money. People would get jealous if someone was successful and they'd boycott the business.

I asked Billy Beauchamp, a strong, smart young man of perhaps twenty-two years of age, why he wasn't working at the diamond mines making $65,000 a year. He said he did work there but he quit. "It's just not worth the hassle. When I came home, everyone asked for money and I gave it to them because it's not the Dene way to say no to family. If you have money and they don't, you give them some. Even after I'd given it all away, no one believed me. They said I was holding out on them and they stopped talking to me." Wow! No wonder the old adage – money is the root of all evil – popped into my mind.

At my last Board meeting, one of the Directors commented on the amount of travel I was doing. He said, "They say you're travelling too much." I read this that he was either jealous because he'd like to do the travelling, or that he was complaining that I was spending too much of the company's money, which brings me to a very important point. There were two components to my job: the day to day management of the company's affairs in the community, and the development of new businesses, which happened in Yellowknife. That's where the movers and shakers of the North conducted their affairs. Being new to the North, I had to spend time in Yellowknife getting to know the players, developing and nurturing business relationships while, at the same time, flushing out potential business partners and opportunities for future joint ventures.

I recommended to my Board that we should create a new position of Business Development Officer (B.D.O.) based in Yellowknife, especially now that De Beers was coming on stream with their new mine at Snap Lake. "No. That's the General Manager's job," was all my Board said, and they refused to discuss it further.

The community constantly complained that they didn't do as well on business deals with the last two mines, as did the other Dene bands, and that this mustn't happen again with De Beers. In their simplistic thinking, they blamed the mines and told me I should go see them and get more contracts! I made the mines aware of the community's sentiments and they concurred, but added that Lutsel K'e didn't form as many joint ventures as did the other bands, and that was the reason they didn't get as many contracts.

BHP Billiton and Rio Tinto (the two existing diamond mine operators) also pointed out that some of their three and five year contracts were coming up for renewal, and they'd be happy to open the door and work with me to increase Lutsel K'e's participation. With De Beers gearing up on their Phase One Snap Lake project in the next twelve months, there was a one year window of opportunity for us. We needed to search out potential, willing service providers; negotiate joint venture agreements with them; and develop meaningful "aboriginal value added" components for consideration in the bid process. That's precisely what I was trying to do, in spite of the resistance and handcuffs from my Board. It was a frustrating and a thankless task, but I knew what I was doing, and in my gut I knew that I must persevere, regardless. The challenge was to somehow get approval for the "B.D.O." position before the window of opportunity shut tight.

Flying High

I worked with an air charter company in Yellowknife to create a new for-profit business: our own "airline." It would be an alternate provider of air services to the community, competing with the incumbent, Air Tindi, which was owned and operated by a Métis company based out of Yellowknife. Owning and operating a business where we were the major customer was a no-brainer, providing we could structure a deal with a partner to be a win/win situation.

In addition to profits, the community benefited in other ways. Because our partner was an air charter company, it had a wide range of aircraft with different capabilities and capacities that we could use. For instance, if there were six people going out and seven coming in, then the nine seat Navajo would be commissioned for the flight and that's all we had to pay for. If there were seventeen going in, a Twin Otter would be used. With the existing airline, there was no choice; their Caravan could only take a maximum of nine people. If more than nine wanted to travel, the extra people had to lay over for the night and fly out the next day, or even the day after that, resulting in them having to incur substantial extra expense and inconvenience.

We assigned the pickup truck, the one the Fire Crew used in the summer, to the new venture, to ferry passengers and cargo between the airport and downtown, and we hired Matt, the fish fillet expert, as the operations and ticket agent. This extra service of picking people up and dropping them off at their home was greatly appreciated by everyone, because with Air Tindi, you had to make your own arrangements to get to and from the airport.

I was blown away by how excited the community reacted to this new company. Chief and Council announced that the band offices would close for the entire day of the inaugural flight, and that it would be a paid holiday for all. They commissioned every vehicle in the community to take people up to the airport to watch the first aircraft land, and then to take them to the Community Hall for speeches and a feast. There were over one hundred people at the airport, nearly a third of the population of Lutsel K'e, when the headlights of the little plane broke through the dark sky. With heads tilted back and eyes peering up and smiling in the semi-darkness, the proud people of Lutsel K'e waited patiently in the cold air for their plane to land. The Twin Otter flew past the waiting crowd, made a U-turn, came down the runway and roared up to the pad in front of the cheering, waving community. Neighbours congratulated each other. There was much hand shaking and back-slapping. Robert Marsland, the pilot, and Larry, the co-pilot, strode across the fine gravel towards the assembled and took up a position with Chief Charlie, in the centre of a red ribbon that was strung across in front of the crowd. After some welcoming remarks from the Chief to the airmen and a proud summation to the gathering about the importance of this new company to the community, Chief Charlie and Robert snipped the ribbon. Everyone bundled into the waiting, idling vehicles and went off to the Community Hall.

After a few short speeches by the Chief and Joe Broadman, our Member of the Legislative Assembly, the feast began. Robert brought with him from Yellowknife, thirty large buckets of Kentucky Fried Chicken and two dozen boxes of fresh salads. Community members provided bannock and tea.

Lutsel K'e had other business interests, but as they were located out of town, most people didn't know about them. The airline, on the other hand, though only a simple business arrangement as opposed to a significant asset based venture, was in their face and perceived by them as a real winner. It was a big deal. In fact, many thought we owned the planes! I was embarrassed by their response, their strong clasping of my hands, and the knowing, smiling nods of the Elders as they looked at me from across the Hall. The message was clear – finally, Lutsel K'e had a General Manager who was doing something for them. This raised my spirits and built up my confidence by proving that I could actually make a difference by using my business skills and experience.

Air Services Inauguration Day

Privacy At Last

Phone conversations with Sue were proving more difficult because she didn't have the knowledge base to be able to relate to what I was saying. We chatted mostly surface stuff and put everything else on hold until we could get together at Christmas. But as we did not yet have a buyer for the house, it was unlikely that she would be returning with me in the New Year. That was concerning.

I went back to Ontario just before Christmas for a three week holiday. It passed by quickly and I didn't get as much time with the children as I would have liked. On the two days that we had set aside for them, the roads were too treacherous to travel, with heavy snow and white-out conditions. This gave Sue and I more time together but it was strained. I felt uncomfortable with her and was critical of the societal lifestyles that I saw around me. I was becoming less materialistic before I went up north, but now I was very much less so. It was a simpler world up there in Lutsel K'e; a more black and white world, where one was aware of the real necessities of life and where indulgences were not taken for granted. I bought only what I needed and it amazed me at how little I really needed to live yet still feel fulfilled. Soon after going home, I went to the local Wal-Mart and had to come out of the store because a wave of nausea hit me; my head spun and I felt claustrophobic. I had to go outside for air. The proliferation of "stuff" on shelves and in people's shopping carts was too much. Why was everybody buying all that "stuff," when I was sure they already had it, though maybe in a different colour? So little of it was life's essentials. I felt overwhelmed and heavy. Sue laughed when I tried to explain. Life was also too busy and complicated down there for me; everything too commercialized with so much hype and BS.

I sat through ads on TV and shook my head at the lies and the deceit companies used to sell their products. I couldn't believe that "stuff" actually convinced people to buy their products but it obviously did. Likewise with the politicians and corporations; everyone on TV spinning the truth to gain an advantage. It was all so deceitful and tiring. The culture shock was making me cynical and negative and I didn't like it. The seeds of practicality and pragmatism, which germinate in most of us as we age, had flourished in me over the last six months and were now a giant oak tree of my existence. Sue said I had changed and that she didn't know who I was any more, but sad to say, I didn't care, for I was enjoying my enlightened and unencumbered view of the world. Celebrities, fashions, and brand names didn't exist in my new world.

"You've changed," she repeatedly told me.

"Maybe I have," I replied, "but I can't help it. I am who I am."

I saw changes in her too, but I didn't dare go there and accuse her, knowing that she would resist, and anyway, there was no mileage to be gained from going there. We were civil towards each other but the magic we once had was gone. I silently hoped that it would reappear when we lived together again in Lutsel K'e, but when that might be was anybody's guess as there was no potential buyer for our house in the offing. Maybe Sue might have to wait until spring.

When I returned to the community after the Christmas break, I was more excited than I was when I first arrived because this time, I knew exactly what I was coming back to, where I was going to live, what I was going to work on, and I could sense the luxury of the privacy that I was going to get. I'd always regarded starting a New Year like opening a new book. Being in my own home represented a fresh start, and this home was brand new; indeed its pages had never been turned, nor a word yet read.

The trials and tribulations of last year were now just memories, to be forgotten or treasured, according to how I chose to remember them. The house wasn't totally finished; two rooms were yet to be painted and the wood trim had yet to be nailed, but those were minor inconveniences. I couldn't wait any longer. I needed to start the year off right and that meant being in my own place. I was ecstatic. I could now cook Indian curries, read a book without interruption, and watch CBC, CNN and soccer whenever I chose. I could invite guests to dinner, and sleep in without people checking up on me. I could listen to CDs, watch VHS tapes, and lock my door and turn off the ringer when I wanted privacy. Having such freedom of choice was awesome. The privacy deprivation of the last six months had been stressful yet humbling at the same time. It had taught me to how to be resourceful and resilient and had increased my appreciation for the simpler things in life.

Still in a buoyant, festive mood, I unwrapped the cartons from Quality Furniture and Wal-Mart with as much surprise as a child opening gifts on Christmas morning. I rediscovered what I had purchased last October with much joy. The house became a home as soon as I decided where to put what. I loved my new home and its amenities. There wasn't much personal stuff to unpack, just a few clothes and some groceries. Joe helped set up the TV satellite dish.

When I went to work on Monday, Vince suggested I hold an open house from two to four on Saturday and Sunday for the next two weeks because that was tradition. I refused and was pleased with myself that I had learned to say no. I had waited six months for this privacy and I intended to enjoy it, without delay. I wasn't in the mood to host walk throughs, provide and prepare food and clean up afterwards.

My house was located at the top of the hill, just before the path that led to the scenic lookout over the bay. It made for an ideal rest stop for people taking long walks in the evenings and on the weekends. After a week of answering knocks on the door at all times of the day and night, I resolved to be quite the hermit and keep my doors locked at all times and not answer.

There was a problem though going in and out of the house. The warm, moist air inside did strange things when it seeped out past the door, crept through the lock and met the arid, frigid air outside. The space between the door and the doorjamb iced up into rock hard glue and the lock froze solid. The problem was highly effective in keeping out unwanted visitors because I couldn't open the door easily, but it made me a prisoner in my own home! Maybe I should be more careful about what I wished for?

I spent two hours one morning chipping away the ice with a putty knife and heating up the lock with a BBQ lighter before I could get outside. That was not good. What if I had an emergency and needed to get out of the house fast? Bob should have built a wall across the entrance to the kitchen from the hall and created a cold porch. This was what they did in the North to avoid the icing problem. I couldn't lock up the house when I went to work and so I just crossed my fingers that no one tried the door while I was away. In the summer, I would get someone to build a cold porch.

The view of Great Slave Lake through the large picture windows was spectacular. As I hadn't got around to putting window coverings on, I had a thirty-odd foot unobstructed view of the lake and islands. In the evenings, I snuggled up into a corner on the sofa facing the windows and followed the dances of the Northern Lights as they illuminated the coal black sky. With the volume turned up on Beethoven's Fifth, the great composer provided a most appropriate musical accompaniment to the light show in the heavens. Aurora Borealis listened and skipped in step with each orchestral movement. The sky curtains shimmered and shook to the staccato of the opening bars and streams of white, green and pink light rose slowly to the apex of the heavens, then plunged down, in dramatic great sweeps to the flat horizon, as Beethoven's music crescendoed and faded.

Simultaneously looking and listening to those two natural wave wonders of the world, with only a pane of glass in between to protect me from the hostile elements, was glorious and spiritual. I let myself be consumed by the combination and smiled when their mating was perfect. I could feel the power and beauty of the Universe, as if it was a tangible thing, but I couldn't adequately explain it. It was magical and it became my nightly interest. I couldn't wait to get home from work, have supper and then to relax on the sofa watching the wondrous light show in the sky. I so wished Sue was there with me to experience it for herself.

G.M. House – exterior

G.M. House – interior

Garage Sale on Great Slave Lake

In early December, prior to going away for the Christmas break, Joe and I ordered snow machines from a dealer in Yellowknife. We both chose the Bombardier 550 Grand Touring model and purchased appropriate clothing that was good for minus sixty degrees from Weaver and Devore, the outfitter in Yellowknife. We planned to ride across the lake from Yellowknife to Lutsel K'e, a distance of approximately 250 km, which we were told should take about five hours, if we kept up a steady pace. Joe and Julie grew up on snow machines and were confident about their abilities. Their confidence inspired me to share the adventure with them.

It was Friday night in the second week of January. I had been in Yellowknife on business and had arranged to meet Joe and Julie when they came in on the late flight from Lutsel K'e. We met at the Chateau Nova hotel, where I was staying, and went over to Brady and Sheila's house as previously arranged. Brady was the plumber who plumbed my house over the Christmas holidays. He very kindly offered to put Joe and myself up any time we were in Yellowknife on personal business. We picked up the machines and sleds in Brady's oversized pickup, took them to a warm warehouse that Brady had arranged, and there we assembled the sleds. They were made of plastic and were six feet long, three feet wide and about two feet high.

It was extremely cold, minus forty degrees, when we awoke the next morning and gathered in the kitchen for a cooked breakfast. The voice on the radio said the forecast was for clear skies and cold temperatures for the next two days.

I was thrilled yet apprehensive about the trek across the lake because I'd never ridden a snow machine before, nor had I attempted anything like that. The mere act of donning all those strange clothes had an exciting feel. First to go on were the red, full body long johns with a flap at the back; then the white polo shirt; the black fleece jacket and thermal socks; followed by the full body sky blue skidoo outfit; the neck warmer and face mask. Like a gladiator preparing for the ring, I slid into my boots, donned my gloves and inserted my head into the helmet. I was ready. Let the games begin.

After gassing up the machines and two extra cans each, we rode over to the grocery store, bought a month's supply of food and returned to Brady and Sheila's to load up the sleds. My sled sat higher than Joe and Julie's because I had extra bags from my business trip. It was so cold that when I took off a glove for a few seconds to turn the clips on my sled cover, my fingers numbed instantly and ached for over an hour afterward. The glossy instruction paper, which came with the sled cover, snapped into micro pieces in the sub-zero temperatures. Each time I tried to pick up a piece, it disintegrated at my touch into miniscule pieces that blew away like confetti at a wedding, even defying gravity. It was a fascinating phenomenon.

With sleds packed and extra gas cans securely tied to the back of our skidoos, we were ready to rumble. Joe had made the trip by boat in July and was confident he could steer a course to get us home. He had also talked to the locals about the route and knew where the open water was. Unlike most large lakes, Great Slave was full of islands running in a west to easterly direction, so you always saw land. To make things a little easier for us, Brady took our machines and sleds down to the government dock on Yellowknife Bay in his pickup truck. He also brought down his machine, Sheila's and their friend Rocky's snowmobile, because they wanted to escort us out of the bay. Apparently, it was easy to get lost if you were not familiar with the lay of the land. After a quick demonstration on how to start, accelerate and stop, I was ready for the big lake.

We played "follow the leader" across the Bay at about 30 kph. It was great. I enjoyed the feel of the machine and the exhilaration of the acceleration when I stepped on the gas. I was also comfortable and warm, due in large part to the well-padded cushioned seat, the thoughtful hand warmers on the handle bars and the hot exhaust venting at my feet. My visor though was presenting a problem. It kept frosting over from the moisture in my breath, impairing my vision. The only way I could see was by lowering my head, raising my eyes and peering through the only clear portion at the top of the visor. On our first pit stop, I pulled up my neck warmer to cover my mouth and made sure the two vents at the top of the helmet were open. This improved things a little, but good visibility was still a problem. After heading out across the larger stretches of the bay and onto the lake proper, we increased our speed to about 70 kph. No problem. I was relieved to be at ease because I wondered how I'd feel when going fast across the ice. I didn't want to hold back my friends.

Brady's machine was a mammoth 900 Arctic Cat, which he used to snowmobile in the Rockies, but it was giving him problems. He kept stopping to make adjustments, which slowed us down, but other than that, everything was going well. We checked the sleds periodically to ensure everything was battened down tight. Once, we flew over a bump and one of Joe's running shoes and a few pieces of clothing flew off. Joe and Julie barrelled along without a care in the world, while Sheila and I doubled back to retrieve their laundry. Gunning our machines to over 100 kph, we easily caught up, passed and waved their personals at them. After a good laugh and a repacking of the sled we resumed our journey.

My sled cover was as tight as a Dene drum skin. I was greatly impressed with the acceleration and the ease with which my machine performed. The power under my seat was awesome, and out there on the lake with wide open space and no obstacles, it was pure joy. When we reached Devil's Channel, our escorts turned around and returned to Yellowknife. We settled in for some serious riding. There were now only one set of snow machine tracks on the lake and those must have been from Lutsel K'e trippers we reasoned because there was nothing else between Yellowknife and Lutsel Ké. The surface of the lake was as flat and smooth as a billiard table and when you looked down through the ice, which was about three to four feet thick, it looked as if you were standing on a block of clear glass. There were a few bumps and ridges, but our headlights easily picked them out. We had enough time to slow down if we wanted to, but it was more fun to ride over them at full speed. It broke the monotony. We were clipping along, keeping the needle steady at 90 kph, with short bursts up to 110 kph, just for kicks.

After about an hour, Joe stopped to examine the trail when it split into two. He wanted to think about which track to follow; to compare the landscape to the map in his mind, and to refuel. I pulled up next to him, lifted up the helmet mouthpiece and got off my machine. I turned around to get my gas can and to my horror, there was nothing in my sled. It was just a black, shiny, piece of plastic, the way it looked in the store. "It's gone; it's all gone!" I shouted frantically.

Joe and Julie burst out laughing. Joe repeated what I said, but in the voice of a toddler, who had eaten all the goodies. With arms outstretched, palms face up and shoulders hunched, he pouted and cried, "It's gone; it's alllll gone, everything's allll gone!" Julie continued laughing but I couldn't. I was devastated. I had that horrible feeling of loss you get when you've been robbed. All my groceries, gas can, luggage with my business suit, dress shoes, underwear, toiletry bag, toothbrush, tie, business papers and files – all gone. I wished I were home in Lutsel K'e. No, I wished I were back home in Ontario.

At that moment, I wished I'd never come to the north in the first place. I had had more than enough: enough adventure, enough icy wastelands and enough freezing cold. My knees sagged. I just wanted to disappear and reappear in my bed. Joe suggested we go back to see if we could find the stuff. Ah, now that was a thought, a glimmer of hope. We turned around and sped back.

After a few miles, we saw a single headlight up ahead and as we got closer, a snow machine with its motor idling. Its exhaust vapours created a thick white smoke that drifted straight up into the still, late afternoon sky. It was Vince. He was off his machine and collecting the spilled goods, which looked like a garage sale on ice. He was laughing so hard he was stumbling around in his big snowmobile boots, like a drunken sailor. He said he was just coming along and saw this big black thing in his headlights – my luggage! Joe told Vince the story and repeated his impression of the three-year old complaining to his mother that all his candies were gone. Our eyes were wet with tears from laughter. There were chicken legs here, a roast of beef there and hamburger everywhere. A can here, a box there and Brussels sprouts scattered all over the land, as if they'd been fired from a shotgun. There were at least fifty items to pick up.

After retrieving most of the groceries, the luggage and the gas can, I repacked my sled and was ready to go again. One last laugh at the rice and spaghetti noodles that were now part of the frozen landscape and we were good to go. Joe's parting comments were, "Just wait until the community hears about Al's groceries." No doubt, the spilled goods would be used as a marker for McKinley Point from that day forward and everyone would look out for "Al's groceries" when they went to Yellowknife. I could just see the ribbing that was to come. I wouldn't be surprised if Matt picked up a few noodles, brought them back and demanded, "Five bucks for traditional retrieval."

So now we had three machines and the very best guide to take us home, because Vince was also the game warden for those parts. We hadn't traveled long before Vince stopped his machine, got off and lifted the hood. His machine was burning up. His exhaust pipe was glowing red-hot like a propane torch, and it was melting and twisting the body moulding. We threw snow on it. It was getting darker by the minute and colder, because the winter sun had dropped below the horizon. Up there, the temperature plummeted the instant the sun disappeared. Even when it went behind a cloud for a few seconds, you immediately felt a five or ten degree drop in temperature. Vince had just picked up his machine from the dealer, who said he'd fixed the very problem he was having now. He was not a happy camper.

For the next hour, we stopped every ten minutes to throw snow on the troubled machine. "Give me your foil," Vince hollered. He had just remembered a box of aluminum foil he picked up when he was helping out. I fished it out of my sled and he fashioned it around the side moulding on his machine. This made a big difference and we could now go for a full half hour before stopping and cooling off his mobile Bunsen burner. Up ahead was Ethanol Island. We stopped there, went into a cabin, made a fire, warmed up and relaxed. You soon chilled when you stopped. The rest of the trip was stop and start, but eventually we saw the welcoming lights of Lutsel K'e. And what a beautiful sight it was. It was a little after ten o'clock when we crossed the line between frozen lake and frozen land. We were exhausted but safe and happy to be home.

I had a coffee at Joe's, got back on my Ski-Doo and went home but the key wouldn't turn – the lock was frozen again. I tried to warm it up with my cigarette lighter but it didn't work. I just wanted this day to end and to go to bed because I was feeling exhausted and overheated. I went back to Joe's. "Do you have a room?"

Joe was beside himself. "Do we still have Al's room or is it rented?" he playfully called out to Julie. They couldn't believe what a string of bad luck I was having. We were all so over-tired we were over-laughing. Joe kept teasing, "Its alllllll gone." It had been a crazy day, but now that we were inside in a cozy, safe, warm living room, we all agreed that we wouldn't have missed it for the world. "Let's do it again," Joe suggested, and we agreed that we'd do it in two weeks' time, when I would be back in Yellowknife on business, and Joe could ride my machine in with Julie on theirs.

As Joe made room in his freezer for my goods, I went outside to get them. Horror of horrors. Homer, Joe's huge, well-fed, part Labrador and part "who knows what" mutt was into everything. The mongrel was chomping on the pork chops; he'd already mauled the chicken legs and ripped open the hamburger. He was wagging his tail so much his whole body was swaying. I know. I know Homer – – such a vast menu to choose from. He couldn't decide what to eat next. I was losing it big time. I was angry and physical. I kicked and screamed at him to back off. He backed up a little, but now that he'd had a taste, he wasn't going anywhere but back to the feast.

I gave up and slowly climbed the stairs, wearily went in and calmly announced that Homer was eating the groceries. "What the hell!" Joe screamed. He threw on his parka in one fell motion, slipped into his boots and flew down the steps three at a time. He hauled Homer off the food and shortened his chain, with much effort I might add, for Homer was a brute of a dog. I gathered what was left of what appeared to be "the still edible" goods, brought them inside, re-wrapped them and put them in boxes in the freezer. As we sipped a final coffee for the day, the mood was somber. It had been just too much for one day and we were too weary to talk.

Al & Homer

Joe and Julies house and our snow machines

Icy Frolics and Follies

As if our Great Slave adventure two weeks ago hadn't been enough to last a lifetime, we decided to do it again. Joe drove my machine in from Lutsel K'e and Julie drove theirs because I was already in Yellowknife. We met up at Brady and Sheila's house. Brady once again generously lent us the use of his trailer to store our machines and sleds overnight, and his truck on Saturday to get gas and groceries. Joe felt he had the route well memorized and so turned down Brady's offer of an escort.

We planned to set off in daylight hours, which at that time of the year, meant we had to leave between one and three o'clock in the afternoon, but we got talking, and it was a little after six by the time we headed out.

Our sleds were tightly laced this time with extra bungee cords. I followed Joe and Julie across the highway as they looked for a way down to the ice on Back Bay. We went this way and that, but couldn't find a clear passage down. An hour went by and we were still not on the Bay. At one time, I would have been greatly stressed out by this, and most anxious about what time we would get home, but I wasn't, for I had changed my perspective from worrying about the future to savouring the moment. I just followed Joe and enjoyed the ride. Although it was bitterly cold, I was comfortable and warm with the hand warmers on the handlebars and the hot exhaust on my feet.

We traversed a long, winding trail, about four feet wide, with lots of overhanging branches before we finally sighted the bay. There was a problem though. We were on top of a cliff about fifty feet up and there wasn't enough room to turn the machines around to go back.

"What can we do Joe?

"We have to go down Al; we have no choice."

"I don't think so. There has to be another option. I'm not going down there. That's suicide," I replied. I tried to turn my machine around by manoeuvring it backwards and forwards. Joe revved the throttle and they went over the top, plunging straight down, their packed sled racing behind them, threatening to overtake if they didn't go faster. It was really a free fall. Their machine flew and bumped off the slope and then, in a few seconds, which seemed to me to be at least a minute, they hit the bottom of the hill. Their machine flipped onto its side and they spilled out laughing onto the frozen lake. I made a note to myself to call them Jack and Jill from then on.

They laughed even harder as they groggily struggled to their feet and waved me down. "Go to the left," they shouted. That was because the big mound at the bottom, which they thought was a snow bank, was actually a rock! I was still looking for options. I feared heights and was inexperienced on a snow machine – heck, I'd only been on one twice before. "Go to the left, go to the left", they continued to shout. There was only one way down and it was straight down. How could I possibly go to the left in a free-fall? They went down and it was obvious they were out of control, and now they wanted me to go to the left? Who did they think I was? Mario Andretti?

Umm. I was up there, they were down there, and we had to get to Lutsel K'e sometime tonight. They were not going to come back up to get me, so I had no choice. I looked down, focused on going to the left and picked out a spot where I wanted to land. I took a deep breath and held it, revved the machine a few times, and then gunned the motor and released the brake. My Ski-Doo launched over the top and I screamed all the way down. I missed the rock, slid straight out onto the lake and brought the machine and sled, all in one piece, to a stop. "You executed it perfectly," Joe hollered. I did nothing of the sort. It was just pure luck.

The visibility was good as our headlights beamed the way across the bay. We headed out at a fast pace. After five minutes, we stopped for a coffee break and double checked the trail. I didn't have a coffee as my thermos was bungee-corded to the back of my machine and it must have fallen off somewhere. Whatever! These things happen, especially in the north. But Joe wasn't one to give up that easily. Without a word, he sped off and five minutes later, the gallant knight returned holding the Holy Grail thermos high above his head for all to see. That was so Joe. He had helped me out so many times. He even helped when I didn't need it!

We had to do some heavy duty driving now because we'd lost so much time. Leaning forward and tucking behind the windshield to minimize drag, we increased our speed to a steady 110 kph. I had no idea where we were but I didn't care, for I trusted Joe. My visor frosted up again blurring my vision, so I just followed the red tail light in front of me and tried to look sideways at the scenery as we flew past.

After about a half hour, Joe stopped. "We're in Dry Bones Bay again for the third time tonight," Joe said. "Brady was right. He said it was tricky if you weren't familiar with the land." We set off again and drove for two hours. It was a strange night, fog at ground level but crystal clear in the heavens. And being out there, so far from shore was a wild experience. The shadowy black islands in the distance gave one the impression of being on land, as if we were driving through a valley with hills on both sides. There was something quite odd in the knowledge that we were on Great Slave Lake, one of the deepest lakes in the world, about a mile off shore, racing on a machine but not knowing where we were and yet I was not the least bit perturbed.

An old wooden Bombardier snow car came towards us. Joe slowed down and waved to the intruder to stop and inquired of the faceless, night visitor, "Do you know the way to Lutsel K'e?" I laughed, for it sounded like Joe said, "Do you know the way to San Jose?" The grim reaper pointed silently and deadly with a heavily clothed finger in the direction from which we had come. And then it disappeared into the fog. Joe thought the guy was either crazy or drunk, so we ignored his dire warning and continued the way we were going. Another half an hour and Joe stopped again. This time we got off our machines, pulled up our visors and walked around looking for tracks. There weren't any. But we must have been getting fairly close to Lutsel K'e, because we'd been driving fast for over three hours! As we turned around we saw a most disturbing sight. The sky was quite light. That was strange because there was absolutely nothing between Yellowknife and Lutsel K'e. It must be Yellowknife! But how could that be? Julie and I looked at Joe and laughed. Joe didn't. He was most upset with himself. He prided himself on having an exceptional sense of direction and he couldn't figure out how he could have got us into this situation. He made lame excuses but they fell on deaf ears. Julie and I were roaring with laughter.

"How can that be Yellowknife, Joe? We've been driving for three hours!" I rubbed it in. And I'd been following, trusting blindly in this Northern Ontario man of the land. It was too cold, too dark, and too late and we were too tired to continue our journey, so we headed back to Yellowknife.

I will always remember that night for another reason. The Northern Lights were exceptionally explosive and colourful. It was magical. Huge thick streams of white light cascaded down like water from a great waterfall and swept back up to the heavens in ribbons. Vast swirls of intensified, white light mystically appeared and pushed through the streams, changing into a greenish hue with pinkish glows at the edges, all on an inky jet black sky. The kaleidoscopic show stretched across all the compass points; such a big playing field for the Universe to show off its magic. It was dreamy and ethereal. Beethoven was out there with me again. "Da-da-da-daaa, da-da-da-daaa, da-da-da-da-da-da-da, da-da-da-da-da-da-da-daaaa … I hummed the Fifth into my helmet and it filled my ears in stereo sound.

The celestial mural was enthralling. No wonder ten thousand people came from Japan every year to witness that spectacular display. The last time I experienced such awe was also a natural phenomenon. It was on the Masa Mara in Kenya; thousands of wildebeests and zebras streaming in a zigzag pattern, south to north, dutifully obeying the call of nature to march relentlessly, regardless of consequence, until they had fulfilled their quest.

Joe looked down at his machine and got more frustrated by the second. Julie looked wistfully at Yellowknife and I looked straight up at the heavens. "Just look at that Joe. Isn't that spectacular?" They didn't understand why I was not the least bit concerned about where we were, what time it was, or anything else. I had found a much more absorbing subject than their mundane preoccupations.

In about fifteen minutes, we were back in Yellowknife and booked into a seedy motel room with two beds. As I began to undo the ties on my sled to bring in the luggage and groceries, Joe suggested we try to bring the sleds into the room in one piece. "Are you crazy – they'll never fit – and they must weigh 150 pounds each, at least," I replied.

"Let's try it. What have we got to lose?" Joe insisted. Julie went into the room. Joe and I took the first sled, gave it a heave ho and turned it on its side. The straps held. We had to turn it nearly vertical as we pushed it through the door but it went, barely. Julie grabbed it and let it down as we assisted and shoved it across the floor, past the first bed and up to the bathroom wall, so that it was positioned as an extension of the bed. We did the same manoeuvre with sled number two. It just fit between the end of the first sled and the door, leaving just enough room for the door to close. Another half inch longer and it would have been a no go. It was a very tight fit.

The sleds took up the whole floor and wall space beyond the beds, from top to bottom and from side to side. There was no free floor space whatsoever. I had to crawl over Joe and Julie's bed to get to the bathroom. We were not comfortable leaving the snow machines in the parking lot, because we had read in the Yellowknife newspaper that eighteen machines had been stolen in the last four weeks, but what else could we do? We discussed renting another room for the Ski-Doos, but we finally resolved our concerns by agreeing to take shifts and stand on guard.

It was freezing cold in the room and the snow-covered sleds plunged the temperature down even more. Joe cranked up the thermostat, took off his boots and outer clothing and retired for the night. He was asleep in minutes and sawing logs. Julie slept for a half hour and asked upon waking, "Are you sleeping?"

"Are you kidding? I'm on night duty. I'm making sure no one steals our machines, and besides, I can't sleep with Joe snoring like that." I was over-tired though and with all the fresh air and adventure, my eyes were heavy and kept closing involuntarily. I thought I heard someone tampering with the machines. In a panic, I scampered over the bed and the sleds, cracked open the door, but there was no one there. I must have been dreaming.

Around three o'clock, Joe came back to life. He was sweating profusely – the moisture from our sleds had turned the room into a sauna. I was so tired that I didn't notice. The room was now foggier than it was out there on the ice! In fact, the steam was so dense that

I couldn't see the bathroom. Joe crawled across his bed, across mine and across the sled to the door. As he opened it, steam gushed out like a geyser. He stayed there for about two seconds, left the door open and groggily crawled back to bed. No wonder he jumped when he was at the door – his back half must have been ninety degrees and his front minus forty – what a hell of a jolt to the system at three o'clock in the morning.

I was at the door in my red long johns, having shed some clothing to cool down, trying to fan the steam out of the room, when Joe gave me a start. He was right behind me, just a nose length away. "God, Al. I thought you were Santa Claus there for a minute," he laughed. We returned to our beds but didn't sleep. Julie woke up and Joe told her that he'd just seen Santa. We laughed about that and about getting lost and losing groceries and Homer eating all of my food *ad infinitum*. We were all so tired and silly. We dozed and talked through the haze till six, and then groggy and hungry, we got up, dragged our sleds back outside and set off to find some breakfast.

Around noon we set off for Lutsel K'e, immediately found our way, stopped twice for a pee and coffee break and made it home in five hours. It had been another wonderful, memorable northern experience.

More Than a Marten in the Trap

Not only was Vince the game warden and the renewable resource guy in the community, who trappers took their furs to, but he was also the President of the Development Corporation, my boss and a good friend. Though there were times when things got a little testy between us at work, out of work we were great pals. Vince had the rare ability to leave his work cares on his desk when he left the office. Perhaps it was the trapping stories that we swapped that connected us, or maybe it was because we were roughly the same age and both cherished our children and grandchildren. Regardless, he invited me to his home many times to share the day with him and his family. I was there for Easter dinner, his son's birthday and his wedding anniversary. Whenever we got together, Vince asked that I tell him stories of trapping coons and beavers in Ontario with Roy, my trapper neighbour. It was only fitting then that when the trapping season came, he would invite me to go with him.

It was the first Friday in February. I was locking up my office for the weekend when he intentionally came around to see me. "Whatcha doing on Sunday? Wanna go check my traps?"

"Love to. Should I come to your house?"

"Yeah. Come around noon. And bring Joe if he wants to come," he said with a proud smile. He couldn't contain his excitement. It was written all over his face and in his voice. I saw the little boy in Vince surface many times and every time it made me smile. I liked that aspect of him. When Vince was in that frame of mind, he was great company. Everyone around him felt light and boyish.

It was another glorious Sunday morning in the north. The light covering of snow overnight sparkled in the bright sun, and the icy surface crunched under our snow machines as we drove up to Vince's house on the hill. Vince used a big Polaris snow machine to pull his eight foot sled when he went trapping. An eight by twelve foot insert of blue tarpaulin gift-wrapped the contents of his load – no flimsy plastic clips on Vince's sled. He created a fastener rope that ran around the entire edge of his sled by threading a half inch yellow rope through the holes, which were spaced about a foot apart. He then ran another long yellow rope under and over the fastener rope, going from side to side, and top to bottom, lacing the package in a criss-cross fashion making the load as secure as a fat lady in a corset. He packed an extra can of gas, a toolbox, as well as a supply of various sized Conibear traps and two garbage bags full of rotted fish. He was trapping martens this year.

With mugs brimming full of steaming coffee, and meat and cheese sandwiches neatly packed and strapped to the back of our machines, we headed out, through the Sunday quiet town, past the deserted airport and into the land of the Dene. The transformation was instant. We entered a pristine, silent world of white. I had never experienced such a breathtaking winter wonderland. It was nature at its finest. A serene, happy feeling filled my mind and body. I wondered for a moment if I was in a dream.

Vince's trap lines crossed many small lakes, encircled by dense forests of spruce and birch, all no more than ten to fifteen feet high. The paths were old Indian trails, formed by the footsteps of the Dene over thousands of years. The trails were tight for a snow machine and we had to go slow in parts, sweeping away branches as we passed. It was a very different experience than we had last week, when we drove fast across the lake. It was challenging in a different way, and I was pleased for staying the course and for staying on the machine. There was a lot of steering, shifting of body weight and standing up to stay on the narrow, twisty paths and to traverse the hills and drops without falling off. It was hard work and made me sweat, but the excitement it generated was thrilling and satisfying. I was tickled pink that I'd only veered off the trail twice, and had only run into two little trees with no serious damage to the machine or myself.

We'd been gone a good hour before we came upon the first trap. How Vince remembered where his traps were mystified me for everywhere looked the same; it was one Christmas calendar scene after another. Maybe we were just five minutes from home, maybe two hours. Joe and I had no idea. Maybe Vince was just having fun taking us around in circles, which wouldn't surprise me because that was the type of prank he would do to us gringos.

Vince examined the trap from his machine. There was no animal in it but he nevertheless got off his machine and left it idling. We did the same. Vince explained what he was doing and why. He said he could see from his machine what needed to be done – if he had a marten, if it needed re-baiting, or rebuilding, or if it was just fine. He went to his sled, pulled back the tarp, broke off a piece of frozen fish and re-baited the trap.

He explained how he set his marten traps by first cutting a six-inch wide spruce pole, about ten feet long, and attaching it horizontally with wire at a height of about five feet off the ground, to two trees, spaced about eight feet apart. He then attached with more wire, a homemade wooden box, about a foot long, a foot high and eight inches wide, to the pole at its intersection with a tree. Then he filled the box with rotted fish. In front of the box, he set a Conibear trap and wired it to the pole. He covered the whole affair; box and trap, with spruce boughs and snow.

"The best place to catch martens is in heavily treed spruce areas such as this," Vince said, "And if I were after mink, I'd use the same set-up, but I'd set it near a small stream, or somewhere along the shoreline." He walked backwards using a whisk brush to cover our tracks as we returned to the trail and our machines.

Ten minutes later, we came across the second trap and there was a marten in it, as white as a freshly laundered handkerchief and as stiff as an ironing board. We watched him open up the trap, with difficulty, because at minus forty degrees, everything was frozen solid.

"What happens if you can't get the marten out," Joe asked.

"Then I have to take the whole trap home and thaw it out," Vince replied.

Joe and I inspected the next five or six traps and asked Vince a lot of questions. By the seventh trap, we were content to sit on our idling machines and just gaze at the scenery as Vince did his chores.

We stopped after about two hours, switched off our machines and ate lunch in silence. The stillness was golden. *Maybe we'll never want to talk again,* I thought, but of course after a little while, we did. Vince used the occasion to tell us more about trapping. He had a soothing voice and appeared always to be smiling, even when he spoke.

"Many trappers from Lutsel K'e have cabins on the land where they go for extended periods while they trap, and every trapper has a unique trail so as not to trespass on another's territory. Fewer people trap today than five years ago. Trapping is something you have to love to do, because you don't make much money doing it, and you certainly can't justify it when you consider how much trouble it is." He sipped his coffee, had a bite of his sandwich and continued. "To trap lynx, I'd look for a place where there were many lynx and hare tracks and I'd use a number three trap. I'd fasten it to either a small spruce, or to a long stick buried in the snow. Or I'd set a snare, by making a noose of rope, or wire and suspend it from a fallen tree, keeping the noose open with small twigs, stuck vertically in the snow on either side of the trap.

To trap white fox, the best way is to set up your trap where caribou have been killed on a lake. You leave the intestines on the ice and you set your traps close to them, covering them with snow, or if you don't have any intestines, then pieces of rotted fish might work. I attach a chain to the trap and wrap it around a strong stick, placed under a heavy rock, and then I tightly pack snow over and around it. It freezes and makes for a solid trap." He had an attentive audience so he continued.

"The wolverine is probably the most difficult to get. David Drymeat is the best wolverine trapper in Lutsel K'e," Vince said, proudly sharing accolades with a fellow hunter. "David sets his wolverine trap near his other traps, because the wolverine is a robber. He selects a small tree and cuts it off about four feet above the snow. He then puts a piece of rotted or dried fish on top and sets a number three trap at the foot of the stump, completely covering it with small spruce boughs and snow." He finished his coffee and sandwich.

"Moose hunting is best in the fall before freeze up when there's no wind and plenty of black flies and mosquitoes. They go into the lake to seek refuge from the pests. They can be spotted, approached and shot, using a .30-30, or .25-35, or even a .303 bullet.

The Lutsel K'e community shoots hares, ptarmigan, spruce grouse and ducks and some go out to the islands in May to collect tern eggs for their families. Vince gave more accolades to his sister-in-law, Rosa: "She's a great shot, gets more ptarmigan and hares than anyone." And with that parting compliment, we left the beautiful spruce grove to continue on our way.

At about trap twenty-five, when I was just sitting on my machine gazing at the trees and the landscape, I glimpsed Vince frantically waving and mouthing "Al, Al." I dismounted and waddled over in my big boots in the deep snow as fast as I could to see what he wanted. He motioned for me to go to his sled. He was very animated and with his right arm he pointed for me to hurry, quick, quick, quick. I waddled faster to his sled, untied the rope and looked to see what he wanted.

When I held up the tool bag he nodded frantically, "Yes, yes, yes." I hurried over as fast as I could waddle and placed the bag in front of him. He was bent over in front of the trap and I couldn't see what he was doing. Quickly, he grabbed what I called "the big pliers," shoved them into my hands and motioned for me to put one end here and one end there. He was going to make a trapper out of me yet. And then I saw that his left hand was caught in the trap. His gloved fingers and the steel trap were one. His face grimaced, his head swayed back and forth, and he couldn't speak. I sensed his horrendous pain.

I squeezed the tool and the trap jaws opened, just enough for him to pull out his hand. He waved it about in the air, gently blowing on it, trying to ease the pain and get the blood flowing again. We looked closely at his hand and inspected the damage. The glove was flat as if it had been ironed and it had creases on it. It didn't look good. Drawing a deep breath and tightening his facial muscles, he gingerly pulled his hand out of the glove. There was no blood. He examined his crushed fingers, blew on them and gently tried to rub them back to life. They might be broken but he couldn't tell. He took stock of the situation and realized he was okay. He tried to force the grimace from his face by forcing a smile, but he couldn't fully hide the pain. His distress was obvious in his scrunched up eyes and in the uncontrollable twitching of the corners of his mouth.

Looking up from his kneeling position he said, "What would I have done if you weren't here?"

I thought. *The trap is chained to the stake, which is frozen to the ground. His sled is twenty feet away and he only has the use of one free hand. No one is likely to come by soon and I don't think anyone knows where his traps are anyway, not even his wife – trappers are secretive about them.* "Cut your hand off," I said. He smiled and looked down at his injury. "What would you do?" I pressed him for an answer.

He looked up and said, "I don't want to think about it," and added, "Now we're even. Right?"

"Right," I said, and slapped him on the back as buddies do to acknowledge their friendship. We spent the rest of the day riding through that wonderful white land, without seeing any sign of man. On one lake, we spotted a moose and drove over, but it just stepped back into the bush and disappeared.

At about 4:30 p.m., with our headlights on, we came up over a ridge and onto the bay at Lutsel K'e. Vince had eight marten, which he'd get about eighty dollars apiece for, once they were thawed, skinned, stretched and dried, Joe and I had a wonderful memory of a day spent in the bush with a Dene trapper, and I had the good fortune to repay a friend with the same neighbourly assistance he had given me a week earlier.

Winter wonderland

A marten in the trap

As Long As This Land Shall Last

If ever the Dene were to elect a saint, it may be René Fumoleau. He was enigmatic, caring and the sincerest person I have ever met. He lived quietly at the Seniors Centre in Lutsel Ké, and had Vince not told me about him one day, I might never have met him, and that would have been most unfortunate because he subsequently became a role model for me in my search for a meaningful life. I saw him occasionally buying groceries at the Co-op store and presumed he was just another visitor in town on business for a few days. It was only when I looked him up at the Seniors Centre that I realized he was a resident. Still waters run deep my dad used to say. Those words popped into my head two minutes after meeting the diminutive, bespectacled, septuagenarian.

René was also an accomplished photographer, author, poet, filmmaker and storyteller. He said that his photographic collection, taken over a forty-year period, depicting the Dene people and their old way of life, was on display in Yellowknife at the Prince of Wales Northern Heritage Center and on its web site. I promised to go to there the next time I was in Yellowknife. I invited him up to my house for tea.

In an accent, still very French, my esteemed guest openly shared with me stories of his childhood in France and of his coming to Canada as a young priest to spend the rest of his life in Denendeh (Canada's north,) living with and ministering to the First Nation Dene.

He was born in 1926, ordained a priest with the Oblates of Mary Immaculate in 1952, and in the Spring of 1953 sailed from Le Havre to Quebec City. He laughed as he recalled his journey by train and river for he had no idea of the terrain that he had to pass through to get to his ultimate destination of Fort Good Hope. In Montreal they told him, "You're going up north to Fort Good Hope," in Winnipeg, they said, "Boy! It's up all the way north," and in Edmonton, "It's still far up north." Then in Fort Chipewyan in northern Alberta, they told him "I've never been so far down north!" He laughed and said, "That's because they look at the world differently up there. Nearly everywhere is south of them and so wherever they go, they go "down." In Fort Providence, they told him, "So, you're going down north to Fort Good Hope," and in Fort Norman, "You still have quite a way down." Still laughing, he added, "Some people travel on paper maps; the Dene travel on rivers!"

He moved from Radeli Ko (Fort Good Hope) to Deline (Fort Franklin) in 1959, and eleven years later moved south to Yellowknife. He retired from the priesthood in 1994 and had lived at the Lutsel K'e Seniors Centre ever since.

I poured him another cup of tea as he gathered his thoughts, obviously enjoying the opportunity to reflect and reminisce. He wanted to talk about photography.

"In 1966 I was living in Deline and I thought: *In a few months I will go and visit my mother in France. I have lived in Denedeh for 13 years and I don't have a single photograph to show her!*" He bought a hundred dollar 35mm Pentax camera, "shot" a few rolls of film, and took them with him to France to be developed. He said he was stunned when he looked at the photographs because he hadn't fully realised until then how beautiful Denendeh was. It was an epiphany of sorts, he said, and from that day forward he took photographs wherever he went, until that is, his camera went to sleep after the 1991 Dene National Assembly in Tthebachaghe (Fort Smith.)

It woke up for one week in the fall of 1995 when the Lutsel K'e Dene invited him to a caribou hunt in the Barren Lands. "A few weeks later I pulled my camera case from under my bed and I zipped it open. I looked at the camera for a while and I shut the cover. Two weeks later I gave my camera away and I haven't taken a photograph since."

He didn't seem to have any regrets, moreover, he was pleased that his extensive photographic collection was now highly regarded and in good hands and available to be viewed by the general public.

When René told his stories, I saw a man full of life; a passionate, caring human being with an eye for the sublime and the subtle; a skilful communicator with a strong sense of humour, morality and justice. If there was one predominant thread in his stories, it was to bring about what was fair and just for the Dene Nation, and for the Canadian government to live up to its promises and commitments.

We chatted about his accomplishments in poetry and filmmaking, but it was his book, *As Long As This Land Shall Last*, that he most wanted to talk about next that Saturday morning over tea and biscuits. No prompting was necessary on my part. For the next two hours, René plunged passionately into the subject and spoke at length about what I would call his crowning achievement, but to the humble man, he simply regarded his book as just another opportunity to help serve humanity.

René revelled at story telling. He said that about 1970, he became aware that the Dene around Yellowknife didn't have a copy of Treaty Eight, which they purportedly had signed in 1900, nor did they have a copy of Treaty Eleven, which was signed in 1921. As Ottawa and the Territorial government were continually imposing new regulations on the Dene that interfered with their traditional way of life, which they said was guaranteed by the government in these Treaties, he said he took it upon himself to see what he could do.

The strong-willed benefactor went to Ottawa to study the Treaties. He thought he would be gone for a couple of months, but it took two years for him to finish the project. He researched government archives in Ottawa, poured through the annals of the Anglican and Catholic churches, and investigated everything that might have some relevance. René recalled that at the National Archives in Ottawa, the authorities told him the Treaty signed at Fort Liard in 1922 was lost, but he uncovered it, after laboriously working his way, day by day, through the Public Archives of Canada. The government officials were astonished and most grateful.

To help ensure the First Nations people retain their rights to continue their traditional lifestyles as agreed with the government, René wrote a book entitled *As Long As This Land Shall Last;* an historically accurate and complete account of Treaties 8 and 11. The book documents events before and after the signing of the Treaties and includes the oral testimonies of eyewitness Elders given at hearings conducted by the government. He published the book in 1975.

He said that the oral testimonies of the Dene were vital in understanding what they believed they were agreeing to when they put their X on the English-written Treaties because very few of them could read or write. In 1921 Bishop Breynat was the go between the Dene and the government, and he encouraged the Dene to sign the Treaty. In testimony after testimony, the Elders said they thought they were signing a peace document in exchange for money, and fishing, trapping and hunting equipment. They agreed not to cause trouble with the White settlers, who would be moving into the area, so long as they, the Dene, were allowed to continue to hunt, trap and fish in their traditional ways. The idea of land ownership was a concept they were not familiar with. *We cannot own the land, because the land owns the people,* was their belief. To them, the land was Creator given, as were the sky, the air, the waters and the caribou, and so there was never any question of land title transfer.

It was undeniably clear, René said, that the Treaties and the prevailing understanding of the facts at the time of the signing, as evidenced by the testimonies, assured the Dene that they would be able to hunt, trap, fish and live their traditional lifestyles for "as long as the sun rises, as long as the river flows, and as long as this land shall last." So convinced were they that the Treaty would be good for them, they asked the government to add those words to the document to ensure the longevity of the agreement, but the government did not do that. René repeated the words, "As long as this land shall last," and said, "Surely that means forever, in everybody's language, does it not?

I wished René well and returned with him to his room at the Seniors Centre to buy his book and his little paperback of poems entitled, "Here I Sit."

"As Long As This Land Shall Last" is a fascinating and enlightening read, which creates a greater understanding and empathy for the Dene cause, with regards to the Treaty rights. René said that it was now required reading in some schools and universities for certain courses, and was regarded by the courts as the definitive text on the two Treaties, and that it will be used by the courts forever, as governments wrestle with Dene rights, Treaty entitlements and self-government issues.

It boggled my mind that a "white" person from France would devote his entire life to the well-being of First Nations people living in remote regions in Canada's far north. It was obvious that he had loved and had deeply cared for the people that he had lived with, and that they had loved him back. That was why he had taken it upon himself to study the Treaties, research the facts and write the book. His insight and passion for the Dene people was evident from the dedication inscribed on the inside of the book: "To the youngest child in the Northwest Territories."

And here he was, living humbly and happily at the Lutsel K'e Seniors Centre. What a role model for a life lived with meaning, full of humility and joy. He impressed me more than anyone else I have ever met in my life, and that included some very famous and "important" people. His cheery smile and softly spoken voice revealed his inner peace and joy.

"The pen is mightier than the sword," my dad used to say. How true I thought after reading his poem:

"FOREVER" by René Fumoleau

During a land claim negotiation meeting,
the Minister of Indian Affairs addressed the Dene:
"Your fatherland covers over 1,000,000 square kilometres,
and you possess all rights over those 750,000 kilometres.
As long as the sun shines,
you may occupy those 600,000 kilometres.
As long as the river flows,
you may roam freely over your 400,000-kilometre heritage.
However, your 200,000 kilometres are part of Canada,

and Canadian laws will prevail over your 100,000-kilometre land.
In case non-Dene settle on your 50,000-kilometre domain,
and want to share the resources of your 20,000 kilometres,
my government will protect you anywhere
within the boundary of your 1,000-kilometre region.
Your children too may live forever on your 500 kilometres,
in guaranteed security on your 100-kilometre territory.
Following our agreement about your 50-kilometre tract,
I will provide you with a Canadian flag
which you may fly anywhere on your 10-kilometre property,
as a sign of our friendship treaty regarding those 5 kilometres.
Even if the national interest requires
that you give up the one square kilometre you own,
I will ensure that you will still have enough land
on which you can stand and fly a kite."

High Stakes In the Wood Shop

Jim Sproule, the Wood Shop crew boss, came to see me one morning. He was most distressed and talking about throwing in the towel. He said his crew was staging a mutiny because people in the community said they were underpaid for the dangerous conditions they worked under and they wanted an increase in their hourly rate. He also mentioned a rumour he'd heard that Tyler was coming back in as Crew Boss! I reassured him that I wanted him to continue as Crew Boss because he did a good job last year and had put together a good team. I agreed to meet with the team at 2pm to sort things out.

I knew the devious Tyler Beauchamp was behind this because he had come to see me a few days earlier to tell me he was thinking of starting up a competitive wood shop operation. He had a job at the mines driving truck, but he was currently on a two-month stress leave and was looking for work in the community. He claimed to have started the wood shop operation four years ago, knew how to run it, and now wanted his old job of Crew Boss back. I simply and politely said, "No."

"Well then. You've got to help me start up my own wood shop operation and get me some funding."

"No," I said. "I suggest you look at other businesses the community needs. How about a coffee shop? I can get you a government grant of $5,000 to get you started."

"No, I'm not interested. I only know how to run a wood shop. If I had my own business, would you let me bid on the stake business and any other wood business the corporation got?"

My lips said sure but my brain said *no way*. He was smart enough to know what I was thinking. I sensed Tyler didn't seriously intend to start his own business. He was in one of those awkward moods he got into once in a while, and just wanted to stir things up a little and create some chaos. If truth be known, he was jealous of Jim doing such a fine job. As he left the office, I sensed he was going to get up to some mischief and so I wasn't the least bit surprised at this latest turn of events.

The wood shop was located in a Department of Public Works garage: a metal building, about twenty feet square. A double garage door filled the east sidewall and a normal sized door hung in the west wall. Jim had extended the work area by adding twenty foot sections of framed lumber and tarps to each outside wall of the building, giving him in effect a sixty foot long work shop.

The surveyor stake operation used sixteen foot long pieces of two by four spruce, which, because of its weight, had to be brought in by barge in large quantities. Ten lifts of lumber had come in on the last barge, enough stock for about eight months of production. The operation began by ripping the sixteen foot pieces into four inch wide strips, which were then cut into fifteen inch or thirty-five inch lengths. One end was cut in an inverted V shape to produce a point and these points were then spray-painted a hazardous orange. The strips were ripped again into quarter inch thick sticks, stacked on a pallet and wire strapped for shipment to the diamond mines.

Last winter, we tried running production in the minus forty degree weather because the crew wanted to continue earning money, but it created such a dangerous situation that we shut it down. It was an accident waiting to happen. The bulky clothing – parkas, balaclavas, gloves and frosted up safety glasses were not conducive to safely running a high-speed saw operation. And so we came to an agreement that we would continue to run the wood shop so long as the weather was relatively mild, and then shut it down for the winter.

At 1:30pm, the entire crew appeared in my office for the 2pm meeting. Being half an hour early could only mean one thing. They were deadly serious about something.

Jim and his boys, without consciously being aware of it, had created their own unique social group in the community, which gave them an identity with roughly the same benefits, as did membership in other social circles. They were tight, good buddies, and proud of their workmanship. Over the summer, they had grown into a cohesive, fun, hard-working team.

There was Jimmy Dryblood, whom everyone called Slim. He was about twenty-two years of age, five foot seven and weighed in at maybe a hundred and forty pounds. Slim was not a man of words: he was a silent young man of action, and so most of what I knew about him was told to me by others and from what I had observed. It was strange that I didn't know which particular Dryblood family he was from because I'd lived in the community for quite a while and could tell, almost to the person, which family everyone else was associated with. They said he brought himself up and had always looked after himself. He didn't eat much, especially when he was in between jobs.

Unlike so many in the community who went to relatives for help, Slim was fiercely independent and proud of it, and his pride wouldn't let him be reliant on others. Though he had his down days, when he was angry at the world, Slim was mostly positive and ever smiling, finding humour in most situations. I knew he didn't drink or smoke, but rumour had it that he sometimes dabbled in the black market of selling booze to augment his earnings. He wanted only sure bets. "Every once in a while though," he said, "I'll pick a fight in the community, or at the Gold Range in Yellowknife, just to stay sharp," and proudly added, "But the fights are no big deal – someone gets a bloody nose or a black eye. That's all."

Brian was the son of Nora Campbell. At five foot ten and about two hundred and forty pounds he was bear-like. Looking at him from behind, you'd swear he didn't have a neck because his head rested directly on his round shoulders, like a Christmas pudding on a plate. You'd also say he didn't have a waist, because his upper torso sat directly on top of his legs. This strange physical configuration made his arms and legs appear disproportionately long, in relation to the rest of his body. His lumbering posture and walk must have reduced his real height by at least two inches. He might appear to strangers to be slow and plodding physically, but he was as sharp as a whip mentally, and as productive as any other member of the team. Brian seemed to be better educated than his teammates; perhaps he'd spent more time in mainstream society, and he tended to look at situations from a "southern" perspective. Over the summer, the crew had begun to rely upon him more for decisions and opinions, which on some occasions, resulted in a power struggle with Jim, the crew boss.

Then there was Andy Beauchamp. Just a young lad of about eighteen or nineteen I'd say, but then again he could be twenty-five. It was deceiving how young some of the Dene men looked. Young Andy kept a low profile, was private and usually smiled nervously when I made eye contact with him.

The fourth member of the gang and the longest serving was George Brownstone, another easy-going, happy guy, who smiled a lot. George was about thirty and the tallest of the crew at six foot, and a little overweight at what I'd guess to be two hundred and thirty pounds. It was unusual to see George upset, but when he drank he could get quite morose and angry, particularly when he had no money. He'd been drinking when he came to see me last year and demanded that I find him a job, right then and there, because he needed money that day. He was on the verge of tears and shared with me in great detail all aspects of his financial troubles, as if I were his personal debt counsellor. It was his lucky day, because

Joe had called that morning and needed extra help on the house project. I sent George up and he worked out well.

As did some others in the community, George went on a drinking binge every once in a while and disappeared from view for a week or two. And then, slowly, like a raccoon emerging from hibernation, he began to be seen again, just here and there at first, until he was back larger than life as one of the daily characters around town. I measured George's progress from hibernation by the size of his smile, for when he first emerged, his smile was just a smirk. When fully integrated back into the community, his grin would give the Cheshire cat stiff competition.

And then there was my friend, El Capitan, Jim Sproule, the crew boss: a sinewy, physically strong, forty-year-old, who admitted he could have accomplished much in life had he made better decisions when he was younger. His hard life, creased into his face and seared into his voice, made him appear much older than his forty years. I liked Jim because he took personal responsibility for screwing up his life. He told me many times that there was no one else to blame but himself but he was not looking for pity. He was simply an enlightened man looking for the strength to change his life. With a startling mop of long, thick, black hair, pushed up and under a baseball cap, Jim could be quite a scary character at times, especially when he let down his mane: it flowed over his eyes and ears, dominating and dwarfing his nose and mouth.

I felt compassion and empathy for Jim on many occasions because I knew he meant well and he tried so hard, but his drug addiction at the time was more powerful than his will to be clean. He could put his monkey on ice while he responsibly ran the Stake operation, but when production ended, he couldn't resist the temptation to go to Yellowknife. After he burned through his money, he would return to the community and adopt a sort of grim reaper persona: a hooded, ghostly figure with dark circles under his eyes and an unhealthy pallor to his skin, whom you only saw fleetingly, as he disappeared into the shadows. Funny how you never saw those types emerging from darkness and stepping into sunlight! Jim was a hard worker, and in his own way, tried to be a good crew boss. He listened to the complaints of his workers and that was why they were sitting in my office that morning.

When the crew put their minds to it, the stake shop hummed. They minded their own business and they were tight. Their personal growth made me proud because they weren't motivated when I arrived; they were just a bunch of casual labourers looking to work a day here and there for a few dollars, and to screw the system as best they could. They'd been together for a year now and were proud of their achievements and deservedly so.

The pot of coffee and bag of cookies on the table pleased them greatly and helped establish a comfortable setting for the meeting. "What do you want?" I enquired.

They laughed and Jim said, "Okay. You asked for it." He began by complaining about poor tools and the physical shortfalls of their workplace. Their list of wants was really quite humble, and in truth, fundamentally essential to their jobs, but they thought they were asking for the moon. I listened and wrote down everything.

"We want double ply dust masks, not the flimsy ones we've been using. And we want a hand held eye wash unit for when we get sawdust in our eyes. And we want a hammer tacker, tin snips, a good supply of Robertson #8 bits and a cordless drill. And we want a clock with big hands so we can all see what time it is."

"That's it? I said, astounded with the minimalism of their request.

"Yeah," Jim replied.

"What about a shop vac that uses garbage bags and a proper first aid kit?" George interjected. I didn't know what to say. I didn't realize how poorly equipped they were. I'd never taken the time, nor apparently had sufficient interest to look as closely at their workplace as I should have.

"I'll phone the supplier immediately and you'll have all of these items by next Monday or Tuesday." They grinned, looking as triumphant as warriors coming out of battle. Their reaction humbled me. They asked if I was pleased with them. They said others in town looked down their noses at them as if they didn't have proper jobs. I was honest with them and told them how proud they made me feel. I probably crossed the line by saying that, in my opinion, they were the only ones in town who did "real jobs," and I was extremely pleased with the way they ran their operation.

Brian wanted to know about costs so I took a sheet of paper and wrote down the selling price, the unit wood cost, labour and paint cost and how much profit the corporation made on each stake. I wasn't surprised when he questioned why the corporation made the profit because he felt the profit should be split between the crew. Thinking fast for a reasonable but saleable response, I explained that for the stake operation to keep going it had to be seen by the community as a profitable venture. They were okay with this explanation and to my surprise they didn't ask for increased wages. I was stunned because I thought that's what the meeting was all about.

I shared with them my idea about hiring a Business Development Officer, based in Yellowknife. One of their responsibilities would be to solicit more stake orders from other exploration and mining companies, as well as go after the core sample box business, which was a big item in the north. They grinned continuously as I spoke. And then I shared with them what I had in mind regarding building a new, fully-equipped wood shop, where they could make kitchen cupboards for the new homes that were built every year as well as other wood products for the community. "And we might be able to get a contract to make the boards and bleachers for the new Community Arena," that rumour suggested would be built next year. Brian rubbed his hands – he could feel the dollar bills in his sweaty palms; Slim rolled his eyes; Andy smiled self-consciously; and Jim blinked and grinned a gummy smile.

I promised myself, right there and then, that this would be my number one infrastructure project next year, if I were to stay, because the wood shop represented the only alternative employment in the community for men like Jim Sproule and Slim, and they deserved an opportunity. It was the perfect job for them. Some men didn't want to work at the mines. They wanted to live in Lutsel K'e because of the traditional lifestyle it afforded – they could trap and fish whenever they wanted, and just needed to pick up some work here and there to pay bills. Others, like Jim, had no other option but to live in the community because of their criminal record while others, such as Andy and Slim, didn't function well in the city – they usually got into trouble. Slim fought too much and Andy was too quiet so the more aggressive types took advantage of him.

Jim said they had about two weeks of work left and that he was looking forward to going to Yellowknife for some R and R. "Will you help me, as you did last year, if I get stuck in Yellowknife with no money for the flight back?" he asked.

"No. You should buy a round trip ticket when you have the money, before you go to Yellowknife. Leave the return ticket with Tina at the airport and you'll have nothing to worry about." Such an obvious, sensible decision, but as with so many others in the community, I knew Jim would only buy a one-way ticket. He would want to have the most amount of money possible in his pocket at all times, just in case. Just in case, what? The answer was, "Just in case." I'd questioned many passengers going out on a one-way ticket and they just gave me a silly smile. They knew it didn't make sense, but it was a habit with them I guess. I usually said something like, "So you're leaving us – not planning to return, eh? When they asked, "Why?" I said, "You didn't buy a return ticket." "Oh", they said and laughed.

And then I had this great idea. I had thought earlier of paying the crew a cash bonus at Christmas for their good work over the summer, but instead, I decided to buy a round trip ticket to Yellowknife for them. That way, they could go and have a good time and not worry about where the money was going to come from to pay their fare back. I'd make arrangements for Tina to keep their return tickets.

What a bunch. They'd learned how to survive and get something out of life, even though going to Yellowknife and getting bombed out of their gourds for days on end wasn't my idea of fun and excitement, but it was their choice, and who was I to judge? They were hard working, truly appreciative to have a job, and you could see they were pleased to be part of a group in the community with a common goal and shared aspirations.

I went outside with them and watched as they walked back to the wood shop. Unless my eyes deceived me, they walked taller with more purposeful measured strides. Even Ursa Major appeared to be a good inch taller.

Auction at the Hudson's Bay Warehouse

I first became aware of the old Hudson's Bay warehouse the second week I was there. The revelation came out quite nonchalantly when I was looking for motor oil for the loader. Check the old Bay warehouse, Vince suggested. My ears pricked up. "The old Bay warehouse? You mean, "THE Hudson's Bay warehouse. It's still standing?"

"Yeah. It's down on the shore. Sunrise should have the key." The warehouse was tiny by today's standards – only about 400 square feet with no windows and no flooring. Hand sawed planks set on a diagonal made up the shed. Shafts of sunlight streamed through uneven gaps in the boards, where the caulking had fallen out, partially revealing the contents that were carelessly dumped in there over the years. Situated just twenty feet from shore, the warehouse was surrounded by an untidy accumulation of large pieces of construction materials: foam panels, window frames and the like. Smaller pieces, left over from community building projects, were stored inside. The warehouse was full to the rafters. All I could do was to peer into the room from the half open door way.

Hudson's Bay warehouse

Sustained frustration led to the idea of holding a community auction. After three unsuccessful searches for motor oil, I decided to take the place apart and sort it out. I'd make two piles: items the corporation could use, and one of other "stuff," and maybe an auction would be the fairest way to get rid of the other "stuff." We could donate the proceeds to the Day Care Centre. The directors supported my initiative at the next Board meeting.

Notices proclaiming an auction would be held at the Hudson's Bay warehouse on Saturday at 10 a.m. sharp were posted on bulletin boards all over town. The Fire Crew agreed to assist in manhandling the items and Sunrise agreed to do the paperwork, leaving me free to act as the auctioneer.

"It will be clear and sunny in Lutsel K'e with a high of 12 degrees," the weatherman on my clock radio announced, stirring me into wakefulness. I removed the cardboard insert from the window to let in the fine 12 degree day. That's not bad. We should get a good crowd. After such a protracted dark and cold winter, April's lighter and warmer weather was being received with great enthusiasm in the community.

It was just a little before 10am when I struggled to unlock the oversized and underused padlock on the warehouse door. Sunlight poured in like Christmas shoppers clamouring at a Boxing Day sale. The illuminated dry, dusty stock looked pathetic. Did I really have the gall to ask for a bid on this graveyard of junk? It was 10:30 and I hadn't seen a soul: no Fire Crew, no Sunrise and more importantly, no customers. "Any time is Dene time," they say. I just had to be patient.

At 10:45 Madeline Tonka padded down the shore road in her moose-hide moccasins, and not surprisingly noticed me and nodded. Was she not wondering why I was standing there? As I watched her shuffle off into the distance, my mind wandered and I thought of the Dene and of their struggles as they adjusted to their new way of life. I contemplated their social issues and the pressures being applied for them to conform. How their lifestyles, which they'd practised for thousands of years, were now, all of a sudden, in jeopardy. They were told that they were dubious and unhealthy and their tradition of intermarrying to keep their bloodlines pure was now frowned upon. There was so much to consider.

11:00 and still no one. I wasn't in any hurry – didn't have other plans. Besides, the sun felt wonderful on my dry face and arms after such a long winter. As I stared out at the frozen landscape again, I marvelled at how the Dene survive this brutally harsh climate. Didn't they realize that if they just kept walking south it would get warmer and there would be more of everything for them? Why had they persisted in living in such an impossible, hostile environment, generation after generation? It was the Land of course. They were one with the Land. It was as simple as that.

At 11:30, I decided to call it a day. Maybe it wasn't such a good idea after all. They could all afford to buy brand new stuff when they needed it. Before heading up the hill for home, I popped in to Joe and Julie's for a brief social visit. "How much did you make?" Joe asked, as I sank into his sofa with a mug of coffee.

"Tell me. Do I look like a vacuum cleaner salesperson, or a magistrate? "I asked of Joe. He just grinned.

Around 12:30 Naomi came to Joe's looking for me. She wanted to know when the auction was. "You're too late. It was this morning and everything's gone!" I joked. The look on her face spoke volumes. She was deflated and irritably disappointed, as if she'd missed the Giant Boxing Day Sale. "No, only kidding. It hasn't started yet." A smile broke out across her face as if a salesperson had just discovered what she was looking for under the counter. She regained her composure and said many people wanted to come. "They do?" Here we go again on the Lutsel K'e roller coaster. What to do? "Tell everyone we'll have the auction at 2:00pm then. And tell them to bring lots of money, because the proceeds are going to the Day Care."

"I will," she replied, and hurried off to spread the news.

Sunrise said she got busy but would try to come, but she had things to do first. Four of the Fire Crew said they'd be there.

It was two on the dot when I scanned the motley, unusually prompt crowd of about forty souls: forty beaming, excited faces, waiting for me to begin this "never before in Lutsel K'e" event. I was pumped, but a little nervous, for I'd never been an auctioneer before. The gathering was in a good mood: laughing, joking and obviously serious about taking something home. I'd been to many auctions in my time, but had never seen such a merry group as this waiting for an auction to begin. They were down there and I was up here, on the top step of the warehouse. I was on stage and they were waiting for the show to begin. Without further ado, I welcomed them, thanked them for coming and reminded them that the proceeds would go to the Day Care. Their hearty claps caught me off guard. Why were they clapping? I hadn't done anything yet! They continued to clap and stare with big, beaming eyes.

Four firefighters arrived and began pulling materials out of the shed and piling them up against the outside walls and on the ground around the warehouse. As they did this, I asked the people to think about what they could use, what it was worth to them, and to get ready to bid. The highest bidder wins, I told them. Be sure you know what you're bidding on and the quantity involved, because some things will be auctioned off individually and other things will be sold off as a package.

"OK. Are you ready?"

"Yes" they hollered back.

"OK. Then let the games begin." I realized I said this more for my own amusement, because I was in a humorous and silly mood. Did I get too much sun in the morning?

I began with four good pieces of insulation batting, holding them high above my head for everyone to see. "Who'll bid five bucks for this excellent insulation?" I called out in a strong clear voice, and looked around at the crowd to see if anyone had raised a hand. But all I saw were curious, smiling faces staring back at me, waiting for me to continue. In an instant, I realized they'd never been to an Auction and didn't know what to do. "If you can use this insulation and you think it's worth five bucks, put up your hand." About ten hands went up. "OK, does anyone think it's worth ten bucks? The ten hands went up again. "Fifteen? Anybody give me fifteen?" The ten bidders looked at each other to see what the other was doing. One hand went up. "OK, I have fifteen bucks. Anybody give me twenty?" The successful bidder at fifteen raised her hand. I smiled and the crowd sensed there was something wrong with the picture. "If no one bids twenty then you get the insulation for fifteen," I politely advised the older lady in the blue fleece jacket with coyote trim. She nodded and smiled self-consciously. "Anybody give me twenty?" Two hands shot up. "Anybody give me twenty five?" Three hands went up this time. "Thirty?" Two hands shot up.

I was feeling extremely uncomfortable because thirty dollars was far too much for the old insulation. I took a minute to point to the many stacks behind me and said there was lots of insulation to be auctioned off, probably more than enough to go round for everyone that wanted some.

"I'm at twenty five, who'll give me thirty?" No one raised a hand. Now I was in a bit of a predicament because three people had bid twenty-five. I should have selected one bidder, but not having done this before, I was shooting from the hip, making it all up as I went along. Without further ado, I picked out two other bundles of four pieces of roughly the same quality and gave them to the three bidders.

Because Sunrise hadn't yet made an appearance, I was left to do all of the tasks: collect the money, make change and record the particulars on the clipboard. I put the money in my right hand trouser pocket so that it didn't get mixed up with my own money in my left hand pocket. From that point on I was in high gear. It was obvious everybody was enjoying their day out, and the novelty of entertaining this merry band was such an appealing opportunity I exploited it to the fullest. Raising the volume and pitch of my voice I shouted from the rostrum. "Who'll give twenty for this bundle of good clean insulation? You'll save at least that on your first month's heating bill." The receptive crowd laughed and reciprocated with comments, which the whole assembly found humorous. When they were the highest bidder, neighbours acknowledged their victory with demonstrative body language: hearty pats on the back and exaggerated thumbs up gestures, making them feel as happy as when they won a Bingo.

As the glorious afternoon drifted on, the strong sunshine continued to beat down warmly, relaxing us and melting away our inhibitions. The proceedings had forged a bond between performer and audience. We were as one and were mutually enjoying this special get-together. Everyone was getting a little silly; in fact it was getting downright hilarious. Partners were bidding against each other and some were bidding exorbitant amounts on low value goods, being comically urged on by the throng to bid higher and higher.

Tundra, Harry Erickson's wife, wanted Harry to be put up for auction. She wanted to see how much her neighbours thought he was worth. The crowd laughed heartily when she pushed Harry forward and I came down to get him. He was a good sport and co-operated fully, though feigning resistance and umbrage. We climbed the four wooden steps and turned around to face the crowd. I exhibited Harry to the assembled, having him turn around slowly to fully show off his wares; a servile slave being paraded before wealthy, discriminating plantation owners. Sucking in his gut, he flexed his body and biceps and smiled but alas, it couldn't disguise his true physical condition.

I started the bidding at a hundred dollars. "Who'll give a hundred for this wonderful specimen of mankind?" Everyone shook their heads no. "Come on folks. Think of the little children who are going to benefit from your bid today? Come on ladies. Wouldn't it be good to have another man in the house, give your hubby some competition?" Everyone broke into fits of laughter and shook their heads no. "Surely someone has fifty for this strong, mature, gentleman. Just think what he can do for you – he's all yours for just fifty dollars!" The heads shook again and the crowd roared and shouted out comments about Harry's usefulness, much to everyone's amusement, and in particular to Harry's wife, who was doubled over with laughter and wiping away tears with her scarf. "OK forty bucks, the price of a pizza. Look what you get for forty bucks. Look at him – he'll keep you toasty warm on those long, cold, winter nights. Come on folks, only thirty bucks then, surely someone, anyone must have thirty bucks for this very special gentleman."

I pleaded with Harry's wife to part with thirty bucks, but she gestured no. "Okay. We're at twenty bucks. That's less than ten cents a pound. You can't buy fish for that!" The congregation was ecstatic and joyous when Harry, feigning much embarrassment and disappointment, slunk back to his wife's side. Tundra gestured that she disowned him and Harry responded with the biggest smile I ever saw him beam.

And with every sale, I stuffed the money into my pocket, made change, recorded the transaction and kept the crowd at bay. When I did this, they got restless and impatient. They were always eager to start the bidding again. I was amazed that everything got a bid. When I got to the end of an item and there were just bits and pieces left, I bundled it all together and said, "Okay, who'll give me five bucks," and sure enough at least one hand went up.

It had been three hours since the bidding opened, and we had found homes for all of the insulation, windows, glass, lights, piping, tubing, plumbing and wiring, soffits, fascia and tiles. The last item was a bundle of miscellaneous wood, of all different lengths and thicknesses, and this of course went in short order at a high price because it was such a useful item in Lutsel K'e.

I thanked everyone for coming, for opening their wallets, and hoped that they had as much fun as I did. I told them that on Monday, I'd post the total amount of money raised for the Day Care on the bulletin boards in the community. They walked away with their goodies, as happy as children leaving a Christmas party; nearly everyone had something tucked under their arms.

And just as I was padlocking the now empty Hudson's Bay warehouse, Rainbow came up and pleaded, "Can we have another auction next Saturday?"

Sunrise posted a notice on all of the community billboards on the following Monday that we had made $685 for the Day Care Centre.

A Terrifying Homecoming

I went out of town the last Sunday in May for a week of business meetings in Edmonton and Yellowknife. When I returned in the early afternoon of the following Sunday, I stopped in at Joe and Julie's, as was my custom, to say hi and get caught up on the events of the week. It had been a slow week Julie said, where nothing much had happened. I remembered thinking that was a very pleasant change.

Around 4pm I said goodbye and went home. I unlocked the deadbolt but I couldn't open the door. The second lock: the door handle you twisted when you leave, must have been locked, but I never used that one because I didn't have a key. There was someone in the house. I held my breath and focused on listening. I could hear people in the house: more than one and they were running. I jumped down the four short steps from the porch to the driveway, sprinted across the back of the house, bounded up the stairs two at a time to the wrap around deck, and raced along the side of the house to the picture windows at the front. I saw at least two shadowy shapes dart into the darkened hallway.

I raced back to the front door but it was still locked. They must still be inside. I definitely saw two shapes and they were big. I was out numbered. That was not a good situation. I held my breath and listened intently. Silence. They must be in there waiting to jump me.

Armed with a three foot two by four that I pulled from the woodpile under the stoop, I carefully began checking the doors and windows. The bedroom patio door was unlocked and the bed had been pushed forward. That's how they must have broken in. I slid the door open about a foot, squeezed in, and wielding the weapon with both hands above my head, stopped and listened. There should never have been a patio door in that wall in the first place. That was Bob's error. As if I'd ever want to open the drapes and walk around in my pyjamas in full view of the water and sewage truck drivers doing their pumping! I'd moved the wooden, king-sized bed up against the door and tried to forget about it.

The silence was deafening and threatening. Who were they and where were they? I thought through how I was going to check out the house to find them before they found me. The most likely place would be a closet, but which one?

"Come out, whoever you are," I yelled from the patio door-sill in the most threatening voice I could muster. "Better you come out now. I've got a chunk of wood and by God I'm going to use it." My imagination heard breathing and felt heartbeats. "Okay, you asked for it. I'm coming in." I was confident because I was wielding a lethal weapon and had every intention of using it. But what if they had a gun, or a knife? The thought sent a shiver through my body. Okay, I'd rush them and swing away at their hands. What else could I do?

I took two steps, listened and looked around. The bedroom was a mess. It reeked of urine and faeces. It was so disgusting that I had to put my head outside momentarily to get some fresh air. The hardwood floor was caked with dried red footprints – not just one set of tracks – many, so many they formed a dull red carpet leading from the window to the door. The red stain was even on the trim. What was it? Blood!

The bed had been slept in. I'd made my bed before I left, always had. The duvet and bed sheets were messed up. And the strange red stains blotted the white sheets, the walls and even the ceiling. "Holy cow! What the hell had happened here? That can't all be blood, surely?" I was scared and shaking with fear and anger. All I could think of was cracking some skulls.

I waved the bat from side to side – it felt more lethal by the second. I had an urge to go racing in and just flail away, but being long in the tooth, I had learned many years ago to overcome impulses like that. They couldn't get out without me catching them. This thinking transformed me into a calculated assailant.

I tiptoed across the room to the closet, grabbed the knob on the bi-fold door, and holding the club above my head, slid the door across its tracks in one fell swoop. They weren't in there. I moved into the hallway, stopped and listened. It was as silent as a morgue. The same red carpet ran down the hall and into the other two bedrooms at the end. Should I go into the bedrooms and check under the beds and in the closets? No. The prudent thing would be to close the doors. I could always race back and get them if I heard them making a bolt for it.

Standing at the end of the hallway, I could see into the kitchen and the living room and it looked like a war zone: a bloody war zone but there was no sign of life. That meant they were downstairs with the water and sewage tanks. Perfect. I've got them now I thought and they can't escape. I made up my mind that whoever it was was going to get whacked. None of that namby-pamby legal shit, where the judge hands down some pansy community service chores. An eye for an eye.

I went down the stairs with deliberate heavy feet. There was no one there. They must have been in the bedroom after all! The thought frightened me. I raced back upstairs as fast as I could and checked the bedrooms, but there was no one in the house except me! I was relieved in one way, yet disappointed that I didn't get a chance to use my club.

Looking at the dirt and the mess and breathing in the soiled air made me want to puke. It was a shit home and now it was even shittier. On the coffee table was an array of personal items, which I had kept in the drawers of my dresser. Two bottles of light blue ink and two fountain pens, with caps and lids removed, sat in the middle of a large, thick, dry blue stain. They drowned before I could save them. Also in this pool of iniquity, were my chequebook and two loose cheques, both made out for a million dollars, but no payee? How interesting!

My telescope, binoculars, mouth organ and a GPS tracker were missing. So was my digital camera, the walkie-talkie set my son gave me last Christmas, and the set of hurricane lamps a friend had given me to dress up the place.

I called the RCMP and Peter came over right away. He was shocked at the mess but sympathetic. "It's kids who done this," he said in a broad Newfoundland accent. With notebook and camera in hand, he went with me from room to room, noting the damage and what was missing. Every drawer in the house had been ransacked. The gross smell came from the two toilets, which had been used many times but not flushed. The flush didn't work. I was either out of water, or the sewage tank was full. Every cup, plate and spoon in the house was dirty and either in the sink, or on the counter, next to two empty tins of mandarin oranges, an empty bag of Dad's oatmeal cookies and numerous candy wrappers. Used tea bags and bread and cookie crumbs occupied the remaining counter space.

Now I knew what the stains were. They were berries. Three greasy, empty zip-lock freezer bags lay on the counter and Peter found two more between the sheets in the smaller bedroom and there were two more in the garbage can in the second bathroom: three bags of raspberries, two of blueberries and two of cranberries. I remembered distinctly how many I had picked and packed.

The top dresser drawer was full of shaving foam. All of my private papers; bank statements, Visa statements, bills and the like, had been removed, mixed up and haphazardly shoved back into the drawer.

The once beautiful blue moose hide slippers, which Madeline Drymoose had crafted, were stained beyond salvage with deep blue ink.

My mind was numb, my brain pooched – nothing was working – I couldn't think – no ideas came. My emotions were frozen. I could not relate to what was happening. All I knew, and it was more of a subconscious feeling than a thought, was that this was my last day in that horrible place. It would be pure insanity to stay. There were no other words to describe it.

Constable King called from the kitchen. "I think you'd better come and take a look at this." He went through the garbage can under the sink and had spread the contents out on the floor. Among the mess were photographs; bits of photographs; a hundred or so tiny pieces of ripped up photographs of my children and grandchildren. They had been under the magnets on the fridge door. It felt like someone hit me between the eyes with a two by four. I couldn't believe it. My knees sagged and my spirit drained as if someone had pulled my plug. I felt like a sack of straw. "What cretin would do a thing like that? Why are my kids involved?" Tears poured down my face.

The sympathetic policeman didn't have any answers. "It's better I leave now. I have everything I need," he said, politely excusing himself. I thanked him and locked the door. Why would someone cut up pictures of little children into hundreds of pieces? Wasn't it enough just to rip them in half? What must they have been thinking? Why? Why? The photos were the only connection I had with my children. I looked at their dismembered images and my heart felt as if it had been ripped out. Whoever did this was sick. I just wanted to go to sleep to get out of the nightmare. But not in that house. I was never going to step foot in there again. Someone else could get my things.

Joe laughed when he opened the door and I asked if I could sleep there, but he got angry like I'd never seen before when I told him what had happened. He was physically distraught and started swearing about the community. Julie fed me and we sat around until late talking about it. "Neighbours must have known what was going on. Why didn't they call the cops," Julie asked. Drained and despondent, I hit the sack and looked forward to the unconsciousness of sleep.

It was ten the next morning when I staggered into the living room for a cup of coffee and a talk with Joe. Even though it was a statutory holiday, Julie had gone to work – she worked long hours. I had planned on working too, but now the thought sickened me. When Sunrise called Joe to see where I was, he told her what had happened and said I'd be in touch in due course. "Tell Al I went home," was her message.

"That's all she said?"

"Yeah, that's all she said."

Talking it through with Joe helped. The right words put things into better perspective and brought emotions under more manageable control. It wasn't my house or my furnishings after all, and the Corporation would surely pay me for what was stolen.

But it was the photos where the hurt was excruciating. I tried not to think about them, but try as I might I couldn't stop the ragged images of little children flashing in front of my eyes. My heart wanted me to feel, not to think, and with the flashes, came the uncontrollable welling up in my guts and the tears.

By noon I was emotionally drained again, but I was beginning to come to grips with the situation and to think about what to do. I could just get on a plane. I realized that. I would have to pack, take care of loose ends, get organized and make arrangements. But where would I go? We had just sold the house and Sue was coming in three weeks. What a dilemma!

And there was another wrinkle. As I had the only house in the community with two spare bedrooms, I had agreed with Julie to take in two twenty-year old girls for three months, while they completed their co-op work term in the community. They would be arriving in two days. It wouldn't be fair for them to go into a house in that condition. What if they were my daughters! And chances were that there would not be any other accommodation available in town for them on such short notice.

"What a perfect solution Al," Julie said. "You won't have to worry about "break and enters" for the next three months. And you get paid by your house sitters. How sweet was that?" she added, trying to inject some humour to lighten the load.

"Be better if the rent went into my pocket," I replied. "I'd bring in cleaners for a day to do a real clean."

When I called the two people who did house cleaning in the community and told them what had happened, they declined to help. They had plans. "It's a stat," they said. Their lack of empathy and co-operation surprised and infuriated me.

"Come on," Joe said. "We can make a start and the girls can finish." Phone calls to rustle up some heavy-duty cleaning equipment proved futile. People were away camping or sleeping. The school janitors didn't answer their phone. We were wasting valuable time when we could be cleaning. The little squeegee was useless but it's all we had. We made more frantic calls. There was either no answer, or the response was, "Sorry, we don't have anything like that."

Joe worked away at the mud with the squeegee, and I was right behind on hands and knees, wiping and smearing the pigment stains with old rags. By the time Joe called it quits at four to go home and start supper, he must have made at least a hundred trips to the sink to squeeze out the dirty water. I continued cleaning, squeegeeing the floor, wiping the berry stains off the furniture, walls and trim, in between loading the washer with bedding, picking up broken furnishings and trash and putting the house back in order. By five o'clock it looked neater but it was still filthy.

Getting out of the house and going down to Joe's for supper was a much-needed break and proved to be refreshingly therapeutic. The reminiscing over supper about the strange happenings and unusual escapades we'd experienced since we arrived reminded me that I had really come for the adventure, and that realisation set in motion a gradual change in my mindset. I began to look at events from a totally different perspective. Putting the photos to one side, I could see that this development was just more of the same. "It's not boring, that's for sure," Julie reminded me. "You said you wanted adventure. You've got to be careful what you wish for."

"Did I ever," I readily agreed.

"And you knew there were risks associated with going into an unfamiliar place."

"Yes, I did." I had to admit. I just wished I hadn't put the children's photos on the fridge, that's all.

By seven, I was back at the house and at the chores but in a totally different frame of mind. The cleaning had to continue for the sake of the students, but it was not bothering me as it did before supper. I now accepted that it had to be done and that's all there was to it.

Time heals so the old adage goes, and in this case it did. With each sunrise, I got emotionally stronger and had a sense of warming back to life from being in a stupor. My reaction to the whole mess was morphing from one of abject horror to one of hilarious disbelief. Socializing with business colleagues in Yellowknife helped. After many good laughs, I left their company feeling buoyed and even more resolute to stay the course, at least for a little while.

"I gave the house keys to your students and I've seen them around town, smiling away with that stunned naive grin all students wear for the first week, so they seem to have settled in," Julie informed me when I dropped by for my ritual coffee after returning to the community.

They moved in all right, and had immediately taken over. There were dirty dishes in the sink, clothes hanging on door handles and draped over the backs of chairs and on the arms of the sofa. As I picked up the towel from the bathroom floor and pushed aside the bottles and packets on the counter to make space for my toiletry bag, I laughed and wondered if this was going to work out. What price was I prepared to pay to have house sitters for three months? And the place was even messier than when I left!

Soon after five, the girls came chuckling in, bubbling over with youthful enthusiasm and excitement, their faces as bright as a pair of five-year-olds getting out of the tub.

Over a hasty, hearty spaghetti supper, which I treated them to, we began the process of getting to know one another. Neither of them had noticed the dirty floors, walls, or trim, nor the stained ceilings, but they did apologize for leaving the house messy and promised to be neater in the future. "We didn't know for sure when you were coming home!" was their excuse. Once I'd explained about the house invasion and pointed out the dirt, we all agreed to do a clean-up on the weekend, but it was obvious their only motivation was driven by politeness to please their host.

On the following Wednesday, three of the directors – Vince, Mickey and Jessy – attended the Board meeting. They had heard about the break-in. Vince opened the meeting with the Lord's Prayer and then asked me in an accusatory tone, "Don't you have content insurance? Why didn't you get a house sitter?" Two well-prepared, well-rehearsed comments designed to immediately shift the blame from the community onto me, which caught me off guard.

Impulsively I replied, "I'm not impressed and I'll be resigning once everything is settled with the police. I thought the corporation would reimburse me for my personal losses."

"No, we won't do that," Vince tersely advised. No one said a word. Mickey and Jesse looked nervously at Vince for direction. Although I was sure they felt bad about the break-in and the fact that I was missing some things and they probably even expected me to resign, they didn't say a word. I think they just didn't know what to say. Any words at that juncture would have been acceptable but silence wasn't.

I left the room angry and disappointed. Vince returned to the agenda and continued with the meeting. It was business as usual for them, but not for me.

Over the next three days, I stayed home and pondered what to do. Sunrise called now and then and asked if I could sign a cheque if she came up to the house. "Sure, come on up," I replied, but other than that, there was no more communication with work.

Peter dropped by the house one afternoon. "Have you quit?" was his greeting after I unlocked and opened the door.

"Not in writing but I've told them I'm going to."

"Well let me tell you what I've found," he said, as we made our way into the living room for a social visit. Sensing this might take a while, I offered him coffee and he accepted. "The place looks better than when I was here last. Who cleaned it?"

"You're looking at him."

"Why do you stay?"

I didn't immediately respond because I didn't have a quick answer. While I was thinking about it, Peter proudly took out his policeman's notebook, flipped through the pages to find the start, and began to interpret his notes in the fashion that he was trained in.

"On the fifth I went to the school. This was very productive. The Grade 5 teacher was wondering who owned the digital camera he took off one of the students. He caught the boy when he turned quickly around from the blackboard to see what the class was laughing at. The kid was apparently taking photos of him when his back was turned and was sharing the images with his classmates. The child's name was Samuel. The teacher also had your mouth organ."

"Good work Peter. I know Samuel and it doesn't surprise me," I replied. I didn't say anymore because Peter was on a roll and I didn't want to interrupt his train of thought.

"I spoke with the other children in the class and they were very open with me. Many of them had been in your house. I have the list of names here if you want them."

"Carry on, I'll get them later."

"After supper on the fifth, I went round to Samuel's house and spoke with his mother. She at first feigned indignation and doubted that Samuel was the culprit, but when I told her what the other children in the class had said, she reluctantly agreed to let me in and took me to Samuel's bedroom. There I found your walkie-talkies and spyglass. They're down at the station for evidence. On the sixth, I returned to the Grade 5 class and spoke individually with those who admitted to being in your house. Do you want me to go through all of their responses? They all said much the same – they just went to your house to play."

"No. Who cut up the photos? That's all I want to know."

"I was just getting to that. All the children answered my questions without hesitation and what they told me corroborated each other's story. Gareth cut up the photos. He's another ten-year-old."

"I don't know him," I replied.

"You will. You'll meet the nine under-twelve-year-olds next Monday in the gym, when we have a hearing, and the three over-twelve-year-olds will meet with you individually, as called for in the Young Offenders Act." In a small community such as Lutsel K'e, twelve children represented the whole community. Peter said most of the children had used the house four or five times. They came after school to play. The younger children had used it as a playhouse, others had ordered movies on the TV satellite account and there was a strong indication that older teens had visited later in the evening when the younger children were safely tucked up in their beds.

Peter continued with his report. Although he wasn't able to get any concrete confirmation from the neighbours that they were aware of what was going on, he said, "My sense is that it was public knowledge throughout the community. With that much traffic coming and going, many adults must have known, but no one reported it."

The helpful and sympathetic policeman said there was a good chance that some of the other missing items were still in the community, and that it was safe to assume many adults knew about them, but he didn't think the GPS unit would be found. It had probably already been sold in Yellowknife, in some bar for cash.

The next day, a Tuesday, Freddie, a past Chief and respected Elder in the community, came to see me. He was a little sheepish and said he wanted to tell me something off the record and didn't want anything he said to be repeated and that he didn't want any trouble.

"Go ahead." He smiled slyly and told me he went into my house. He waited for a reaction but I didn't give him one. "Go on."

"There were children in your house. I shooed them away."

"Go on."

He then said, with the air of a Good Samaritan, "I found some of your cheques on the coffee table. They were made out to certain children. I put them in the third drawer of your bedroom dresser. The names on the cheques will tell you which kids were involved. I just wanted to tell you this."

"I found the cheques and we know who was involved and the RCMP are laying Break and Enter charges against the three who are over twelve," I replied to his confession, but I didn't give him absolution. And it felt good. Good, because I had stepped out of character and resisted the urge to say, "Thank you for this Freddie." Being overly polite, even in such a ridiculous situation such as this, was an unwanted legacy from my British upbringing, which I continually struggled with. I had to think about it. It didn't come easy. I didn't ask him what he was doing in my house in the first place, why he didn't call the cops, or why he didn't let Vince know. I didn't want to hear him, or speak with him after that because I didn't want to hear his voice anymore and his lame excuses.

Feeling uncomfortable with my vacant, cold look, he turned and walked away, feeling I'm sure, more uncomfortable than he did when he first approached me, and certainly more uncomfortable than I.

When something like this happens in a small community, everyone hears about it quickly because it's the topic of conversation at supper tables, at least for a few days. At the Co-op, I met some of the parents of the children involved, but no one brought up the house invasion, nor did they apologize directly for the involvement of their child. But there was a sorrow in their eyes and in their over-friendly demeanour; a sorrow and regret far stronger than any words could possibly convey. I sensed it and it saddened me. Everyone else I met wanted to discuss the event in great detail and took their leave by apologizing on behalf of their community.

Over the weekend, I thought about how I was going to handle the meeting with the children and decided that I would be tough on them, knowing full well that the guardians would be uncomfortable even if the children weren't.

Everyone was there at five minutes to seven when I arrived at the school gymnasium. Peter had arranged the chairs in a huge semi-circle in the middle of the spacious floor with three chairs at the front; one for himself, one for Andrea Laverly, the Justice co-ordinator, and one for me. In front of the chairs was a table, upon which were articles from the house.

My running shoes squeaked on the recently mopped floor breaking the uneasy silence in the cavernous hall, as I walked through the gym, past the seated backs of uncomfortable adults and children. It was the type of expectant silence you only hear in a courtroom, as the assembled await the entrance of the judge. No one turned around to look nor did those on the opposite side raise their heads as I walked through. Peter and Andrea maintained the peace by nodding as I took my seat. On the table were about a dozen pieces of the ripped up photos, the berry stained moccasins, the walkie-talkie set, inkbottle as well as various other items.

With his trained eye, Peter looked around the room to ensure everyone was seated and ready for the proceedings to begin. He broke the silence by announcing the reason why we were there and stated, in a regulatory and judicious fashion, that this hearing was part of the provisions of the new Young Offenders Act.

Every child had to be accompanied by a guardian, which in this case were mothers and grandmothers. Peter and I were the only males in the room. By now, Peter had the full story down pat, and even though he had no need of his notes, he pretended to consult his little blue book periodically, giving the hearing a gravity it might otherwise not have had. He proceeded to retell the events in chronological order, not missing any detail. There was no sound other than Peter's voice and the odd cough, and no discernible movement, until he handled the stained moccasins.

Chairs rattled and echoed through the gym as the adults shifted uneasily in their chairs. Their jaws dropped and a distraught look appeared on their faces. I don't know if Peter planned it this way – saving the best for last – but this was the only item on the table that educed a strong reaction. It was a desecration in their eyes.

Peter looked at the children and told them that they must face Mr. Henry and tell him what they did when they went to his house and to answer Mr. Henry's questions. With that, Peter turned the session over to me.

I was in no hurry to get this over with. On the contrary, it was my thinking that the longer I kept them there, the more they might remember it. It felt like a courtroom. I took my time, going from left to right, studying every face of the women and children in the room. A few children looked up. Some faces revealed confusion; others, the innocent guilt of a child. Speaking to the group at large, I recalled the sequence of events and shared with them how I felt.

When I got to the part about finding the ripped photographs in the garbage, I lost it and had to leave the room for a minute. Upon my return, I spoke to them of my anger, my disgust and my feelings of personal violation. My voice was loud and admonishing. I spoke slowly so that every word would sink in with full effect.

"I came here to help," I said and asked rhetorically, "Is this how you repay me? I will be leaving soon because of this," I added. To the children I said, "You're lucky I'm not your father, or grandfather because if I were, I'd put you over my knee and teach you a lesson." The room filled with negative energy. The guardians looked up and glared at me. I didn't care. This made me feel better, because now I knew I had their full attention and was connecting at last. The Dene don't discipline their children the way we do in my culture. They shout at them and feel this is all they're expected to do as parents. And then they quickly forgive and forget, rationalizing that they're only children.

Their reaction strengthened my resolve and I sat bolt upright in my chair and looked around again at each adult and child. I was stern and looking for retribution. There was anger and hurt in my face and voice. I made eye contact with anyone who dared look my way. A few children did, but not one guardian dared. Experience had taught them not to. Most children only looked at me fleetingly and then, frightened by my demeanour, cast their eyes downward to stare at the floor. One child was nervous and hid her head under a blanket on her mother's lap. She hadn't come out since we sat down. One little boy looked bewildered and just stared blank faced at me with a timid, half-smile. It was now 7:35 and the children were beginning to get restless with all this adult talking. Some looked around the gym, wide eyed, wondering when the next basketball game was going to begin. Now that I'd had my say, my heart began to soften and my sternness to dissipate. I looked at all the little faces and thought, "They're just kids. I have grandkids just like them. I know they made a huge mess, but they're just kids." And Dene children are so friendly and loveable. They are so naive in some ways yet street smart, but the bottom line is they are just kids. I felt sorry for them.

It was not the Dene way to confront issues as blatantly and dramatically as we did that night. Peter began with the child on his left, a ten-year-old girl called Sweetgrass. He asked her a number of questions. "Did she go into the house? How many times? What did she do there?" She whispered a few answers.

I addressed her and asked. "Why did you go into my house?" Her answer was so quiet it was inaudible. She was looking down at her shoes.

Peter jumped in and said in an authoritative policeman's voice. "You must look at Mr. Henry when he's speaking to you and you must speak louder." She looked up briefly, then back down at her shoes. I repeated the question.

She pointed her finger at another girl in the room. "Because she did."

"Did you know it was wrong to go into my house?"

"Yeah."

"Why did you go in if you knew it was wrong?"

She shrugged her shoulders and raised her eyebrows. "I don't know."

"What did you do in my house?"

"Play."

"Who cut up the photographs?" As soon as I spoke those words, my eyes welled up and an involuntary shake seized my body. Again I excused myself and looked sideways at the wall on my way out so no one could see my tears, but I sensed they felt my pain. Their auras of anguish made the air heavy and stifling. I went to the bathroom, blew my nose and splashed water on my face. I returned and sat down.

Peter asked Sweetgrass to answer Mr. Henry's question. "Gareth," she said in a matter of fact manner. "He cut the pictures." I looked down the line and picked out the boy everyone was looking and pointing at. *Right, you little shit, just wait 'til I get round to you*, I pledged to myself.

It was unfortunate Sweetgrass was the first child to receive my heavy handed lecturing, sermonizing and discipline, because she was obviously just a pawn, but I had promised myself that every child, without exception, would be spoken to harshly until they were on the verge of tears, so that they'd remember this day forever. Her tears came quicker than I thought.

And so it went with each child. When I mentioned that it was lucky for them that I didn't have any guns in the house, because some very bad things might have happened, it didn't seem to register with them, but it did with their guardians. I'm sure my statement triggered many traumatic memories. More dirty looks, because I was trying to frighten their children.

I asked them about the inkpots, the GPS unit, the berries and the walkie-talkies. They freely mentioned names and pointed fingers. They used the walkie-talkie sets as an alarm system. Little eight-year old Lucy was positioned at the end of the driveway as a lookout to give the alert should an adult show up on the scene.

And now I came to the master burglar, the architect of this fiasco, ten-year-old Samuel. He looked straight at me, so confident, brazen, angelic yet cocky. He answered my early general questions honestly, but when I probed and asked him deeper questions about how he felt when he broke into my house, he began to shrug his shoulders, look down at the floor and went dumb. I carried on regardless because I wanted him and everyone else to hear what I had to say.

"Why did you go into my house? Did you want to see me? Why did you break in? Have you ever broken into other people's homes? What were you after – money?" And all he did was shrug. "Have you ever been to a jail? Do you know what it's like in there?" I know he did because his father was incarcerated at that very moment for multiple Break and Enters. "Do you want go to go to jail when you grow up?"

This brought an instant, but quiet, "No." His response heartened me. I'd hit a nerve.

"Well jail is where you'll be going if you were an adult and you did this. Do you understand what I'm saying, Samuel?"

There was no vocal response but I sensed he was listening. "We are all responsible for the decisions we make, do you understand that?" More shrugs. "When you decided to break into my house you were not an innocent child anymore. Many in this room were, but you weren't. You are responsible for us all being here tonight. Do you understand that?" Still no words but he was listening. "That's why we have laws to send people to prison who break the law. Think about it, Samuel. Do this again when you're an adult and you're going to jail."

His mother was glaring down at the floor throughout my sermon. I felt sorry that she was subjected to this indirect humiliation, for everyone in the hall knew of her circumstance, but it couldn't be avoided.

Next to Samuel was a boy and then a girl, who both just went into the house to play, and then next was Gareth. Was he trembling? Was his stomach tied up in knots? What was his mother thinking about?

"Did you cut up the photographs?" I asked sharply but in a quiet, serious voice. He nodded yes, looked at the floor and drew imaginary circles with the point of his running shoe on the shiny gym floor. His mother sat stone-faced by his side. "Why?" He didn't respond in any way.

"You must look at Mr. Henry when he's speaking to you and you must answer Mr. Henry when he asks you a question," the mediator policeman cautioned the young offender.

"Why, did you do that?" I asked again. Realizing that he had to respond, the young lad brought his shoulders up to his neck and let them fall in a defiant "I don't know" gesture.

"I want to take you back to that afternoon when you were in my house. You're standing in front of the fridge, looking at the pictures of little boys and girls. What are you thinking about, Gareth?" He raised his shoulders and let them drop again. "Did the happy smiling faces make you feel resentful? Were you jealous these children were happy? Do you feel loved, Gareth?"

You could cut the air with a knife it was so heavy with tension and anger. Anger directed at me for my troubling remarks to their children. "What were you thinking when you went to find a pair of scissors to cut up the children? Did you feel better when you'd cut them up? Were you smiling when you did it?" There was neither a glimmer of a reaction on his face nor a shift in his physical composure. He just continued to make tight circles with his shoe and shrug his shoulders.

"Why did you do that, Gareth? Did you think you could hurt the children by cutting them up? Have you thought about what you did since that day? Are you sorry?" All the little shit did was shrug his shoulders, and draw faster and smaller circles on the floor. How I wanted to go up to him, shake him and force him to look me in the face.

After a long pause, where he had ample opportunity to say something, I broke the peace and said, "You're a troubled child. Do you know that? You need a lot of counselling son before you grow up because if you don't change, you're going to hurt someone, and you'll be spending a lot of your life behind bars." I knew I was stepping over the line, but I didn't care. I felt I had every right to say whatever I wanted to say. And I didn't feel rushed to say it. I knew Peter and Andrea, the Justice co-ordinator wouldn't interrupt me until I'd had my say. Peter, because he was on side with what I had to say, and Andrea, because she was in a state of shock. I'm sure she never expected that it would turn out like that. But that was it. I had nothing more to say.

Peter and Andrea purposely gave me more time, in case I suddenly thought of something else I wanted to say. After a long pregnant pause, I moved on to the boy sitting next to Gareth and continued on as before. Finally, after an hour and a half, I finished addressing the children.

The Justice co-ordinator said a few words about the Young Offenders reconciliation process, and suggested that all the children come up to my house the next night to clean and do any jobs I gave them. They all enthusiastically agreed, except Samuel and Gareth, who refused to take their eyes off the floor. Peter suggested that each child come up to Mr. Henry and apologize for what they did.

I spoke to the children. "What you did was wrong. You've all told us tonight you knew it was wrong, but you did it anyway. And that's why we're here. Whenever you feel something is wrong you mustn't do it, even if it means losing your friends, or not having friends for a little while. This is why we have a conscience. It tells us what we should and shouldn't do. You must listen to it. There, that's all I'm going to say. I want you to leave here tonight and only take the lesson with you. Forget about the rest because it's not important. I forgive you. That's all that matters."

The children politely lined up in single file, approached me and said, "I'm sorry I went into your house, Mr. Henry." I gave them a big, sincere hug and said to each one, "I forgive you." They acknowledged their relief and thanks with a smile of gratitude; the type of innocent smile only a child can give.

A few adults gave me their regrets and thanked me for speaking to the children. Most of the guardians left the gym holding their child's hand. I noted this, and for some reason, it resonated deeply within me. Maybe it was the message that these pairings were parts of families, and that the kids were only little children after all. My reaction caught me off guard, and I felt on the verge of tears again.

Ethel Petersen said she would make me another pair of moccasins. She didn't. Bertha suggested they have a bake sale, or some kind of fundraising event to pay for the cost of the lost items, but no one seconded the motion, so the suggestion died right there on the gymnasium floor. Samuel came up and went through the motions of apologizing. Was he sincere? I told him that I forgave him and gave him a hug, but he just stood there, hands at his sides, as limp as a wet rag, so unlike the other children, who were so receptive and who hugged me back so warmly. When Gareth stood in front of me he apologized with sad eyes. I could see that he now realized what he did was hurtful. I told him I forgave him and gave him a long, strong hug. He hugged me back and for a fleeting moment, it felt like the hug of my youngest grandchild. I hugged him stronger.

Most of the children came up to the house the next night and picked up every piece of garbage around and under the house. They even continued to clean up, all of the way up to the top of the hill. I provided drinks and cookies when they came in, and we had a little party. I so enjoyed their laughter and smiles. They didn't show any negativity or hard feelings towards me, in fact, since that day, all of the children waved and smiled whenever they saw me. They were now my little friends. Three of the mischievous brew wrote letters of apology and hand delivered them to my house. When I opened the door, they were smiling from ear to ear; pleased with themselves for writing the letters. I thanked them for their consideration.

I met separately with two of the three older children, the ones over twelve years old, who were charged under the Young Offenders Act. I was out of town when the hearing with the third child was scheduled. Because they were older and I was meeting with them on a one on one basis, I was more brutal in my questioning and handling. I led them step by step, action by action, purposely dragging out the event so they had to relive it and tell me how they felt and what they thought throughout the whole invasion. One child appeared truly sorry for causing so much grief. The other just shrugged his shoulders, as Samuel did, at every question and refused to speak. His mother just sat there and didn't say a word. Because they were over twelve years old, the courts directed that they must make some form of restitution. One gave me a caribou roast, one gave two bags of frozen blueberries and the third one gave me a slab of musk ox.

I decided not to resign after all because quite frankly, Sue and I didn't have a Plan B. So confident were we that our immediate future lay in Lutsel K'e that we never considered where we'd go or what we'd do after. Decisions could wait until after she arrived. No point cutting off my nose to spite my face, as my dad used to say.

Joe and Julie were speechless when I told them. "What happened? We didn't think there was any way you'd change your mind, this time." I laughed with them. Others in the community were surprised too and pleased because I think they interpreted this as a sign of true forgiveness. Everyone became noticeably friendlier and more talkative than before.

The girls moved out after two weeks, having found alternative accommodation with work colleagues, and that greatly pleased me because I needed privacy for when Sue arrived. I sensed things would be strained between us, as we got to know each other again, and the last thing I needed was to have strangers living in the house. Through pain comes gain. So many lessons learned by all, I mused philosophically.

Disappointments and Partings

We had a buyer for the house and a June 15 closing date. Sue put into storage only what she felt we needed to equip a much smaller house, sold off some of the surplus furniture and fixtures by various means, and consigned what was left to an Estate Auction. She decided to drive her little red Toyota to Yellowknife and I made arrangements with our air services partner in Yellowknife for her to leave her car at their airport lot whenever she was in Lutsel K'e. Sue was excited and as apprehensive as a toddler starting primary school; to be finally setting off on her northern adventure after so many delays and setbacks.

She was excited too with the prospect of starting a new career. Miki had got the go ahead to hire two Fetal Alcohol Syndrome (FAS) Counselors and felt, from what I had told her, that Sue would be an ideal candidate. The applicants would first have to go to Yellowknife for training, all expenses paid, and then they could go anywhere in the north that required their services. It was a serendipitous happening and Sue was over the moon with it. So excited was she that she made the trip, which was normally a five-day trek across Ontario, Manitoba, Saskatchewan, Alberta and then north to Yellowknife in three days.

We met up in Yellowknife and stayed a couple of nights at the Chateau Nova Hotel, to give her a feel for the north and to acquaint her with what the city had to offer. On June 24th, we went to Lutsel K'e.

She laughed at the wobbliness of the house, despaired at its condition, for it was still dirty, and enjoyed the novelty of walking around the strange community in daylight at eleven in the evening. I introduced her to everyone I met and all showed her a great welcoming. We visited on the weekends with Joe and Julie, the cops and the nurses.

Three of Sue's relatives, who were on a road trip across Canada, visited us soon after and for the first month all was well. But the job didn't materialize, and by the end of the second month the writing was on the wall. She didn't like the place and she wasn't going to stay. Despite Miki's urging the Health Department that, in her opinion, Sue would make a good counsellor, they gave the jobs to two band members, who raised their hands and said, "I want that job." And when they didn't work out after the first week, another two Dene hands went up and the owners said, "I want that job."

Without a job, there was nothing for Sue to do but wait for me to come home, in much the same way as Joe did for Julie, but that wasn't sufficient for Sue. I understood how she felt and empathized with her sense of abject dejection and disappointment. If she had got the job, the outcome would have been very different. I understood the dynamics of the north and why being a band member in Lutsel K'e pre-empted all other considerations, but nonetheless, I was very disappointed. If only one person had raised a hand, Sue would have been given the chance to be trained and that would have affected the rest of our lives. But it wasn't to be. We just had to accept what was and go from there.

We found an apartment in Yellowknife and I hoped that she'd find something productive to do there, while I finished my work in Lutsel K'e. As it was, I was going to Yellowknife on business at least once every three weeks, so I made my appointments for a Friday so that I could stay over the weekend and catch the Monday morning flight back. I knew that I would soon be leaving Lutsel K'e, but my intuition told me, loudly and clearly, that it wasn't yet my time to go. Many things were coming together after months of preparation, and I couldn't abandon the ship until it docked, which at the very earliest, would be sometime in the New Year.

Sue and I had been growing apart over the last year and this latest event significantly increased the distance between us. We were now two strangers living in different worlds, bonded by a past in Ontario, but unsure as to how our future would play out. My hope was that she would find a job she liked in Yellowknife, and after that, we could work on a plan to meet both of our needs, whatever they might be. In the meantime, it had to be business as usual for me in Lutsel K'e.

The Performance Review

Although my employment contract called for a performance evaluation after six months, this was month sixteen and I was still waiting for a review. Had I not pressured the Board by putting it on the Board Meeting agenda, month after month, and been proactive in sending each Director an evaluation form with a request that they complete it and bring it to the next Board meeting, I was sure a review would never have happened. I wanted the review because my interest in the job was waning, and I was hopeful that it could be resuscitated if I were to sit down with the Board and have a good heart to heart discussion with them. I wanted to complete everything that I had in the hopper before I left the community, but I was finding it increasingly difficult to stay motivated. I just needed to know that my efforts were recognised and appreciated.

We were in the Boardroom. Vince sat at one end of the big brown conference table to chair the meeting. I sat to his right, and next to me was George. Jessy and Mickey sat on the opposite side. There was a strange tension in the room. No one spoke, so unlike the other Board meetings that I had attended, where there was much social chitchat and laughter. I sensed that a discussion had recently taken place, perhaps within the last half hour that had put the Directors in this weird mood. It was obvious no one wanted to be there, except for me of course. I noted the look of seriousness on their faces, but I wasn't disturbed by it. I was ready to handle whatever they threw at me.

Vince recited the obligatory opening prayer and we took our seats. Before he had a chance to review the agenda, I asked everyone, "Did you bring the form?"

"No," they responded, almost in unison.

"No problem. I have extras," and handed out copies. The evaluation form was a simplified managerial evaluation; ten questions evaluating the skills and abilities of a typical manager with a maximum mark of ten points per question. Vince was clearly irritated. There was no doubt that he had hoped to defer the evaluation yet again by perhaps advising his Board not to bring the forms, but he could see I was not to be put off this time. I knew him well, and so did the others. You could tell by the look on his face that he was upset and irritable. He was smart too. He saw how determined I was and knew that he might as well cut to the chase and get on with it.

"We're here today to evaluate Al's performance. We have to keep our cool and not let things get out of hand. Okay!" he cautioned, looking down at the form the whole time.

Not let things get out of hand? Where was he going with this? His words were intriguing and I found them amusing in a strange sort of way, not at all threatening. "I can assure you Vince that I will take everything that is said as constructive criticism and the meeting won't get out of hand because of me."

He held the form with both hands and stared at it. "I'll go through the form so everyone knows what it means when it's time to do the rating. Is everyone okay with that?" All said yes. He began his dissertation by spending the next thirty minutes explaining the meaning of every word on the form. Words like "productivity, effectiveness and efficiency."

I wondered why George was there because he'd just replaced David and he had no idea what I'd done, but then again, as a Director, he was entitled to receive an honorarium for attending.

It was interesting to watch what did *not* happen. After Vince explained the meaning of a question, he asked the Directors to circle the number on the form according to how well they felt I had done. There was no response. No one asked Vince to elaborate on a meaning, yet no one wrote down anything. Vince noticed this too. His face mirrored his discomfort. But he ignored his observations and pressed on, continuing to define the meanings of words and all the while, asking the members to circle a number.

The thought occurred to me that the words on the evaluation might be inappropriate – too business-like. Maybe I should have used other words, and then it dawned on me that there might be another problem. Maybe the members couldn't read and Vince didn't want to reveal this to an outsider. It wouldn't be Dene to do that. The Directors were all Elders and they hadn't had the schooling that the younger Dene got today. I felt horrible. It was never my intention to catch them out, to make them uncomfortable, but this is what I sensed they were feeling.

The diminutive, plump, grandmotherly Jessy looked up at me every once in a while, through her dark tinted glasses, and then returned her gaze to the piece of paper in front of her, as if it were an alien object.

Mickey looked up periodically too, but with him, I think it was more for air. He was at his best when he was out on the land, not sitting in a stuffy Boardroom evaluating the General Manager. This was the last place he'd rather be. Despite his ageing years, Mickey like Harry, our Fort Reliance boatman, was physically strong yet I suspected his hearing was weak. When he spoke, he came so uncomfortably close to my face, that I could see every tiny blemish and pimple on his nose. And the "in your face" feeling was intensified by his manner of speaking. Mumbling and muffling, he spat his words out, as if that was the only way he knew how to release them. I dreaded speaking to him. I cringed when I felt his spit hit my cheek, and I couldn't wait to get to a bathroom to wash it off. Mickey never took a shine to me. When I went to Fort Reliance last year, he asked what I was doing there. "You're not Dene," he said.

"Vince invited me," I replied. He snorted and walked away, not even remotely aware that his behaviour came across as racist. A few of the elders spoke a little English, but not clearly, for they had never learned to write, yet I could usually tell what they meant but that was not the case with Mickey. I always had trouble understanding him.

Vince came to the end of the explanation phase. "What do I do now" was the message his face telegraphed, as he looked up from the desk at me. But it was his call. Taking another quick scan of the virgin forms in front of each evaluator, just in case he missed seeing someone draw a circle, he switched to Plan B. He placed the form on top of the other papers he'd brought for the meeting, and pushed the entire discard pile away from him, and looked at me. "You've worked too much overtime," he bluntly stated.

Now that the leader had set the stage and given the green light, Jessy chipped in and said, "You've been travelling too much."

Mickey, not to be outdone, muffled, pointing a thick accusatory finger, "I've been watching you. You aren't in your office as much as you should be."

George went on about how much money our airline partner was making off the new airline service. All four unanimously supported one another's comments. George rambled on about air safety and about the "accidents" – a blown tire and an engine problem. He said that at the Fort Reliance Spiritual Gathering the pilot took off against the waves. "Really George! I didn't know you could fly." I didn't intend to say it facetiously; the words just came out. But when Vince frowned, I remembered that I'd promised not to let the meeting get out of hand. Jessy used the opportunity to complain about her luggage being damaged and lost and Mickey said that the airline lost his wife's leg (her cane) one time, and she couldn't walk for a week.

After another five or six silly complaints about air travel, I pushed my chair back, took a deep breath and said, "My recommendation then is that we pull the plug on the new company and go back to using Air Tindi. There are obviously too many problems. No one seems satisfied with the service and quite frankly, I don't need the hassle." My statement brought an immediate reaction, not in words but in looks. They stared at me in disbelief. Obviously, they expected me to vehemently defend the air services operation. Vince recommended that we add this to the agenda for discussion with the Chief and Council and let them decide what to do, and all of the members agreed. We waited for Vince to continue. I sensed his brain working feverishly, struggling to figure out where to go and what to say next, so I helped him out.

"As this is my Performance Evaluation, would it be okay if I said a few words?" Vince nodded for me to continue.

"I came to Lutsel K'e as your General Manager sixteen months ago to look after the corporation's business and to create some new companies for you. When I arrived, the Corporations weren't making any money, were they?" I looked around the room for a response. Everybody had their head down, staring at their uncompleted homework, but they slowly nodded their heads in agreement. "And now the Corporations are making money, are they not?" More nods. Without the nods, I would have got up and left the room because I'd given a lot of thought as to what I'd do if I felt there was no recognition of my accomplishments at the meeting, and that's what I had decided to do. Sometimes in life, a small gesture can be more powerful than a thousand words, and in this case it was the nod. That was all I needed.

"We have three new joint ventures; one in air services, one in land surveying and an accounting one I'm working on, and a couple more in the hopper." More quiet nods. "The stake operation is making money and there's great morale among the team. I'm pleased with what is happening. It hasn't been easy." No nods, but that was okay. I understood. "I'll be leaving the community in the New Year, but I would like to continue working for you in Yellowknife. I would like to be your Business Development Officer. The knowledge and understanding that I've gained from living and working here will help me to do a good job for you."

I'd discussed the need for a BDO based in Yellowknife with the Board many times before and had told them of my interest, so this was not news to them. I scanned their faces for reactions but found nothing perceptible. They must surely have had an opinion, but no one was willing to reveal it. They continued to stare at the foreign object in front of them and wait for Vince to lead the way.

"Let's table that for our meeting with Chief and Council," was all Vince had to say. A minute elapsed before he spoke again. "In future, you must get approval from me on all travel out of the community, and you must continue to work just four days a week to use up your lieu time."

It was so bizarre. I then realized what was concerning him. Company policy called for lieu time to be paid out when a person left the company, and he wanted to make sure I wasn't owed any money when it came time for my departure. He didn't want the corporation to have to pay more, regardless of what the dollars were for or what benefits had ensued. Julie said it was the same with her and the band council. With that, Vince thanked everyone for attending and closed the meeting with the Lord's Prayer. His last words were, "Can we pick up our cheques before five?"

Upon reflection, the whole exercise seemed to be geared to not admitting that I had done anything beneficial, so there would be no basis for a salary increase. I think that is what Vince had cautioned them about prior to the meeting, even though I'd never asked for an increase. It was as if Vince was under the impression that a performance evaluation always resulted in an increase in salary, and that's why he had been stalling the review for as long as he could.

Being the General Manager of the Development Corporations meant that I was also on the Board for three outside companies, and had to travel to Yellowknife periodically to attend Board meetings. When I now informed Vince of an upcoming Board meeting, he requested that he attend as a guest. My colleagues on the other Boards thought it inappropriate, but conceded from an aboriginal political standpoint. Not only was Vince now able to visit his family and friends in Yellowknife more often, and to shop, but he also benefited financially by picking up per diems for meals and honorariums for attending out of town meetings.

Whatever

Julie and Joe returned to northern Ontario at the end of October when Julie's contract with the Band ended. The Band had not appointed a successor and was experimenting instead with different people and different ways of doing things, but this was not going well – too many toes were being stepped on, and too many egos were competing for power. The politics were getting nasty.

Their departure also affected my personal sense of comfort and enjoyment. Life was not the same without them. I missed their ever-smiling faces, their good humour and their role as my sounding board to bounce issues and ideas off. And we, the people, weren't the only ones to miss them. They were missed most by their dog, Homer. That was clear to see, and the only reason Homer was still around was because Joe changed his mind about shooting him. When Joe left, he gave him to a neighbour as a guard dog, but that didn't work out, so another neighbour took and fed him. But it was obvious he wasn't getting the same attention and stimulation that Joe had given him. I had spent so much time at Joe and Julie's house that to Homer, I too was family and in his doggy mind, I knew he wondered why I wasn't looking after him. I wished I could, but it would have been cruel to tie him up at my house all day, while I was at work. How could I explain this to a dog? He needed to be downtown, where he could be stimulated and greeted by the kids going to and from school and by the noise and activity of the ravens and the community at large. For a short while after Joe left, Homer greeted me with great enthusiasm, wagging his tail so hard his bum shook from side to side. This pleased me and made me smile, but it also made me sad, for he seemed to be saying, "So you've finally come for me?" And then after a loving pat and a rub, I'd turn and leave, feeling his gaze burn my back.

I'm sure my visits reminded him of the good times: the boating to the islands in the summer when he'd sit up front with the wind blowing his fur and his nose twitching with the scent of fish; the evening trips to the river where he ran around in the bush following the scents of who knows what creatures; and of course, the smorgasbord meal that he would never forget when he helped himself to the hamburg and pork chops from my sled. It was heart wrenching to watch him decline in health and happiness over the weeks. He got thinner and depressed. I could see it in his eyes and by the way he lazed apathetically, so unlike the Homer of old, who would be up on his feet prancing around, even when he was tied up. I made a conscious effort to avoid seeing him, but every once in a while our paths inadvertently crossed, and when that happened, he just raised his eyebrows in distant recognition and feebly wagged his tail. Many were the times I thought it would have been best had Joe served him a bullet for his last meal.

In mid-January, mining companies that have operations out in the barren lands – the tundra – contract with a supplier to build a forty-foot wide, single lane, five-foot deep ice road from Yellowknife to Contwoyto Lake in Nunavut, Canada's newest Territory. Built over land, streams and lakes, the icy highway had spur roads to service the various mines along the way. The road is open for approximately six weeks a year, and about 6,000 trucks use it to haul goods that are too bulky, too heavy, or too hazardous to fly in a plane. Tankers bring in enough fuel over the six-week period to feed the mine trucks for a year as well as to provide the energy source to heat the remote facility and to run the processing plant. Specialized flat beds bring in monster-sized trucks, equipment and machinery while vans provide the mines with other goods.

Crews from various communities, including eight men from Lutsel K'e, were picked up by small aircraft on skis and taken to the site where they either stayed in a camp, or in a tent equipped with a bush stove. They worked a two-week in, two-week out cycle and made a lot of money. Their job was to pump water up from below the ice to flood and build up the road to the required depth necessary to carry the behemoth loads. In addition to the eight men (two four-man crews) working on the main ice road, Lutsel K'e also provided thirteen other labourers to help maintain the ice on the airstrip at the De Beers Kennady Lake facility and to work on the DeBeers Snap Lake spur line off the ice road. I posted the Ice Road Job Application notice on all bulletin boards in the community. It was very specific. It read that the hiring would be done in late December and that this year, the mines were insisting that two of the eight men working on the ice road at any one time had to have valid driver's licenses. Within five minutes of the notices going up, my phone began to ring.

"Am I on the ice road? I was on it last year so I should be on it this year."

"Is it the same crew as last year?"

"Can I switch with Toby and work with Fred?"

Even though the volume and the nature of the calls were disruptive and exasperating, they didn't upset me because I knew what the problem was, was empathetic to it, and was determined to just go with the flow. Most men interested in these jobs would not be able to read. They would have heard through the grapevine that the notice was up and were calling to ensure they were in the running for a job.

One of the callers was Dino Brokengoose, whom the ice road contractor told me last year not to send again, because despite being reprimanded many times, he kept falling asleep in the truck. I didn't have the heart to tell him when he called, but of course I knew that at some point I must make up some plausible excuse as to why he wasn't selected. Tim Traber said he had a letter at home from me guaranteeing him a job on the ice road this year. Where did they get this stuff? As if I would be bamboozled by those antics.

But there were lighter moments that tended to balance the scale. It wasn't all doom and gloom, dark and foreboding. I was enjoying everything that was happening in a sort of bizarre way because I was learning more about life, myself, other people and other cultures. Even though I'd lived in Lutsel K'e for seventeen months, and was part of the community fabric in many ways, the fact was that I was not Dene. This meant that I could observe all of the happenings objectively without being sucked into the vortex.

I stopped having expectations and settled instead for "whatever." When things went wrong, I didn't get upset. I just looked at what could be done and moved on. It was amazing how much that simple change of mindset helped. I no longer worried or got anxious about outcomes. I felt mentally lighter and freer. And in thinking about my personal situation with Sue, an element of the "whatever" crept in too, and that was helpful in releasing some of the pressure I had sensed regarding putting a Plan B together. We both had a responsibility to figure out what each of us wanted for the future. I would be okay with "whatever" she came up with, whether it included me or not.

Matt told me one day that, "Rabbits and frogs fall out of the sky as a gift to the Dene people. I know you don't believe me but it's true. I've been out on the lake in winter and right out of nowhere there were rabbit tracks going in just one direction. They just appeared out of nowhere." I didn't laugh, nor did I say a word.

I thought about some of the preposterous religious beliefs that I once held and how vehemently I had defended them and how I felt when non-believers ridiculed me. Matt truly believed in what he was saying and I found that I could sincerely respect that without feeling an urge to challenge him.

"It's the same with frogs. When it rains, tiny frogs come down with the rain and jump about. The Creator sends the Dene people whatever they need. That's why I never worry about money. Money doesn't die. It just changes hands. There's always money and I always get it when I need it. I'm getting $5,000 to buy a boat," he said proudly. I knew that. Julie had told me before she left that he was one of the lucky ones to get a $5,000 Harvester grant from the government, to help buy trapping and fishing equipment. "Why don't you buy Joe's boat? He's only asking $2,000. You'd have $3,000 left to buy all sorts of stuff," I said. Although Joe had left the community, his boat was still for sale and I was trying to sell it for him.

"No way, man. I want a proper boat. This is what I'm getting," and he pulled out of his back pocket a brochure showing a gleaming monster of a boat priced at $17,500.

Decisions At Last

For four days, the Lutsel K'e Dene band had been holding its Annual General Meeting at the Community Hall. Chief Charlie had promised to convene a special meeting with his councillors to discuss the Development Corporation's request for direction on the Business Development Officer position, the future of the air services company, as well as on some other issues, but now the Chief and council were going to Yellowknife on Monday for another week of meetings.

The diamond mines contracted out their non-essential services to third parties specializing in particular services, such as catering, or janitorial services. Under the Participation Agreement that the mines signed with the Lutsel K'e Dene Band and with other aboriginal groups, preference in the awarding of contracts was given to aboriginal owned companies providing that service.

To participate in the process, aboriginal groups created joint venture businesses, 51% owned by them, with reputable companies that specialized in a particular service; the minority partner providing the service knowledge and skills and the aboriginal partner the labour force, wherever possible. It was an economic development initiative for the aboriginal communities. The concept was that over time, there would be transference of skills, both managerial and clerical, to the band members, so that they could offer these services independently at some point in the future.

I had to be proactive, because we needed to make some key decisions if we were to take advantage of the window of opportunity with De Beers. The balance of their Requests for Proposals would be coming out early in the New Year and it was essential we had some joint venture arrangements in place by then. I was working on three of them; one with the North Slave Métis to create a catering company; one with a land surveyor to develop a mapping and land surveying business; and another with our chartered aircraft partner, to provide the mines with air transportation. I wanted to put these together for the community before I moved on, and firmly believed that I had a good shot at it.

I booked the boardroom at the Yellowknife Inn where the Chief and Council were staying and set up a meeting for the following Tuesday at 7:00pm. Vince and I flew out on the noon flight on the Tuesday. We had prearranged to meet Jessy and Mickey, two of our Directors, who were already in town on other business, in the Hotel foyer at three.

Jessy was sitting in the lobby when we checked in at two, so I used the opportunity to bring her up to date on what we were going to present to Band and Council. I told her we needed her presence for a quorum. She assured me she'd be there and asked if she could get her per diem now because she wanted to play Bingo. "No, we'll pay after you've attended the meeting. I'll call Sunrise in the morning, ask her to cut you a cheque and we'll put it on tomorrow's flight. Okay? She said that was fine.

Vince and I waited for Mickey in the lobby from three until three thirty. He didn't show. At six o'clock, as I was striding through the hotel lobby with arms full of papers to go to the meeting room to get set up, I saw Jessy in a small crowd of happy people. I quietly went up to her and reminded her that we needed her presence downstairs at seven. She said not to worry. She'd be there. But at seven, she wasn't. Nor was she there at eight, nor at nine, when the meeting adjourned. She told me the next day that she got so absorbed in the Bingo that she forgot.

There were nine of us at the Board table in the lower level office, which we had booked for the meeting; seven were from the Band and Council: the Chief and six councillors, and just Vince and I from the Development Corporation. After Chief Charlie opened the meeting promptly at seven with the Lord's Prayer, I asked if anyone had seen Mickey. A few people laughed and someone shouted, "Mickey's old lady won $4,000 on Bingo last night so don't expect him." Another voice chimed in, "Mickey was on cloud nine when I seen him at five. He wasn't feeling any pain, let me tell you." At that point, we, the Development Corporation, didn't have a quorum, but it didn't matter because we needed Chief and Council to give us some direction and we weren't going to let a technicality stop us from hearing what they had to say.

And then Mickey sauntered in. "Thanks for coming," I said gratefully as he pulled out a chair. "What cloud you on, Mickey?" someone shouted and everybody in the room gave him their full attention. They hooted and cheered, including me, but then I felt sad for him. He looked so lost, tired and bewildered. He too joined in the laughing but you could tell he had no idea why he was laughing. The attention had caught him off guard, as if he'd just walked into a room to find his friends staging a surprise birthday party for him. I knew why he was there. Despite being partially pickled, he was sober enough to know that if he just showed up and sat through the meeting, he'd get his honorarium.

Chief Charlie was behaving out of character. He normally took the reins and ran the show, but not that night. He was unusually quiet. He sat well back in his chair with his arms folded tightly against his chest. Normally, he'd be perched on the edge of his seat, resting his elbows on the table, raring to go. His behaviour initially surprised me, but then I remembered what Julie had told me earlier in the week, and everything began to make sense. She said the community had given him a difficult time at the Band's Annual General Meeting. They accused him of being too bossy and not listening to the membership. More than a few people had called him Little Hitler. He was obviously licking his wounds, taking a low profile and turning over a new leaf with a new persona, keeping in mind the upcoming elections. That was unsettling, because I was relying on him to encourage the rest of Council to agree with our recommendations. They normally went along with whatever he said. Many happenings in Lutsel K'e were of a political, strategic, or opportunistic nature and many were predictable. So I wasn't surprised when Gertie Sproule, a past Chief, stepped up to the plate and played her cards.

It wasn't a pleasant meeting. Gertie did most of the talking. In her opening remarks, she said that it was obvious that my spouse and I didn't like living in Lutsel K'e and that we wanted to live in Yellowknife instead, and that's what this meeting was all about. I countered by briefly summarizing the benefits to the Development Corporation and to the community of having a BDO based in Yellowknife, but my words were not heard because the ears of Council had been deafened. I could tell by the nodding of heads around the table as Gertie spoke that they were with her on this, one hundred percent.

George Petersen jumped in and added his two cents worth that the mines should do more business with us. "Exactly, George. That's precisely what I'm talking about and what this meeting's all about," I said excitedly, sensing half a chance for a breakthrough. "But we need someone in Yellowknife to develop stronger ties with the business people there. It takes a lot of time to put joint ventures together and it can't be done from Lutsel K'e. There's a lot of competition for partners. Other bands are well represented in Yellowknife and that's why they have more joint ventures than us. I can only do so much, living in Lutsel K'e." I looked to Chief Charlie for support but he purposely avoided my plea. I scanned the room to see if anyone might be interested in my continuing this talk but I didn't see what I needed. So I stopped talking and let Gertie continue. She had them all under her control and no one was going to step out of line.

After a few minutes, Gertie finally stopped talking, gave me the floor and asked that I officially make my presentation. "The main reason we are here tonight is to get Council's support for a new position for the Development Corporation; that of a Business Development Officer based in Yellowknife. There were other issues we wanted to run by you, but because of time constraints, we'll handle those ourselves at a later date." I paused and looked around the table at the silent, attentive faces. They appeared to be interested in what I was saying, but then appearances can be deceiving, especially in the north. "I've been up here long enough now to know how things work and you need a BDO to live and work where the action is, and that's in Yellowknife. Whether that person is me, or somebody else doesn't matter. But I want you to know that I'm interested. And I'll be available because I'll be leaving Lutsel K'e sometime in the New Year. With my knowledge of the community and the contacts I've made in Yellowknife, I know I can develop some good joint ventures for you. I'm working on three at the moment that I hope to finish before DeBeers puts out its tender in the new year. And I've spoken to BHP Billiton and Diavik about their obligation to give you more business when their existing contracts expire. And I'm working on a partnership with an accounting firm in Yellowknife to handle the bookkeeping for our air services operations, as well as for the many little businesses in Yellowknife who need this service." I paused and thought about what I was going to say next, but then I realized that I'd got carried away and had probably said too much about myself. "I'm not asking you to give me this job. All I'm asking is for you to support us in creating this position. That's all." I stopped speaking. There was nothing more to say.

Gertie immediately used the opportunity to disparagingly voice her opinions. "Business Development has always been part of the General Manager's job and I don't see any reason for changing this. You go to Yellowknife a lot I'm told, so I don't see why you can't meet with the people when you are there. We can't afford two people. And we don't need any help from the Dogribs, Yellowknives, or the Métis. The mines are obligated to give us business. Remember that!" *Whatever, Gertie. Whatever!* I ignored her caustic comments and simply stated, "The BDO position would pay for itself from new business it would generate. We could pay a salary, or a commission based on sales or profits. I'd be willing to work on a one hundred percent commission basis."

After much banter back and forth without getting anywhere, Gertie concluded the meeting by saying, "This is Corporation's business. We should not be involved. You decide what you will," and with that, she adjourned the meeting. In retrospect, I should not have been surprised with the outcome, because politics always underpinned the running of Band and Council, especially when Gertie was involved. It was safer for Council not to give advice, or to make decisions for the corporation, if they had an option, lest they be blamed by the community for some future event that might happen.

I was in my room by ten getting ready for bed when the phone rang. It was Mickey. "Can I pick up my cheque?"

"Mickey. I'm in a hotel room. It's ten o'clock for God's sake. I don't have your cheque. You'll have to wait till I get back to Lutsel Ké tomorrow."

"Oh yeah," he replied, but he didn't know what time it was, nor even what day it was.

Over the weekend, I developed a PowerPoint presentation for the Board, covering all outstanding issues, and decided to press them hard to stand up and be counted. I had taken the horses to water. Now it was time for them to drink.

When the Board met the following Tuesday, I said my piece. All, including Vince, spoke enthusiastically about the need for more joint ventures and fundamentally agreed with all of the recommendations on the table. They looked to Vince for direction. *What the hell*, I thought. *What have I got to lose! Maybe I can shame them into action.* I looked at Jessy. "I'm disappointed with you, Jessy. You were the one who said let's take the items to Council, yet you went to Bingo instead. How would it be if we all did that? You must stand up and be counted if you want to be a Board member. We need to work together as a team." She squirmed a little in her seat but offered no response. I continued to chastise each of them for not having any backbone.

"You have to make these decisions. I can't. And I will tell Chief and Council and anyone else in the community who asks why nothing has happened. I will say that it's ALL your fault." I looked around the room. It was like ground hog day again. How many times had I been in this situation with the same type of challenge? It was now second nature to me. "This is the last Board meeting of the year and probably the last one you'll have before your Annual General Shareholder's meeting with the community in January.

The community is not going to be kind to you guys unless they see some positive things happen. I'm not concerned about what they say about me. I do my best every day and that's good enough for me. I wouldn't vote back a Board that did nothing! Would you?"

There was the usual shifting of bodies in chairs and the clearing of throats, as my words entered their ears, shocked the neurons in their brains, and released uneasy feelings that heated up their bodies. They looked imploringly at Vince for assistance but he just nonchalantly packed up his papers. Another déjà vu moment.

I began to stack my papers too, expecting Vince to adjourn the meeting at any moment, but he didn't. He sat up straight, moved his body closer to the table, uttered a little nervous cough and said, "Okay then. Let's make some decisions." From that point on, the proceedings went smoothly and quickly. On my overtime, the Board directed that I be paid for half of it, and for me to take whatever time off that I needed in order to use up the balance, and as soon as possible.

"How about I take my Christmas vacation from December 2nd to January 5th? That will use up three weeks of lieu time and give me two weeks of annual Christmas leave." Vince nodded his approval and the rest of the Board smiled and relaxed.

"And let's approve this BDO position based in Yellowknife," Vince said. More broad smiles and nods from the team around the table. "Al, you write up something to put in the paper and figure out the pay and that stuff, and have Sunrise post the position in the Yellowknife papers with a December 31st closing date for applications." Vince was on a roll. He seemed to be relishing this chance to be the hero, making the big decisions and being captain of the ship.

"And let's approve a Christmas bonus. $2,000 for Board members, $1,000 for Al, $750 for Sunrise and $500 for Matt." Each proclamation was greeted with muted oohs and aahs from the now ecstatic faces sitting around the table. There were a few other items on the agenda that required decisions and Vince complied effortlessly. He adjourned the meeting and the members filed out of the room, relieved and joyful. Seldom had I seen them in such a light-hearted mood. The Christmas festive season had started early for some.

I prepared the newspaper ad and sent it off to the press. I also prepared my cover letter and resume, placed it in a file marked "BDO Applications" and gave it to Sunrise with the following instructions, "Put all applications that you get in this file but always keep mine on top. If Vince wants to see who's applied, and I'm not back from vacation, give him the file."

Before leaving for vacation, I met with the Chief and advised him that I would be leaving the community on March 15th. I also told him that my Board had approved the BDO position and that I'd be applying for the position. He smiled, leaned back in his big, black, leather swivel chair, which was his normal reaction to news that he found interesting, and said, "Have a great Christmas Al and we'll see you in the New Year then."

The fundamentals of the new bookkeeping business were in place and just needed a few more meetings to get it started. Its first business in the new year would be to handle our air services bookkeeping, which I was outsourcing because no one in the community wanted to do it over the long term. I was tired of training someone new every month.

Sunrise prepared my pay and my $1,000 Christmas bonus, which netted out to around $700 after taxes and I took it to Vince for signing. He came into my office and asked, "Why isn't the cheque for $1,000?"

"Its $1,000 gross but you have to deduct payroll taxes," I explained.

He smiled his usual wry smile and said, "But then you're not getting a $1,000 are you?" I showed Sunrise how to gross up the amount of the bonuses so they all netted out to the gross figure.

On the day that I was leaving for my Christmas break, I arose early but ran out of water at 7:30 for my shower. I immediately called and left a message on Rose's machine for her to send the water and sewage trucks to my place when they opened at 9 a.m., because I was leaving on the 11 a.m. plane. I just figured that it would be prudent to get the sewage pumped out of the tank before I left for an extended period of time. I then called Matt and asked him to pick me up last instead of first for the trip to the airport.

The sewage truck arrived at 10:10. The driver hooked up the hose and turned on the pump. It blew instead of sucked. He had turned the valve the wrong way. The kitchen sinks bubbled up, blowing water into the air. I raced into the bathroom. To my horror, the toilet lid was up and the contents of the bowl were spewing out with much force, all over the shower curtain, the floor and the wall. I raced outside and swore at the operator to shut the damn thing off. He didn't. He climbed down out of his truck to see what all the fuss was about. When he saw the kitchen sink with water blowing out of it like a whale, his jaw dropped, and he raced back like a madman to his truck and moved the handle from Blow to Suck. I had less than ten minutes to clean up the mess before Matt arrived to take me to the airport. I was livid. Who needs this! I couldn't believe that I was still there taking that shit.

My "whatever" philosophy obviously had limits. I was not a happy camper when I met Sue in Yellowknife to go back to Ontario for the Christmas break.

The 10,000 lb. Ice Cube

I returned to the community after a Christmas break of five weeks. Sue stayed in Ontario with family for a few more weeks as she needed more time to decide what she was going to do, but she wasn't going to stay in Yellowknife she said.

I purposely didn't stay in touch with Sunrise over the holidays, and whenever thoughts of Lutsel K'e drifted into my mind, I consciously banished them, for I wanted a complete rest and change of pace. It was only when I boarded the plane in Yellowknife that I let myself begin to think. Was my house still standing? Or did it blow over the hill in a winter storm? Had it been broken into again?

I started to think about other matters; how to create the presentation for the Development Corporation's Annual General Meeting the following Tuesday; how the accounting for the air services company was coming along, and if Sunrise was still my Admin. Assistant. These thoughts didn't stress me, as they would have done a year ago, because I now had a different attitude, clarity of mind and renewed energy. I was ready to take everything in my stride and wrap up everything before I left on March 15th.

It was a mild nineteen degrees below zero when I stepped off the plane … they said it was minus fifty the week before. I brought in more goods than I took out because of Christmas presents and groceries. Matt dropped me off last and said he'd come back in an hour to drop off the truck. Well, the house was still there. What a relief! It hadn't fallen down the embankment nor had it burnt down to the ground. And judging by the untouched snow around the house, it appeared that it hadn't been broken into, at least not in the recent past.

I put the key in the lock and it turned. Thankfully it worked. Great, because that meant the cold porch that Joe built last year did what it was supposed to do. I entered the house, and just like that, the insanity of the north returned. It was at least twenty degrees below in there. My breath vaporized as I exhaled. The ice-cold, hardwood floor cracked as I walked to the fridge. The liquids in the fridge were frozen. I checked the kitchen tap and it wouldn't turn. In the bathroom, one toilet bowl was cracked in half and the water in the tank was a big block of ice. As I descended the steps to the basement in my big, insulated winter boots, the stairs made a disturbing crunching sound, as if they were going to snap at any moment. The sewage and the water tanks were frozen solid and the cast water pump was split.

And then I realized the enormity of the situation. I had a 10,000 lb. ice cube, instead of a water tank sitting in my basement. I shook my head and thanked the Universe for the serendipitous event that led to my getting the sewage tank pumped out before I left on vacation, or else I would have another 10,000 lb. block of something that wasn't ice!

The fuel gauge read "below empty," but there was fuel in the tube when I shook it. I must have run out of fuel but that made no sense because I put in $500 worth just before I left and had turned down the thermostat in every room to fifteen degrees.

Matt arrived with the truck. He thought it was hilarious. "You should have asked me to house-sit," he scolded.

"Yeah. Guess you were right, but I thought everything would be OK," I replied. I didn't tell him of course that I felt more comfortable leaving my house empty than having him, or anyone else house-sit while I was away.

I called the Co-op, made arrangements for a fuel delivery later in the day and went to work. To my great surprise, Joe and Julie were back in the community. The Band had called her before Christmas and asked her to come back to straighten things out. They had come to terms with her on a one month contract and had flown her and Joe back just before Christmas. She'd worked through the holidays and was initially planning to leave in mid-January, but now she was considering returning full time, if the Band agreed to her terms and conditions. What a godsend. The Universe had once again intervened and looked after me. Joe and Julie had been so helpful when I got sick and needed a warm place to stay, and here they were again, offering me my old room back at the end of the hall, until my igloo thawed out.

The neighbour, who took Homer, gave him back to Joe, for as long as he was going to be in the community. It was just like old times. I told Joe the story about my early musing regarding having to live in an igloo, when I was doing my research on the north. He laughed and said, "Gotta be careful what you wish for Al. Wishes do come true. Particularly up here in the north. Julie and I are back, aren't we?"

"You wanted to come back, Joe? I thought you'd had enough."

"Just needed a rest I guess. But we didn't get much of that before they called and pleaded with Julie to return. We missed the place. How about you?"

"Yeah. It's strange how this community grows on you. But I'll be leaving soon, Joe … on March 15th. It's time for me to be moving on. I can feel it in my gut."

We went back to the house and after inspecting the furnace, Joe offered the opinion that the problem seemed to be a furnace malfunction. There was fuel and power but the furnace wouldn't kick in when he pressed the restart button. It activated but didn't fire up. I was relieved in a sense, because this would make it an insurance claim. If I'd simply run out of fuel, I'd be on the hook for the repair bill, which I was sure was going to run into thousands of dollars.

I listened to the messages on my answering machine. The last two were from John, the janitor at the Seniors Centre, and were recorded ten minutes apart and all in the last half hour. John wanted a cheque that afternoon. He was waiting for me at the front door of the office when I arrived for work. "Can you not wait until tomorrow John? That's when we'll cut the payroll cheques."

"No. I was waiting for you to return. I haven't eaten for three days because I don't have money." I went inside and was greatly relieved to see Sunrise sitting there. She prepared John's cheque. Jim Sproule came in to see if the cheques for his stake crew were ready. I smiled and told him that I had no heat in my house and needed to address that before I could get to calculating wages, which I promised to do first thing in the morning. He was cool with that.

On my desk was a folder marked "Business Development Officer (BDO) Applications," containing five resumes. One was from Joe Broadman, our ex-Member of the Legislative Assembly, three that came in the mail, and mine. I marched over to Vince's office, made small talk about the holidays and with great pleasure, placed the resume folder in front of him. "We have five applications for the BDO job."

He smiled, slowly opened the folder and riffled through the stack. "Any good ones?"

"I can't say Vince. Haven't had a good look at them yet. But as I'm applying, it wouldn't be fair for me to assess them." And added, "One of them's from Joe Broadman."

"Is it now? How interesting!" He pulled back away from his desk, lifted his head up to look me full in the face and with raised eyebrows and a smiling twinkle in his eye said, "I'm not surprised. I heard Joe was looking for a job in the community."

We discussed who he'd like to have on the interview selection committee and he picked Annie Beauchamp and Lorraine Basker. I called them but they were both out of town for the week, so I wrote them a letter. It was just a formality really, because I'd learned to get something on paper in situations like that to validate my actions. The letter simply stated that they had been appointed to a candidate selection committee for the BDO position and for them to get in touch with Vince to arrange a convenient time for the review and interviews.

Sunrise told me the other pickup truck had been in the shop for two weeks and that Larry was working on it, but she didn't know what the problem was, or when it would be fixed, and that Bernard had rented the passenger van for two hours last week, but hadn't returned the key and now was out of town. *Whatever!*

At that time of the year, the sun came up around eleven in the morning and went down around three. For a couple of hours on each side of sunrise and sunset, there was a strange twilight, a half light, which took an outsider a little getting used to. It was strange at first, walking about in the dark when my brain said it should be light, but I quickly adjusted. It didn't affect me, but it did some people, especially many of the young teachers. They got severe mood swings and deep depressions, which of course didn't help them to adjust to living and working in the north. Miki suggested they sit under ultraviolet lights in the evenings to get their daily dose of Vitamin D.

It was noon and a beautiful day. The sun was a ball of orange fire blazing away just above the horizon, casting long black shadows on the flat, bright white snow. Because it was so low in the sky, it shone in your eyes and made you squint. Many in the community wore sunglasses or goggles when they went out on the land at this time of the year.

The lake was completely frozen to a depth of four to five feet, making it an open playground for snowmobilers, as well as a highway for those hardy souls wishing to make the trek to Yellowknife to visit relatives or to shop for groceries.

They said that last week there were hundreds of caribou in the Stark Lake area, which was just about a mile south east of Lutsel K'e, and that this was the first time in many years that the herd had come so close to the community. Jerry Tibbet had shot four a few days ago, and Julie had got a hindquarter from him to take back when she left next week. I got a side of ribs and a shoulder. We had to clean them up because the meat didn't come to you as it would from a butcher. This included removing bits of hair and blood and pulling off mucous membranes. I cut the ribs into three pieces about 14" long, wrapped them in a garbage bag and put them in the freezer with the shoulder.

The PowerPoint slides for the Corporation's Annual General Meeting on Wednesday were ready and Sunrise had made arrangements for Taylor to chair the meeting. She'd also arranged for the translation equipment, for Jessy and Tundra to do the interpreting, and for Stu Frobisher to provide the janitorial services. She also ordered a cold cut and cheese buffet from the Yellowknife Co-op. We brought in Kentucky Fried Chicken last year, which was a big hit, but we wanted to do something different this year. Business associates had kindly provided coffee mugs, T-shirts and fleece jackets for door prizes.

I was looking forward to the meeting for another reason – the chance to get some new blood on the Board; people who might stand up and be counted and be willing to carry the ball until my successor was hired and in place. But Julie advised me not to raise my hopes too high. Always the optimist, I reminded her that sometimes you do get what you wish for, and that this would be one of those occasions, but inwardly, I sensed she was right.

The house furnace problem was caused by a plumbing mistake. Brady should have installed a two-line system – fuel in, air out, but the air out line was patched into the fuel in line, causing a vapour lock. Willy Wolf had recently been hired by the Lutsel K'e Housing Authority as an oil burner mechanic. I showed him the house situation and he immediately went to work, bleeding the fuel line and turning off the water lines except for the in-floor heating system, which he said would be okay, because they were made of plastic. *Whatever!*

The house was now in recovery mode. I checked it periodically and the water and sewage tanks looked to be okay. I certainly hoped so or else I'd have to empty 1,000 gallons of water with a coffee can, one tin at a time, and dump them into the sewage tank. I dreaded to think what the total damage would be when everything thawed out. Willy said the copper header pipe between the kitchen and the two bathroom walls would have to be replaced, but he was not sure about anything else. I would just have to wait and see and cross my fingers. He said he'd speak with a plumber he knew in Hay River to see if he would come to Lutsel K'e to do the repairs because he didn't have the time to do it. Brady wasn't available.

In the meantime, I continued to live with Joe and Julie, in my room at the end of the hall, just like old times, eating Joe's daily meat and two vegetable meals at five o'clock sharp and after supper, throwing sticks for Homer.

The ice road scheduling was proving to be a nightmare. What should have been a simple scheduling exercise turned out to be exceedingly complex. Although the crew schedules were posted all over town, we might as well not have bothered. All day long, the phone rang. "Do I go out this week?" "Am I on the list?" "Can I work here instead of there? Fred says it's OK if I switch with him." "Can you put me with Dino? Me and him did good last year."

Sunrise drove around town picking up the crew going out to take them to the airport and provided a taxi service to the returning crew. Many times, someone couldn't make it at the last minute, resulting in her having to drive around town to find a qualified, warm body replacement, because it was critical we send the right number of crew as there were no extra people at the frigid base camp to cover absentees.

Wives constantly called me at the office and at the house in the evening to check on the arrangements to ensure their men folk didn't miss the plane, or to ask whether so and so was coming back today, or they'd call to get the site satellite phone number because they wanted to speak to their partner about little Jimmy not listening to his mother.

Whenever I felt frustration coming on, I simply reminded myself that although some might not be able to understand a one paragraph notice on a bulletin board, they could survive in a white wilderness for days at a time on next to nothing. They could track, shoot and skin bears, wolves and caribou, as well as fix snow machines and boats, and ride out storms on the lake. How much more important were those skills and abilities than mine? I did book work. They did real things and they did them in real time. This type of thinking always flipped my perspective and humbled me. I respected and acknowledged the differences between us.

Joe and Julie went home to Sault Ste. Marie and I agreed to house sit for them, or until the Band hired a replacement for her. If the Band agreed to her terms, she would return the following month. The arrangement worked extremely well for us, especially for me as I had a warm, comfortable place to stay while my house thawed out and the Band got a house sitter they could trust.

The Corporation's Annual General Meeting, that was originally scheduled for November, rescheduled for the second Wednesday in January, was now rescheduled for the first week in February, because the Chief and Council were out of town. My PowerPoint slide presentation was all set to go. It revealed the big picture and that was what I assumed was important to the community. No one cared about details.

Sunrise had been absent from the office a lot of late, because she had recurring babysitter problems. Her sister Delilah and brother,

Mark, usually babysat, but they weren't always available and she had no back up.

My very capable but unreliable assistant also missed at least an hour of work a day, running here and there on errands for her parents, but I was okay with that. How could one not be supportive of a son or a daughter helping out their aged parents? And besides, the Co-op store was only open during office hours! Regardless, I much preferred to have Sunrise as my helper than anyone else. It was difficult to find people in the community with basic office skills. The Band employed most of them but even Julie had a difficult time with employee absences and refusals to work.

Chief Charlie had lent the Band truck to Lorraine to go to the bush to visit some relatives who were winter camping and she got it stuck and they couldn't get it out. The Band wanted to rent the second pickup truck from the Corporation; the one in the shop that Larry had been working on forever, so pressure was brought to bear on him to get it repaired quickly. He fixed it within two days.

The Band accepted Julie's terms. They passed a motion when Gertie was out of town. She wouldn't be a happy camper when she returned and found out what had transpired, but Julie didn't care. The news was greeted warmly by the community. Gertie was now Chief and Council's problem.

The house was warming up and the tanks beginning to thaw, but the Hay River plumber was not interested in coming to Lutsel K'e. I befriended Willy and out of compassion, he agreed to do the job in the evenings and on the weekends. The copper header pipe, between the kitchen and the bathroom walls, had broken at the bends, so Willy had to cut large holes in the drywall in all of the affected rooms, so he could gain access to the joints to solder them. This entailed removing the kitchen cupboards. He also had to replace two toilet tanks and many pieces of cracked plumbing fixtures throughout the house.

The house was ready for me to move back into in the second week of February. Half of the wall in the kitchen was missing, but once the kitchen cupboards were re-installed, it wasn't that noticeable. My successor could repair the wall.

Chief Charlie gave me the names of the three new directors: Charlie Beauchamp, Norton Brokengoose and Rainbow Tibbet. He said he was hopeful that with my new Board more progress would be made!

The BDO Selection Committee didn't get together. Vince handed me back the file of applications and instructed me to have the new Board deal with it. *Whatever!*

Dried Meat to Go

Since coming to Lutsel K'e, I had acquired a liking for dried caribou. At first, I wasn't fond of it because it was too different to the foods that I was familiar with, but now I could say with strong conviction, that I craved it; almost as much as I craved Indian dishes. There was something exotically pleasurable about the texture and taste that filled my mouth when I chewed it. As my saliva softened up the meat, releasing the trapped juices and flavours, my taste buds went into overdrive, similar to how they behaved when I ate lamb, or lobster dripping in warm garlic butter. I had to take some with me when I left the community next month. It would be my souvenir of Lutsel K'e.

The air was so arid in the north that meat or fish left out in it dehydrated to a bone dry condition within forty-eight hours. It wasn't important where you hung it. In your house, or on a clothesline, you could always count on it being ready for eating in two days. Elders preferred to smoke their meat over wood fires, and sometimes brought in different woods, such as hickory, from outside the community. Seldom did they season their meat, other than with salt and pepper.

I approached Tim Traber for the meat. He was pleased to hear of my intention and suggested I use a two pound hunk of caribou shoulder, that he could let me have. I wasn't going to smoke it, but I was going to season it, and heavily. I decided to use up the Indian spices I had left in the cupboard, along with the honey, soy sauce and whatever else I could find that would be an interesting ingredient. My mouth watered at the thought of combining northern fare with oriental seasonings in a gastronomic, culinary delight. I put the slab of meat in a plastic bag in the fridge because they said you had to use fresh meat.

The next step was to get the meat cut properly. Miki recommended I offer the job to Madeline Beauchamp, the much-respected Elder and mother of Chief Charlie. Miki made an arrangement with her to come to my house the following night for the princely sum of forty dollars.

At the appointed time of seven o'clock on the dot, an odd couple appeared at my door. Their silhouettes were comical; one was tall and skinny, the other short and fat. Their punctuality didn't surprise me because Miki was a stickler for timeliness and she was the one picking up Mrs. Beauchamp in the Health Centre truck.

Madeline was the taller one. She wore a thin, floral headscarf, hooded green nylon coat with a black fleece jacket underneath, the customary long, cotton floral skirt of an Elder and a pair of well worn, yellowing moose-hide moccasins. Her only exposed flesh was her face and ankles. It was at least forty degrees below in the doorway. Miki, bundled in a bulky, light blue hooded parka, looked as wide as she was tall. The winter clothing completely hid her face and draped down to her insulated, booted ankles. The top of her head barely reached Madeline's shoulders. Mrs. Beauchamp was tall for a Dene Elder, at about five foot eight I would guess, and yet she only weighed maybe a hundred pounds. There wasn't a gram of fat on her spry frame.

As Miki and I spoke, Madeline waited silently; head lowered, eyes fixated on the floor. She continued with this pose as Miki gave her some last minute instructions. Satisfied that the Elder felt comfortable being in my house, Miki took her leave, and I took Madeline's scarf and jacket and put them over the chair in the hallway.

The lady butcher moved two steps forward, past the freezer in the hallway, and decided this was where she was going to cut the meat. She squatted on the floor and motioned that she was ready to begin. I brought the wrapped meat to her on a plate. She removed the plastic, pressed long, sinewy fingers into the roast, turning it over a few times in her hands and smiled, obviously pleased with the quality she had to work with. She asked for a sharp knife and some garbage bags. Actually, she never spoke, for she had never learned to speak English, but I could tell from her hand gestures what she wanted. I gave her a knife and a pack of garbage bags. She ran her finger over the blade and shook her head in a "no good" motion. I gave her another one to try. She nodded, "This one's okay. It'll do."

She spread two layers of garbage bags on the floor in front of her and was ready to work away at her craft.

I switched on the hall light to give her more illumination, but she motioned for me to turn it off; she was obviously more comfortable working in twilight. And so the only light in her work area came from the two lamps in the living room and the ten halogen bulbs under the kitchen cabinets.

As she squatted on the floor, I stood in front and watched her every move. Starting at the top in the middle of the roast, she carved down, nearly splitting the meat in half, but she stopped at what I would guess to be about an eighth of an inch from the bottom. Bending the meat slightly apart and working from the bottom up, she made a short horizontal cut sideways, again at maybe an eighth of an inch, and working the meat expertly with her hands, carved up towards the top but not through. This produced the first layer. She continued as with her first cut, silently and at a steady pace. She never stopped, nor looked up. It was plain to see that she enjoyed her work.

A half hour later, what had been a six-inch square chunk of meat was now a six foot long, continuous thin piece of caribou. She doubled the meat over neatly in layers and raised it up in her hands, in an offertory gesture. With a warm smile of satisfaction, she motioned for me to take it. I accepted the gift, returned her smile and placed the piled meat on a large platter on the lid of the freezer. I extended a hand to help her up but she didn't take it. She arose unassisted with ease: she just rose up and stood all in one motion, despite her seventy plus years. I had better luck with my offer to help her with her jacket and had no problem giving her the two clean, crisp twenty-dollar bills. She slipped them nonchalantly into a pocket of her jacket. When I motioned that I would drive her home, she gestured, "No, it's a good night. I walk." I thanked her again and watched her stride briskly down the dark driveway and mysteriously disappear into the foggy night.

After picking up and discarding the garbage bags, I took the bundled meat to the kitchen sink, rinsed it thoroughly in cold water and set it aside to drain. I put the plug in the sink and poured in the mixture of soya sauce and honey that I had made the previous night, and then immersed the meat. Heavenly aromas wafted up my nostrils when I added the crushed fennel, anise and cardamom pods. To give it a lighter, sweeter taste, I sprinkled in basil, oregano and mace, a tablespoonful of ground cinnamon and two crushed bay leaves. For the East Indian flavour, I stirred in the magic powders of ginger, garlic, cumin and coriander and topped off the concoction with a copious dash of sea salt and black pepper. I worked the meat well and let it marinate in the juices overnight.

The next day, with three kitchen chairs and a twelve foot, wooden banister rail, which was never installed on the stairwell to the basement, I created a meat drying apparatus and hung sections of the meat across the rail to dry. Garbage bags on the floor caught the drips. They said it took forty-eight hours to dry enough for chewing, and if I wanted it dry enough to snap in two, then to leave it for seventy-two hours. I decided to leave it for ninety-six. It was going to travel a long way and the drier the better.

It turned out so exquisitely that I couldn't find words to adequately describe the heavenly taste and texture. I was also pleased with its paper thin quality and flatness, thanks to Mrs. Beauchamp's expert cutting. The pieces stacked so neatly that I only needed six zip lock freezer bags to package all the meat.

A Most Important Meeting

The Development Corporation's Annual General Shareholders' meeting was slated to begin at 7 p.m. at the Community Hall, but of course at seven o'clock, the Hall was empty, which was fortunate because we were having preparation problems. I'd been waiting since November for this meeting so what was another few hours! It was fortunate that Dene time meant anytime because I needed another forty-five minutes to get set up.

The laptop with the PowerPoint slides was in the back seat of the truck, which Matt had, but no one knew where he was. The projector apparently was still in my office – Sunrise had forgotten to bring it to the hall.

By 7:30 we'd tracked down Matt, retrieved the laptop and brought the projector from the office but two more wrinkles surfaced: we couldn't find the projector screen and the electrical cord for the laptop wasn't long enough.

The meeting room was arranged thus: fifty six-foot long tables were butted together to form a large rectangle in the centre of the hall. Chairs were placed on the outer sides of the tables so that the community was looking in and up at the head table, which was positioned at the front of the hall in front of the stage, upon which the door prizes were displayed.

The Chairman, Board of Directors and the General Manager sat at the head table, in front of the projector screen. Additional chairs were placed at the back of the Hall and alongside the two opposing walls. The buffet was set up against the back wall of the room, behind three rows of additional chairs. The translation table, where the two lady interpreters sat, was located on the left hand side, when looking from the head table.

By 7:45, when the first wave of shareholders swarmed into the room, we were almost ready. We'd tracked down the projector screen and secured enough extension cords, but the electronic Bingo machine wasn't set up, and Sunrise wasn't ready to hand out the Bingo cards and raffle tickets. We wheeled out the Bingo machine from the storage room and squeezed it in on the back wall of the hall, by the side of the buffet table, and decided to pull out the numbers manually, because no one knew how to operate the machine. We sent word out to find Richard, the regular Bingo caller, but to no avail. Maybe he was out of town.

By 8 p.m., about fifty people had arrived and were helping themselves to the buffet. Sunrise did a good job in getting the food delivered on time and in setting it up. There were cheese and meat trays, veggies, fruit, dessert, cookies and Tim Horton donuts, all tastily displayed. But, there were no serving utensils ... she couldn't find any. Beverages consisted of tea, coffee and soft drinks. I took a plate and one look at the picked over food and instantly lost my appetite. I always had a problem with the Dene hand eating tradition; all those fingers picking up this and that and putting them down because they'd spotted something bigger or riper.

At 8:10 p.m., Taylor Petersen, our Chairman for the event, asked Alan Tibbet the Elder to say the Lord's Prayer and open the meeting. Sunrise had been around the Hall ensuring everyone had a Bingo card and a raffle ticket, the most important aspects of the evening to everyone in the Hall, except me, for I wasn't eligible to receive a raffle ticket at an event such as this – you had to be on the band membership list.

I felt good about the presentation though because the Corporations had had a good year. My first slide showed the consolidated numbers for all of the companies; revenues and profits. So far so good. There were many smiles but no comments. My second slide showed the numbers for each of the corporations. More smiles and no comments.

At 8:30 it was time for the first of eighteen door prize draws and for the first game of bingo; $50 for one line. As I hurried to the back of the hall to take a seat next to the Bingo machine, the crowd stirred and got excited. Bingo had that effect on them.

I put my hand through the hole in the cloth at the back of the machine and grabbed a ball. Leaning into the microphone, I announced, in a very affected, deep British accent, slowly and clearly, "Under the B." I hesitated for a few seconds, and then said "eight." Riffles of pleased expressions rippled through the crowd as winners covered their B8 squares. I repeated the selection, stressing every syllable, "B… eight." I sensed that I had won over the gathering; they were enjoying the way I was handling their revered game.

I selected a second ball and using the same technique stated in a deep BBC voice, "Under the…O…Thirty…Six. O…Thirty…Six. Before I selected the third ball, I looked around the room at every face in the place and was overwhelmed by the intensity. Everyone was into the game in a big way and was gleaming at me, in full expectation that tonight was going to be their lucky night. I would be their lucky mascot, along with their pictures of grandchildren, rabbit's tails and carved animal figurines, which were laid out on the tables in front of them. I continued to pull balls out of the dark, cloth cloaked machine and proclaimed the lucky number to the hushed contestants until someone hollered "Bingo," which broke the holy silence. People updated each other on how close they had come to winning while they awaited the outcome of the verification process.

Returning to my seat at the head table, I continued with my show and tell, and revealed other details; number of people employed, amount of gross wages and so on. At 9:10 p.m. we had three door prize draws and another round of Bingo; this time for two lines. When I recommenced the slide show, I presented the results of our various joint ventures. Gertie Beauchamp complained that the joint ventures didn't employ as many community members as they should. Vince took the lead and responded, "The problem is that all of the Dene bands are training truck drivers, so we have hundreds of trained truck drivers in the Territories, but there are only so many trucking jobs at the mines." *Right on Vince.*

He then said, "Our people should be learning different trades and skills, which the mines need. But no, everyone wants to drive a truck because you don't have to do much to get your Class three license." I was shocked by his candour. No one rebutted his remarks, so the meeting continued. And then the inevitable happened. The Elders began to speak about drugs and drinking in the community and about not getting paid as much as other communities paid their Elders. It was impossible to keep the discussion on the agenda at hand so I sat back, listened and enjoyed the oratories.

In due course, the soliloquies ended, and I immediately jumped in and used the opportunity to bring the meeting back to the agenda. It was 10:15 p.m. and time for another draw for two door prizes and the "All of the four corners game." As I hastily made my way to the back of the room, everyone came back to life. Chairs were noisily repositioned to face the Bingo caller and there was much chatter, as they checked each other to see how many open squares their neighbours had. It was a déjà vu experience of the auction.

This was round three and I sensed the crowd was in my corner when it came to Bingo. I pulled out more balls and announced winning numbers. As I strode back to the head table to reconvene the meeting, it seemed that this might be the perfect time to speak about the new Business Development Officer position. And, if I could get their attention, I would suggest that I might be the best candidate for the job. My thinking was that if I could garner the support of a few Elders, then my Board's Selection committee might be swayed in my favor. Looking around the room, while waiting until I had their undivided attention, I picked out a couple of key people who I thought might just listen to what I had to say and might be supportive if I could button-hole them.

"Last year, if you recall, I recommended that we hire a person to develop new Businesses, but we didn't. We're now looking for that person again so that we can get lots of business from the mines. I searched the faces in the room for a positive sign that someone out there understood and agreed with what I was saying, but I didn't see what I was looking for.

"I came to Lutsel K'e two years ago to run your development companies. As you saw earlier this evening, your companies did well last year and should do well from now on. No one was looking at me and I sensed that they were bored, but I continued, nevertheless. "I've built a lot of excellent business relationships in Yellowknife with the mining companies, especially with the De Beers people, as well as with potential partners. There is a lot of new business to be had, but you need someone in Yellowknife to take advantage of these opportunities for you. I would like to be that person."

The room was quiet – either they were listening intently, or just being polite – I couldn't be sure of which. I hoped that someone influential was listening and might make some comments in my favour once I finished my oration. "I will be leaving Lutsel K'e next month but I could continue to work for you in Yellowknife. I am available. Doesn't it make good sense for me to keep working for you?" I thought a question might elicit a reaction but once again, no one gave the response I was looking for.

Tundra raised her hand and moved to a microphone on the table. Taylor acknowledged her and she asked, "Do you pay rent? They asked me to ask you this."

I leaned into the microphone and said, "No."

"Do you pay utilities?"

I said, "Yes." That was it. There were no further comments or discussion.

Harry Petersen, the Elder with whom I shared that infamous boat trip to Fort Reliance, raised his hand and was recognized by the chair. After clearing his throat with a heavy cough, he moved his bulky body closer to the table, stretched a hand across and grabbed the microphone. In a deep, gruff voice he complained, "When we gonna get coffee shop. I ask this every year but you don't do nothing."

"A coffee shop is a wonderful idea, Harry. If someone would like to run it, the Development Corporation would support them 100%. But without this person, the coffee shop isn't going to happen. Is anyone interested in running a coffee shop?" I scanned the room for a raised hand. All avoided my eyes and looked down, silently, at the table in front of them. "The offer is always there folks. I hope one day someone will step forward because you need a coffee shop.

It would be healthy for you; especially for the Elders. And I think an operator could make a good living from it."

There was much grumbling in the pews and I knew why. They felt I should build and run the coffee shop. It was obvious they didn't like my answer but it was too bad.

Harry then made a resolution, passed by the membership, for the Corporation to look into putting a gas station on an island in the middle of the Great Slave Lake, halfway between Lutsel K'e and Yellowknife, so people could gas up midpoint on their journey rather than having to take extra cans of gas with them on their boats and skidoos!

Nellie made a resolution, passed by the membership, for the Corporation to get more contracts from the mines!

Gertie questioned the profitability of our airline arrangement and threw out big numbers she figured our air chartering partner was making in profits. "Those are gross sales numbers, Gertie. When you deduct the cost of the planes, pilots, maintenance, fuel, hangar and terminal fees, there's only a fraction of that number left for profit," I replied. Gertie sat back in her chair and humourlessly folded her arms. There were no further questions.

The meeting continued with little input from the floor and at 11:10 p.m. it was all over, except for the Full House Bingo, the last of the door prizes, and the pulling of the ticket for the Grand Prize: a trip for two to Yellowknife return, courtesy of our air services company.

Alan the Elder wrapped up the evening with the closing prayer and the membership went home: eighteen with door prizes, four with Bingo winnings and one with a return trip for two to Yellowknife.

Time To Go

My last day of work was March 15th. I had given the Chief, Council and the Board of Directors six weeks' notice and had hoped that they would appoint a successor before I left, but they hadn't. Nor had they selected a candidate for the Business Development Officer position; in fact, the Selection Committee hadn't even met let alone reviewed the applications.

I knew that I wouldn't be offered the B.D.O. job because the other applications were from band members and they would take precedence over me and I was now okay with that.

Though everyone in the community knew almost everything that was going on at all times, very few people talked to me about my leaving. That didn't surprise me, and in an odd sort of way, I was greatly relieved because I was sad to be going and preferred not to discuss it. To me, this event was much more than my just quitting a job, for I was leaving my community and my extended family. When I first arrived, people asked how long would I be there. "I don't know. A year or two maybe, but not forever," was my stock reply. "Not forever" turned out to be twenty-one months according to the calendar, but in terms of the experience it afforded me, it had been a mini-lifetime. The experienced, well-intentioned businessman who came seeking adventure was not the same person who would be flying out. The man with questions had become the man with answers, for I now had a stronger sense of who I was, and I knew what I wanted to do. I felt as alive and as hopeful as I did when I was nineteen and leaving home and family for a new life in Canada. I could smell, taste and feel the future, yet I had no idea what it looked like, or what I would do. Leaving a comfortable life in southern Ontario, surrounded by family and friends, to living monastically in an isolated and physically hostile land, in a society so very different to mine, had been the most life altering chapter of my life. I wasn't concerned that Sue and I didn't have any definite plans as to what we'd do next, if indeed we'd still be together, because I had a strong intuitive sense that we'd both find our paths and everything would be what it was meant to be. Trusting in the Universe did that.

Nor did I know where I belonged, and that too didn't bother me. I knew I didn't want to live in a big city again and I certainly didn't want to get sucked back into mainstream living and thinking. Maybe I didn't belong anywhere. Was that possible? Were there people out there like that? Maybe I'd just go from one situation to another, having an adventure here and there, and helping out where I could.

My old confused version of spirituality; remnants of religious dogma brainwashed into me as a child, had been replaced with an appreciation for the wonder of the Universe and for everything in it. As well, I felt a vital energy for living in the moment, as practised by the Dene. And as to life after death, I figured that as no one knew for sure what happened, not even the Dene, why bother speculating on what might be. Life was too precious and was to be lived and savoured, moment by moment.

Many times over the past two years, I recalled that magic moment of awareness from three years ago, when I was on the deck contemplating the fleeting nature of ice and life, and its significance to me had only grown stronger. I now saw life as an hourglass. Moments yet to come were in the upper chamber, moments passed in the lower one, with life happening fleetingly in between; as one moment of time dropped from top to bottom. None of us know how many moments are left in our upper chamber, but for all seven billion of us on the planet, as well as for the trillions of other sentient beings out there, we all have sixty less moments of life left every minute. All it took to shift my consciousness from mindless daydreaming to an acute awareness of the preciousness of the present moment was the mental image of that hourglass. It became my trigger and I was pleased that it appeared randomly but with regularity, whenever I reverted to old ways of thinking.

The Dene's "one day at a time" approach to life, which initially disturbed and caused me much grief, was now well entrenched in my psyche and at the core of my new philosophy. I initially struggled with it, because it conflicted with what I was taught at school, in the home and in the workplace. I was advised that in order to get ahead I must take charge and orchestrate events in my life and to take great pains to plan for every eventuality. Perhaps that is a prudent approach for young people starting out, but at my age I needed a more liberating view.

I now took life as it came and accepted setbacks as a normal part of life's journey. I believed that the universe and everything in it was evolving as its destiny prescribed, and being able to accept and be comfortable with *"whatever,"* without any emotional analyzing, was energizing. And not having a house, nor any possessions of consequence to fret over, made me feel light and unencumbered. I relished the freedom of knowing that I could go wherever and whenever, in response to *"whatever."*

Being the General Manager had stretched my abilities too, far beyond any previous job had ever done. To many in the community, I was the person of last resort and the resolver of personal dilemmas. I had to dig deep into the archives of my experience to see if there was a suitable solution, and to my surprise, there usually was. But more to the point, I realized that the personal satisfaction I got from helping others was more meaningful to me than managing a business. My latent senses of compassion and empathy, so deeply buried when I was a businessman, were awakened and fed and had risen to the top of my emotional cup, like cream. Helping others is what I wanted to do when I left the community.

Winter sun over Great Slave Lake

CHAPTER 4

Manifesting the Gypsy's Prophesy

Costa Rica

Sue returned to Yellowknife and we deliberated on what we might do and where we might live; we just needed something to occupy us while we figured out a long term plan. The close intimacy that we once had was gone, and we both knew it and avoided talking about it. Instead we took on the semblance of good friends and went about our business.

I accepted an offer from the North Slave Métis Association, based in Yellowknife, to do a four month consulting contract, starting April 1st, and Sue decided that she wanted to live in Edmonton. We gave notice on our lease and I found accommodation in a private house. We drove the twelve hour journey down to Edmonton and found a suitable apartment.

Sue got a job that she liked and settled in. I joined her on August 1st upon completion of my Yellowknife contract and a month later. I went to Costa Rica to write and reflect.

When I was a child, I collected postage stamps from all over the world, as did every kid in those days, and Costa Rica was my favourite country because I was fascinated with the variety of birds: parrots, toucans etc., and animals: monkeys, sloths, iguanas, etc. depicted on their stamps. I never imagined back then that one day I would go to this country to see the birds and animals for myself yet that was what happened.

In Lutsel K'e, I'd written daily and diligently in a journal that my daughter gave me before I went up north, and in other journals that I had subsequently purchased. My main reason for going to Costa Rica was to convert the journals into a story as a legacy for my children and grandchildren. The idea to write this memoir came many years later.

I flew into San Jose, the capital city, and got a room in a guest house in the suburbs for the first two weeks. Immediately, I got into a daily routine of writing from 7 a.m. to around 2 p.m. and then I walked into town for a break, found a place to eat supper, and did a little sight-seeing along the way. The writing was fun and as I relived the Lutsel K'e happenings I began to view my experiences as more a part of a personal journey than just episodic adventures. The reflections allowed me to see how I had changed in response to challenges and to write the story with a deeper meaning than I would otherwise have done.

Before heading to Cahuita on the south eastern coast for the last two weeks, I took off for three days to enjoy Manuel Antonio,

Montezuma, and Monte Verde, where I saw all of the birds and animals on the stamps and many more besides.

Arctic Art

When I returned to Edmonton, I enlisted with a job placement agency and looked at a couple of jobs, but none appealed to me until a three month placement in Kugluktuk in Nunavut, as the Interim Finance Officer for the Kitikmeot School Board, came up. I accepted the offer and soon after the new year, was on my way to Yellowknife for furtherance to Kugluktuk to begin yet another mini-chapter of life in the north. In the meantime, Sue was enjoying her employment and well on her way to becoming established in the big city.

Kugluktuk is located inside the Arctic Circle and was extremely cold and still dark when I landed around two in the afternoon. In July it is the land of the midnight sun, but in January it is the land of no sun, and we would have to wait until early March for the blazing orb to appear above the horizon for the first time in the year. I had half a duplex to myself and enough furniture and fittings to be comfortable.

It didn't take long to get acquainted with everyone and the requirements of the job. There was a knock on the door soon after supper on the first evening that I was there. It was a guy called Douglas and he had the most beautiful stone carvings for sale. I bought a couple of pieces as gifts for Christmas and birthdays. About ten minutes later, there was another knock and this time it was Gary with more exquisite carvings that I couldn't refuse. And fifteen minutes after that, came Roy, then Ann and many others. I had never been into art but these carvings for some reason moved me. I found them to be beautiful on many levels; they were so detailed and lifelike and I loved the white stone that they were made from.

The knocks on the door continued the next night and each night thereafter until the artisans accepted the fact that I wasn't going to buy any more. I had bought twelve pieces by then and was concerned about being overweight on my luggage and how much extra that would cost when I left the community.

Douglas came into my office one day to show me two mini polar bears that he had just created. They were exquisite and I bought them instantly, but more importantly, he told me something that resulted in my developing a long standing relationship with the artists of Kugluktuk. He said that the only way for them to sell their art was when someone new came into the community, such as cops, nurses, visitors or people on business. How could that be when the art was so incredibly attractive? I was vaguely aware that Inuit art was a most sought after and expensive form of collectible art so why wasn't their art part of this market?

I discussed the situation with my younger son, Dean, and we began to research the whole Inuit art scene. We learned much: its beginnings in the 1960's, how it had evolved since, and where it was at today. It seemed that the bulk of the art was coming from the Baffin Island area of the Arctic, in eastern Canada, and that the grocery stores in those communities – the Arctic Co-op and the Northern Stores – were the major buyers and distributors to art galleries in the south and to the world. I asked the managers of those two stores in Kugluktuk why they were not buying.

Kugluktuk

Carving shed

I didn't get a satisfactory answer, but they both told me that they were not interested, and not likely to buy in the future. One manager told me that it was too logistically difficult and expensive: they would have to fly the art to Yellowknife and then to Edmonton and then on to Toronto and that made it cost prohibitive.

To cut a long story short, my son and I decided to build a new business, a web-based art gallery to showcase and sell art from Kugluktuk – www.gallerycanada.com – and that's what we did. My son created the website, secured the domain name, and I set about buying up as much art as I could before I left the hamlet.

I so enjoyed meeting the artists and marvelling at what they had created out of various types of stone, as well as from different parts of animals, such as musk ox horn, caribou antlers, whale bone, walrus teeth, animal hides and furs. As I handled the art and felt its texture and shape, I thought about what it was that I was holding; the manifestation of an imagination, brought about using only the most rudimentary of tools and I was in awe.

Kugluktuk art was very different in colour, detail, composition and theme to carvings and sculptures found in the Cape Dorset, Iqaluit and other eastern Canadian communities, and that was exciting to learn about. We had art that was truly unique and not available anywhere else in the world!

Most Kugluktuk carvings were 'white stone,' sculpted from Dolomite; a hard, white rock found on islands in the Coronation Gulf of the Arctic Sea. Extracting the stone was very dangerous and physically demanding work. The carvers could only get the stone in the two summer months, when they could take a boat out onto the Arctic Ocean. They then had to scale an island cliff, or descend a riverbank to locate a suitable piece for carving. Using spikes, crow bars and drills, they pried off whatever chunks they could and then transported them back to their house work area, or carving shed by boat and ATV.

Other Kugluktuk stone carvings were fashioned out of darker stones from the embankments of local rivers. Most Inuit carvings from the Baffin Island area and sold in galleries in the south were carved out of soapstone, or serpentine; a hard, dark stone, that was readily available to the carvers from community Co-op stores and local quarries.

There was a snag to the marketing. We needed to provide customers with a government "igloo" tag to authenticate that their purchase was indeed created by an Inuit, but only the Co-op and the Northern Stores had been issued them. I contacted the Department of Indian Affairs in Ottawa, explained what we were doing and requested the tags. They told me to get them from the Arctic Co-op but when contacted, their answer was no. I went back to the government, and after a year of phone calls and personal visits, we finally got approval and a supply of tags.

Before I left the community, I arranged with Dave, a teacher from the south who was working at the high school, to have the "Grizzlies," a fundraising arm of the school, to act as our agent. We needed someone in the community to transact business with the artists on our behalf, in return for a commission. The arrangement worked great and we received a steady flow of new products for many years until Dave left the community.

Drum dancer by Douglas Akoilak

Musk ox horn swan by Isaac Klengenberg

Going Home

I returned to Edmonton and took the TESOL (Teaching English as a Second language) course and toyed with the idea of going overseas to teach. I applied for many positions, but I was not eligible for most of them as I did not have a university degree. My interest waned somewhat with the rejections, but it was still an option for the future. Informed sources said that if I was to go somewhere under my own steam and knock on doors I would pick up a job for sure as the schools were always in need of replacement teachers.

There was never any question that I would settle down in Edmonton, for there was nothing of interest there to keep me, except for Sue, and given our flagging relationship, that was not enough. So, "where to go and what to do" was the big question that rattled around in my head every morning as I showered, shaved and got ready for the day.

Writing descriptions for the art pieces as well as other narrative content for the web site kept me busy for a while and I enjoyed these tasks. However, it wasn't long before the mental "hourglass" began to pop up with high frequency, indicating that that it was time for me to make a decision. I researched and fleshed out more work options, more consulting contracts in the Arctic, but as I thought about everything, the only thing that I really wanted to do, was to go home and see my children and grandchildren again. Nothing else mattered. It was an emotional pull, not a thoughtful idea, and that put me into a new head space. I had a sense that I had turned a page and was now at the start of a new chapter, maybe the last chapter, and that this chapter would be light reading and enjoyable.

The grandchildren

Lost Amigos

About the middle of June, I packed up my van with most of my clothing and a few personal effects and drove to London, Ontario. I arrived feeling refreshed, glad to be home, and eager to spend the rest of the summer with family.

I lived with my youngest son for a couple of weeks and then got a place of my own: a neat little furnished cabin, not far from the beach at Port Stanley on Lake Erie. My modest home at Lost Amigos, one of eight cabins, was perfect for me, and even came with a small TV, cable and internet, but my children were not as enthusiastic. Compared with their relatively big homes, I was living in a shoe box! I would guess that the outside dimensions of the place were about twelve feet by twelve, but the four rooms – kitchen, bathroom, bedroom and lounge area, were arranged so strategically that not an inch of space was wasted, and that pleased me greatly, for I was now aware of my carbon footprint in the world and any-thing that minimised, reduced, or recycled was to my liking.

Lost Amigos was idyllic. Set in a clearing in a heavily wooded area, it was peaceful yet filled with the beautiful sights and sounds of nature: deer emerged from the trees every evening in the farm-er's field across the road, a variety of birds visited the local trees throughout the day, and the breeze from the lake continually rustled the leaves in the trees overhead, refreshing the air.

Over the last couple of years, I had been reading books on Buddhism and other spiritual subjects, and had begun to do a little meditation. Upon arising each morning, I would sit outside on the patio on a little straight backed chair, and do a simple breathing meditation for about twenty minutes. It was so easy to be present and mindful, and to appreciate how wonderful it was to be alive. Sometime later in the morning, I would walk up the country road and down the beach cut off to the shore, for an hour of swimming, lazing and reading. Then I would stroll back along the sand and up a road back to the cabin. As I strolled, I reflected and thought about the past and the future.

It seemed to me that my life had been a quest; a continuous journey, with many objectives and diversions along the way, but it had all boiled down in the final analysis to a search for truth – to find personal fulfilment. And as I strolled in the sunshine, I realised that I felt fulfilled. I was at peace with the world and content with who I was. The inner peace and joy that I always intuitively knew were out there were in me. There was nothing missing.

Many times in the past few years I wondered where my journey would eventually lead. Now I was home, and in my gut I knew that this was it; this was my destination, just as Bilbo Baggins felt when he returned to the "Shire." People must have thought me strange indeed when they asked about my plans for the future, and I told them that I didn't have any. I just went with the flow. And if they pressed me further, they would be even more confounded when I told them that I let the Universe guide me on my life journey. And that was the truth. What always worked best for me when I needed to make a decision was when I relied on emotion and intuition to guide me, rather than rational thinking.

In September, in a friendly, but brief telephone conversation with Sue, we decided to each go our own way. She was settled in Edmonton, and had no plans to return to Ontario, and I had no desire to go anywhere else. She arranged with the storage company to have our household effects shipped out to her, and I was okay with that. I did not want any "stuff," except for a few personal items, which she packed up and sent. In some strange way that I do not totally understand, having even less made me feel as if I had even more. Perhaps my psyche considered the increased sense of freedom and simplicity that came from having less was greater than having more. I relished the feeling, and felt even more "alive" and "conscious." But then again, maybe I was manifesting my "destiny dream" as prophesied by Madame X in her little tent, so long ago now, for it certainly would be easier to travel down the pot-holed path with less. Dreams do come true.

Lost Amigos

EPILOGUE

When I was at Lost Amigos, I was in a strange place, mentally and emotionally. I was at peace and feeling totally satisfied. That I had no plans did not concern me because I sensed that the Universe would send me what I needed, when I needed it, and it did. Sometime in late fall I became aware of a volunteer sending agency called CUSO International. I don't recall now who told me about them, but it was serendipitous, because it resulted in me finding my passion: a new path on my life's journey to self-actualization. It gave me the opportunity to help others, less fortunate than I, as well as to quench my thirst to experience and explore other countries and cultures.

I applied online, attended various workshops and sessions at their headquarters in Ottawa, and in March of the following year, was on my way to Dhaka, Bangladesh for two years as an Organizational Development Adviser with SAP-Bangladesh, an NGO working with the abjectly poor in remote rural and coastal areas of the country.

I sometimes wonder how the rest of my life would have unfolded had I not gone out on the deck that bright April morning to watch ice flows melt on the river. I find it so profound now that a seemingly, innocent event could have impacted my life so dramatically, but it did. What if I was in a different frame of mind at the time and didn't connect the dots between fleeting ice and fleeting life? Maybe I would still be there, cutting grass, playing golf and asking myself, "Is this all there is?"

Now I see a larger purpose to "life" – the period between one's birth and death – that I didn't see before. To me, it is to attain inner peace and joy by finding your passion, and treating life as a journey of self-discovery, growth and self-actualisation. It is about experiences and learning and being all that we can be, by doing our best each and every day, for ourselves, as well as for others. It has nothing to do with the material world.

During the months at Lost Amigos, I spent a lot of time reflecting on life, my life's journey, and the lessons I learned from the Dene; from my readings on Buddhism; and from Eckhart Tolle's books, "A New Earth and the Power of Now," and how the enlightenment that came from those lessons, had shaped my life going forward, allowing me to finally find the inner contentment that I had so craved.

The biggest agent of change was in living and working with the Dene, in their land and in their world. What I learned from them transformed many of my life perspectives and philosophies, and that impacted how I viewed and lived life going forward. The Buddhist teachings and the wisdom contained in Tolle's books reinforced and clarified those learnings for me. In the "Awakenings" section that follows, I use Buddhist and contemporary terminology to describe particular situations, so that the reader might better understand the gist of what happened. At the time of course, I did not know what was happening, and nor was I aware that others had had similar experiences.

AWAKENINGS

I developed a deeper *"appreciation for the gift of life – for having been born and for still being alive."*

Prior to going North, I had taken "life" for granted and not given it much thought, but being in the presence of the Dene over a prolonged period of time, enabled me to look at the world through their eyes, and I felt in my gut that this view was wholesome and true. Their regard for Mother Earth, Father Sky and Grandmother Ocean, and for the animals and birds as their brothers and sisters, struck a chord in me. The Dene respected and cherished the land, the water and the air, and their reverence energised me – made me feel "alive"– and caused me to think more deeply about my humanity.

Putting aside religious beliefs, there is no reason that we know of for there to be anything. Why a Universe at all, with billions of galaxies, and billions of stars in each, and a planet earth, teeming with billions of different life forms, one of which is us, homo sapiens? And yet here we are. We are a part of the Universe, created from the same atoms as are all other life forms, but because our brains evolved faster than other species, we stand alone in intellect, and thus have been able to dominate and use the rest of the Earth to our advantage.

And everybody reading this is a descendant and heir to that evolutionary phenomenon. You and I are here today, and that in itself is a fluke, for the chance of us ever being born is infinitesimally low, so low in fact that we should never have been born. Had any one of our forefathers, or mothers, going back tens of millions of years to the dawn of evolution, not had another child, for whatever reason, we would not be here. But you and I are. What an incredible gift is that?

And with our evolution came the unique ability to see and appreciate, through our senses, the wondrous Universe that we are part of. I became awed by it and by everything in it. With this perspective on Life, I was able to feel calm and content, and to experience the joy of "being" at an incredibly deep level that I wasn't able to before. There was a paradigm shift in my values, from "wanting more" to "wanting less," and being "content with what is."

Living in the moment: Mindful Awareness: Stillness

The North is a dangerous and unforgiving land, and if you are not mindfully aware at all times, you can get into trouble very quickly. It seemed to me that living consciously in the moment was the natural way to live, and must have been the way our ancestors lived, in order for them to have survived. Living unconsciously, the way most of us do in the developed world – multi-tasking listening, watching and doing – is I think a relatively new phenomenon in human evolution, in response to the technologically complex world that we have created over the last fifty years or so. Our new world is such a busy, loud and active place that any personal "down time" is now viewed as a commercial opportunity to sell you something; you're not even alone when you go to the bathroom, or wait for a plane at the airport! Mainstream society doesn't want us to be still and living in the moment; it wants us to be engaged and spending money unconsciously.

I will forever remember the delicious quiet and stillness of the North, and in my heart I still yearn for it. It is easier for the Dene to live in the moment, in mindful awareness, because they have lived that way from birth. They lead simpler lives and they spend more time out on the silent land by themselves hunting, fishing, picking berries, camping, etc.

For the better part of sixty years, I, my mind that is, had been unconsciously preoccupied for much of my waking hours in planning for the future, or in analyzing the past. That was my conditioning and training and what I did for a living, but it resulted in a semi-permanent state of mind that was not mentally or spiritually healthy, and was, I think, the major reason why it took me so long to find inner peace. I was always thinking, instead of being; a mind-stream of thought that never stopped. Even though I am retired, leading a simple life, and consciously aware most of the time, I find it more challenging in the South to sustain a mindful presence than I did when I was in the North.

Doing our best is all that matters

Of course I didn't realise it at the time, but the longer I stayed in the Dene community, and the more challenges I endured, the greater the transformation taking place within me. There were tough lessons: the delays on the house building, the break-in, the "ice cube," etc., but through them I learned a better way to be. The challenges taught me patience, resilience and forgiveness, and along the way, I shed my ego, let go of attachments to the material world, and began to interact with my fellow man on a different level.

What I can only describe as "loving kindness," which I later read about in the Buddhist teachings, began to fill my heart, but where it came from and why, I don't know. There's no doubt in my mind though, that this change precipitated many other changes in my philosophy and spirituality that contributed to my sense of well-being.

For instance, I decided to eliminate setting "expectations," because it seemed to me that they usually resulted in disappointment. I figured that most people did their best, given their circumstances and the situation of the day, so why be dissatisfied with the outcome, just because it didn't meet expectations, which were after all, just arbitrary thoughts. My being dissatisfied didn't change anything, in fact, it always seemed to make the situation worse. So, instead of setting "expectations," I encouraged people to do their best, and from then on, no matter how much or how little progress we made, I was always pleased with the efforts at the end of the day.

My decision to accept *"whatever"* when things went wrong, came out of frustration and a sense of hopelessness. It was only later, when reading the wisdom of the Buddha teachings, that I realised that my *"whatever*, was in reality unconditional acceptance of what is. And what a transformation that was, for I had been conditioned since birth to internalise everything, and to always look to assign blame when things went wrong.

When I left the North, I felt reborn − as if I had been totally re-invented − and it was wonderful. I didn't have any specific plans yet I was excited about the future and had faith in the Universe to send me more opportunities to further my enlightenment and enjoyment of life, and it did.

Being happy is a state of mind

I read about what happens in the brain every moment of wakefulness, and was surprised to learn that everything is just a thought, and that every thought is unique to each individual, for thoughts are dependent on one's life experiences. Every sensation from our senses is converted in our brains through chemical and electrical reactions in our synapses, and revealed to us − we feel, see, hear, smell, taste and sense. Everything we experience in life is imprinted in the archive portion of our brain, regardless of whether we can recall the details, or not. When we think about something, our brain accesses our memory data bank to see what is in there regarding the subject matter, retrieves it and cobbles it all together and produces a thought; an answer.

We are a product of the environment that we grew up in. Our values, beliefs and opinions are all based on historically archived experiences. If I had been born in a different country and brought up in a different culture with a different religion, I would manifest the values and habits of that culture and religion. Of course I didn't realise this when I was in my late teens and confused about life. My

Victorian style upbringing and religious conditioning, based largely upon intimidation and righteousness, resulted in me feeling fearful, insecure and holding rigid life views. All of that changed when I had a life crisis – the news that I was to be a father. That event was so traumatic that it overrode much previous conditioning and fuelled my desire to succeed in business.

Twenty years later, because of work successes, I developed a new persona: a big corporate ego with big dreams and high expectations. And then another crisis – the need to adapt to the Dene way of being or leave the community. It was only later in life, when I learned about the difference between living consciously versus unconsciously, that I realised that I always did have a choice. I didn't need a crisis to change. I can be present and look at the thought, the idea or the opinion that my brain produces, and then decide if I want to react to it, or choose a different option. That's what had happened many times over the years, but when it was happening, I didn't realise the process at work.

Our journey to enlightenment and a better world

Fundamentally, all seven billion of us, human beings, on the planet, regardless of our life circumstances, want one thing out of life, and that's to be happy. Would anyone choose to be unhappy? We are all born equal, but into unequal circumstances, that are not of our own making. Man is still in its infancy in terms of evolutionary development, and has a long way to go, before we, as a species, become all that we can be. Much of the unhappiness in the world results from differences in ideologies – political and religious mostly – which are a legacy from our past, and result in thinking that is intolerant, righteous and selfish. There is no absolute truth. We only think that we are right and others are wrong. Our perception of the truth is based on our limited conditioning environment.

The world today is a very competitive place where making money and winning seem to be the name of the game of life. Just look at the myriads of TV shows aimed at every demographic segment of society that you can think of, and at the insane adulation and monetary awards afforded to winners. We obsess over film and TV celebrities, try to emulate them by buying their products, and we even make them a part of our lives by following their every move on the internet, television and magazines. This predilection with "successful people" and money is not a healthy scenario for the average Joe, and to my mind, is a major cause why there are so many unhappy people in the developed world with mental health issues, such as addictions, depression, low self-esteem, etc. And it isn't just the average Joe, whose quality of life is affected by this obsession with money – just look at the governments of the world that are despairing over low economic growth and high national debt.

I competed in the corporate world for twenty years and won, if achieving career goals and making lots of many is how success is defined, but at what cost? I didn't achieve inner happiness, nor did I contribute much to other people's joy; on the contrary, I was dissatisfied with life. Doesn't it make more sense to have happiness as a life goal instead of the pursuit of money and other material things?

The materialistic society that we live in today has only been around for the last fifty years. Living and working in a concrete jungle, where most of our time is spent working, shopping, spectating and competing, is unnatural and delusionary. We get swallowed up by it, and forget that we are only human. There will be future crises, as there always has been, that will result in a change in our societal values. The pendulum will swing back, and our extreme predilection with money and fame will be modified, and the pursuit of happiness will take centre stage. I have no doubt that our society will look a lot different fifty years from now.

When one considers how much more we know about everything today than we did a hundred years ago, and how the quality of life for the average person has improved with time, we can be hopeful that in future generations, the "ideological differences" problem and "the fame and money" obsessions will get resolved, and man, as a life species, will become much more enlightened and happier.

About the Author

Awakening in the Northwest Territories, is my first published work. I am penning two other books for Boomers: one on International Volunteering and one on Budget Back Packing, for publication in 2014. For the last ten years I have been an International Development volunteer in Asia, India, South America and the Caribbean, and I now reside in Southern Ontario.

Thank you for reading my memoir. If you enjoyed it, please consider writing a book review and posting it on amazon.com or at http://www.awakeninginthenorth.com

EXTREME!

Pirate!

From Navigation to Amputation

Anna Claybourne

A & C Black • London

Fact Finders is published by Capstone Press,
a Capstone Publishers company.
151 Good Counsel Drive, P.O. Box 669,
Mankato, Minnesota 56002.
www.capstonepress.com

First published 2009

Library of Congress Cataloging-in-Publication Data

Claybourne, Anna.
   Pirate secrets revealed / by Anna Claybourne.
   p. cm. -- (Fact finders. Extreme explorations!)
   Summary: "Describes the life of pirates, including their
ships, weapons, treasures, and food"--Provided by
publisher.
   Includes bibliographical references and index.
   ISBN 978-1-4296-4557-7 (library binding)
   ISBN 978-1-4296-4621-5 (pbk.)
   1. Pirates--Juvenile literature. I. Title. II. Series.

G535.C55 2010
910.4'5--dc22

2009028175

Produced for A & C Black by
Monkey Puzzle Media Ltd
48 York Avenue
Hove BN3 1PJ, UK

Editor: Susie Brooks
Design: Mayer Media Ltd
Picture research: Lynda Lines
Series consultants: Jane Turner and James de Winter

This book is produced using paper that is made from
wood grown in managed, sustainable forests. It is natural,
renewable, and recyclable. The logging and manufacturing
processes conform to the environmental regulations of
the country of origin.

Picture acknowledgements
Alamy pp. 24 (Marion Kaplan), 25 (North Wind Picture
Archives); Art Archive pp. 4–5 (Bibliothèque des Arts
Décoratifs, Paris), 7 (Private Collection), 11 (Private
Collection), 22 (Royal Palace, Monte Carlo, Monaco/
Gianni Dagli Orti); Bridgeman Art Library pp. 13 (Private
Collection/Look and Learn), 29 (Private Collection/Look
and Learn); Corbis pp. 6 (Bettmann), 9 (Richard T.
Nowitz), 16 (Tria Giovan), 17 (The Mariners' Museum), 19
(Bettmann), 21 (Bettmann), 26 (Bettmann), 28 (Richard T.
Nowitz); Getty Images pp. 1 (Howard Pyle), 18 (Jean Leon
Jerome Ferris), 27 (Howard Pyle); iStockphoto p. 14; MPM
Images pp. 4, 8, 15; National Maritime Museum, London
pp. 10, 12; Science and Society Picture Library p. 20;
Science Photo Library p. 23 (John Burbidge).

The front cover shows a skull and crossed cutlasses,
which often appeared on pirate flags (MPM Images/
Tim Mayer).

Every effort has been made to contact copyright holders
of material reproduced in this book. Any omissions will be
rectified in subsequent printings if notice is given to the
publishers.

Printed in the United States of America
in Stevens Point, Wisconsin
092011
006366R

CONTENTS

Pirates ahoy!

Look out! PIRAAAATES!!! A few hundred years ago, everyone feared pirates. These ocean raiders roamed the seas, chasing ships, capturing crews and stealing cargo. If you didn't do as they ordered, you might be gruesomely murdered or forced to walk the plank.

"Calico Jack" Rackham was a famous pirate known for his stylish dress sense.

Yes, pirates were seriously scary. But they weren't just a bunch of brainless bullies. They had to find their way across vast oceans, keeping their ships afloat and their weapons working. They had to find food and water, cure diseases and treat injuries.

In fact, pirates needed a lot of skills and insider knowledge — from reading the stars to **amputating** limbs.

cargo goods carried by ship   **amputate** to chop off

The golden age

There have always been pirates, and they still exist today. But most of the pirates in this book lived in the 17th and 18th centuries – the "golden age" of **piracy**.

To capture a ship, pirates sailed up close to it and leapt on board, weapons at the ready.

Axes were handy for chopping through ropes and cabins, as well as attacking victims.

Cutlass

Pirates

Spear

piracy robbery at sea

5

Sailing the seas

To attack other ships, pirates needed a ship of their own. Small, narrow, speedy vessels were best for chasing and catching their victims.

Pirates loved capturing big, wide ships called galleons, carrying treasure or other valuable loads. These were slow to get moving, and once they were moving, they were hard to stop or turn around.

A small, light ship, such as a ketch or a barque, could move and turn much faster. In one of these, pirates could easily speed up to a bigger ship and **manoeuvre** into a good position to board it.

Scary flags

Pirates really did fly frightening flags, to show other ships that they meant business. Often this was enough to scare their victims into surrendering.

Here's a selection of real pirate flags.

vessel a boat or ship   **manoeuvre** to make a skillful movement

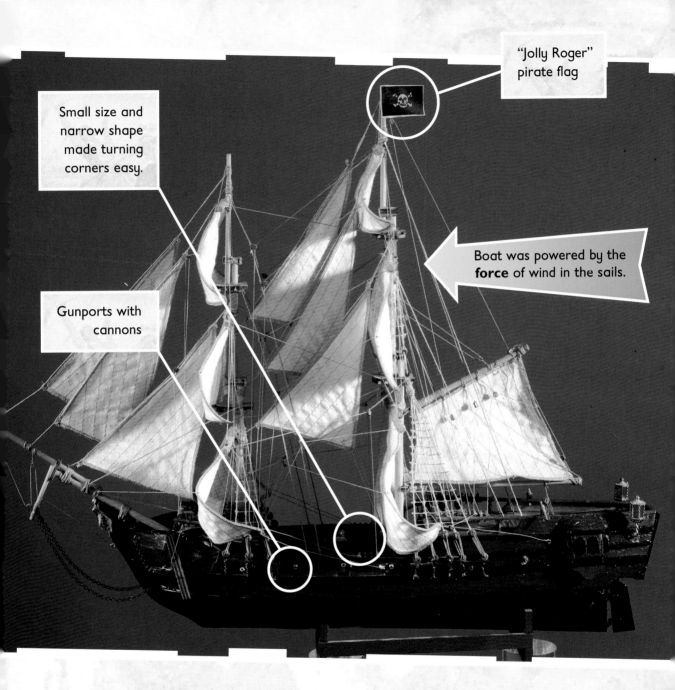

"Jolly Roger"
pirate flag

Small size and
narrow shape
made turning
corners easy.

Boat was powered by the
force of wind in the sails.

Gunports with
cannons

This is a model of the Black Falcon, *the ship of 17th-century pirate William Kidd.*

force a push or a pull

7

Which way, Cap'n?

How did pirates find their way? In the days before handy **Sat Nav** systems, they had to use the Earth's **magnetism** and their knowledge of the stars.

North Star

These constellations are known as Ursa Major (Great Bear) and Ursa Minor (Little Bear). Ursa Minor contains the North Star, which indicates north.

A compass was essential pirate kit. It's a magnetic needle balanced on a point. The Earth's magnetic pull makes the needle swing around and point north. Once you know where north is, you can also work out south, east and west.

Seafarers also used the positions of the stars and **constellations** to work out their direction and their **latitude** – how far north or south they were.

Sat Nav a navigation system that uses space satellites   **magnetism** a kind of pulling force

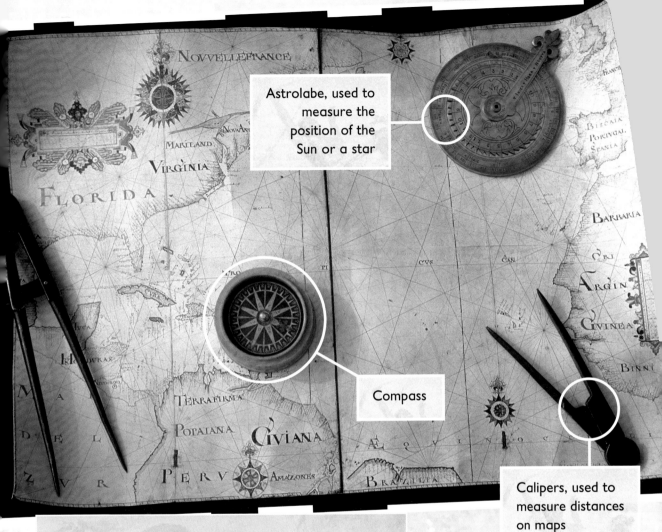

Astrolabe, used to measure the position of the Sun or a star

Compass

Calipers, used to measure distances on maps

Star patterns

The stars in a constellation can be huge distances apart. But seen from Earth, they seem to form a meaningful shape or pattern.

This old map shows the Atlantic Ocean, the Caribbean and part of North and South America. This region was where many famous pirates hunted their prey.

constellation a group of stars **latitude** distance north or south of the Equator

Tools and technology

Pirate gadgets from 400 years ago might seem old-fashioned to you. But in their day, many pirates were technology lovers who snapped up the latest inventions as soon as they could.

This ship's telescope dates from 1810.

Swinging the lead

Pirates used a lead weight on a string to measure the depth of the sea. This was such as easy job that "swinging the lead" now means messing around and skiving!

The telescope, invented in 1608, used curved glass **lenses** to magnify faraway objects. It helped pirates to spot their victims – and their enemies – before being spotted themselves.

In 1595, John Davis invented the backstaff, which used the Sun's shadow to measure the angle between the Sun and the **horizon**. In the 1730s, the sextant was invented to do the same job for the stars at night. These instruments were used with maps and charts to help pirates work out where they were, when all they could see was sea.

lens a shaped piece of glass used to bend light

A sextant used mirrors to make the Sun or a star appear to line up with the horizon.

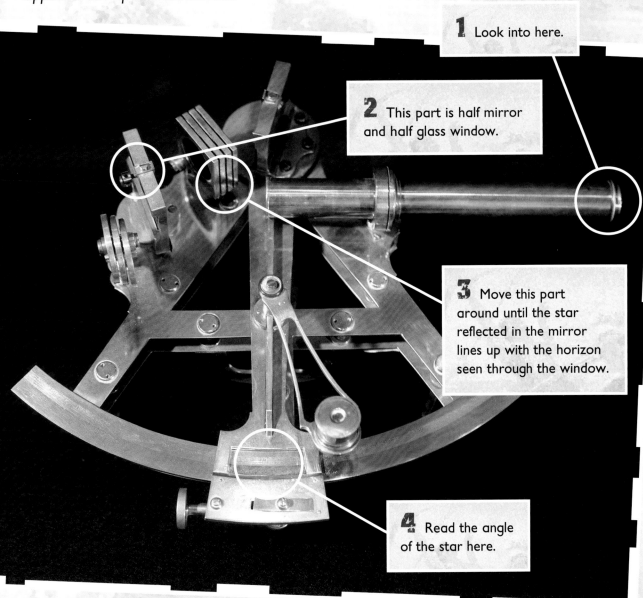

1 Look into here.

2 This part is half mirror and half glass window.

3 Move this part around until the star reflected in the mirror lines up with the horizon seen through the window.

4 Read the angle of the star here.

horizon the line where the edge of the Earth seems to meet the sky

Cutlasses and cannons

A good pirate prided himself on his sharp cutlass or well-oiled flintlock pistol. Over the years, pirates' weapons developed and improved to suit the task of capturing enemy ships.

The cutlass was a classic pirate weapon – a small, sharp sword that could be used one-handed, leaving the other hand free. Its short length made it easy to use on a crowded deck.

Blades were often made of steel, a very strong metal made of iron combined with a chemical called **carbon**.

Battle ballistics

Ballistics is the science of firing things like cannonballs. To shoot accurately, pirates had to set the cannon at the right angle, and take into account the wind speed, the speed of the ship and the speed the cannonball would fly at. Tricky!

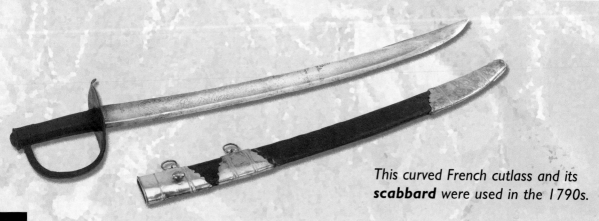

This curved French cutlass and its **scabbard** *were used in the 1790s.*

carbon a chemical found in coal, diamonds and living things

1 A "powder monkey" pushed gunpowder into the cannon.

2 Cannonball went in next.

3 Taper was lit to fire the cannon.

4 Holding the "cascabel" (the back end of the cannon) helped to aim it.

It took a team of people to load and fire a cannon.

scabbard a protective case for a sword or dagger

Pieces of eight!

So why did pirates sail the seas, risking disaster and disease? To get rich, of course! The most precious prize of all was treasure, such as jewellery and gold coins.

Silver, gold and gemstones are precious because they are rare. Gold stays valuable for a very long time because it doesn't **react** with other substances – so it won't rot or **rust** away.

Parrots in pirate cartoons say "pieces of eight!" – and these really did exist. They were Spanish silver coins. Doubloons were even more valuable gold coins.

Pirates craved gold and silver coins like these Spanish ones.

Buried treasure

One pirate, William Thompson, is said to have buried a huge treasure hoard on the island of Cocos in the Pacific Ocean, in around 1820. No one has ever found it – yet!

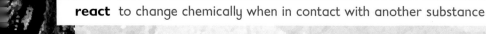

react to change chemically when in contact with another substance

Some treasure was worth fighting for. Clever pirates buried it – or more likely spent it – fast!

It's mine!

Pirates were said to hide their treasure on deserted beaches or islands.

Coins or jewels were kept safe inside a heavy chest.

Iron locks could get very rusty, thanks to oxygen in the air and seawater.

rust a non-reversible change that happens when iron objects react with oxygen and water

15

Grub and grog

There were no fridges, no freezers and no tin cans. But pirates needed a store of food that would last for weeks at sea.

To stop their food going off, pirates **preserved** it. They dried meat and beans, as removing water from food makes it hard for **germs** to survive. Food could also be salted (like bacon), or pickled in vinegar, as these things kill germs too.

Pirates really did guzzle rum, as well as beer. Alcohol kills germs, so these drinks were safer than plain old water, where germs could breed and grow.

Pirates ate dried biscuits called hardtack. They were usually crawling with **weevils**!

Fresh every day

Pirates went fishing too, and stopped at islands to hunt animals and pick fruit. Some kept chickens on board for their eggs, known as "cacklefruit".

---

preserve to treat food to make it long-lasting   **germs** very tiny living things that cause disease

Pirates often had feasts when they stopped on dry land.

Probably a mixture of rum and water, known as grog

Sluuurp!

What's in here? It could be turtle soup, or salmagundi — a meat, fish and bean stew.

Bottles of rum or beer

weevil a type of beetle

Diseases and medicines

Pirates were far more likely to die from a disease than in a battle. They suffered from tropical diseases like malaria, as well as sunstroke, seasickness, animal bites and stings, and worse.

Most ships had a doctor or **surgeon**, and a medicine chest full of medicines and tools. They used herbal remedies, such as tree bark for malaria, cloves for toothache, peppermint for vomiting, and chamomile for headaches.

Doctors also treated illnesses by cutting the patient to let some blood spurt out. Did it work? Unfortunately for pirates, it didn't.

Blackbeard (left) was one of the most famous of all pirates. He once demanded a medicine chest in return for prisoners he was holding.

surgeon a doctor who carries out operations

Pirate James Lind and a fellow seaman prepare a lime to cure scurvy.

Scary scurvy

Pirates often got scurvy, caused by a lack of **vitamin** C from fresh fruit and vegetables. Their skin went pale, their muscles ached and their teeth fell out.

Groan!

Scurvy makes you weak and tired.

Fruits like limes contain plenty of vitamin C — the perfect scurvy medicine.

vitamin a substance essential to the body and found in food

19

Losing a limb

Pirates really did lose eyes, arms and legs in battle, just like in stories. Limbs were also amputated if they were injured or infected.

Even hundreds of years ago, there were artificial limbs to replace missing arms and legs. Properly shaped ones were expensive, though. On a pirate ship, you'd have to make do with whatever was lying around. So pirates sometimes had a wooden peg-leg, or a metal hook for a hand.

This artificial hand dates from the late 16th century. Silver Arm's silver arm probably looked similar.

Silver Arm

Oruc Reis was a Turkish pirate who lost his left arm in a battle in 1512. He was nicknamed "Silver Arm" after the shiny silver replacement hand he wore.

infected diseased by germs or rotting away

In those days, there was no **anaesthetic**, so having a limb cut off hurt – a lot!

anaesthetic a powerful painkiller

Pesky parasites

A pirate ship was an enclosed, tight space, with lots of men all crammed together. It was heaven for fleas, lice, nits and bedbugs!

In fact, a typical pirate was sure to be home to a variety of biting, nibbling **parasites**. Fleas, nits and bedbugs sucked his blood, while mites fed on his skin flakes. Body lice crawled around in the seams of smelly old pirate pants and shirts.

Ships had their own hangers-on, too. Most were full of rats, while small sea creatures called barnacles collected on the **hull** and slowed the ship down.

These sailors are tipping their ship over to clean barnacles off it — a job known as careening.

Worm damage

Many a pirate ship fell apart thanks to shipworms. They aren't actually worms, but a kind of **clam**. They burrow into underwater wood and fill it with tiny holes.

parasite   a creature that lives on or in another living thing

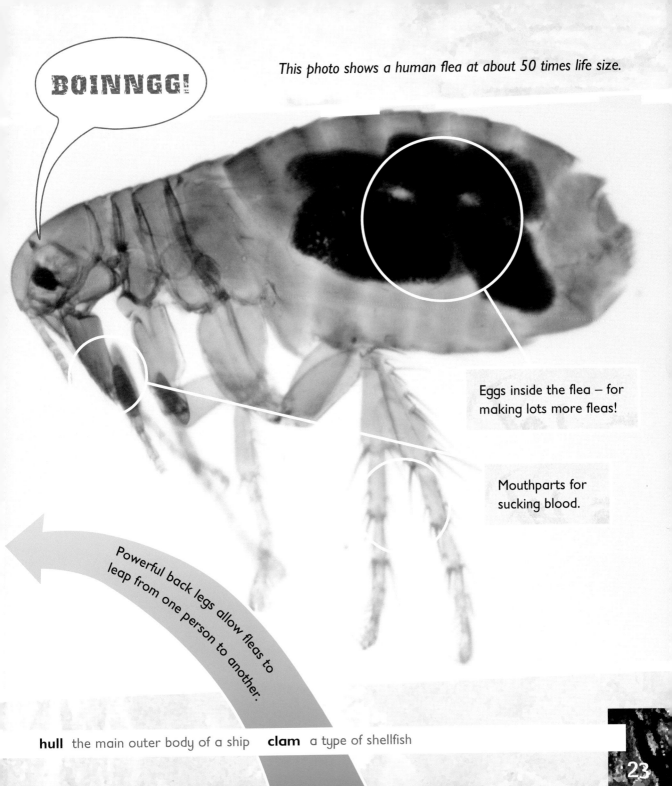

BOINNGG!

This photo shows a human flea at about 50 times life size.

Eggs inside the flea – for making lots more fleas!

Mouthparts for sucking blood.

Powerful back legs allow fleas to leap from one person to another.

hull the main outer body of a ship   **clam** a type of shellfish

23

What's that smell?

If you could step inside a 17th-century pirate ship right now, there's one thing you'd notice straight away. It would stink!

Pirates ships didn't have showers, and modern toilets hadn't been invented. Pirates could wash in the sea, but they rarely bothered. Most pirates didn't clean their teeth either, so they usually had tooth decay and smelly breath.

For a toilet, pirates used the "head" – a hole in a seat sticking out over the sea at the front of the ship. Waves splashing over the ship's **bow** washed away the mess.

Can you imagine sitting on one of these open-air ship toilets?

Sweaty and stinky

Why does not washing make you whiff? It's mainly sweat collecting on the skin. If it's not washed away, bacteria feed on it – and they give off smelly chemicals.

bow the front end of a ship   **bacteria** a kind of germ

Blackbeard demonstrates the many ways in which a pirate could seriously pong.

Bad breath from drinking rum, smoking tobacco and avoiding a toothbrush

Blackbeard wore smoking **tapers** in his hair, which didn't help.

Grimy hair and beard

Sweaty armpits

Phhheww!

Dirty clothes

Unwashed feet

taper a thin candle or paper strip

Sharks and sea monsters

Wild animals were a big part of life for many pirates. They caught them, ate them, and were sometimes eaten by them!

Did pirates really have parrots on their shoulders? It's not clear, but they did capture tropical animals such as parrots and monkeys to sell. European leaders liked keeping **exotic** pets, and paid a high price for them.

Sharks followed ships to eat the scraps — or sometimes dead bodies — thrown overboard. When pirates made their victims walk the plank, the sharks would be waiting.

The sea monster in this illustration looks like a giant octopus (though real ones aren't quite this big).

Sea monsters

Seafarers' stories of sea monsters were thought to be fairytales. But scientists have discovered several huge sea creatures, such as the colossal **squid**, that could have explained these sightings.

exotic from somewhere far away and unfamiliar

26

It wasn't common, but pirates sometimes really did make people walk off a plank into the sea.

Victim is tied up to stop him swimming.

Plank

Sharks might be waiting right here!

Sharks can smell blood a mile away.

squid a sea creature similar to an octopus

27

Davy Jones' Locker

Davy Jones' Locker was what pirates called the bottom of the sea. It was where you were headed if you died at sea, walked the plank, or went down in a sinking ship.

When a pirate died, the body couldn't be stored on board. It had to be buried at sea. Soon, only the skeleton would remain, as the rest was munched by sea **scavengers** such as sharks, shrimps and worms.

When a ship sank to the bottom, it gradually became coated in seaweed and coral. But any treasure on board could stay shiny for hundreds of years, waiting to be found.

Archaeologists bring up gold and silver coins recovered from the Whydah.

The wreck of the Whydah

In 1717, pirate Sam Bellamy captured a treasure ship called the *Whydah*, but it then sank. The wreck was located in 1984, and divers rescued piles of treasure from it.

scavenger an animal that eats dead, rotting bodies

A ship sank fast once it had begun to fill with water.

A sinking ship could suck people down with it, so the crew had to get off fast.

Water sloshed to one side, making the ship tip even faster.

Yikes!

The lucky ones might escape in a rescue boat.

archaeologist someone who studies people and objects from the past

Glossary

amputate to chop off

anaesthetic a powerful painkiller

archaeologist someone who studies people and objects from the past

bacteria a kind of germ

bow the front end of a ship

carbon a chemical found in coal, diamonds and living things

cargo goods carried by ship

clam a type of shellfish

constellation a group of stars

exotic from somewhere far away and unfamiliar

force a push or a pull

germs very tiny living things that cause disease

horizon the line where the edge of the Earth seems to meet the sky

hull the main outer body of a ship

infected diseased by germs or rotting away

latitude distance north or south of the Equator

lens a shaped piece of glass used to bend light

magnetism a kind of pulling force

manoeuvre to make a skillful movement

parasite a creature that lives on or in another living thing

piracy robbery at sea

preserve to treat food to make it long-lasting

react to change chemically when in contact with another substance

rust a non-reversible change that happens when iron objects react with oxygen and water

Sat Nav a navigation system that uses space satellites

scabbard a protective case for a sword or dagger

scavenger an animal that eats dead, rotting bodies

squid a sea creature similar to an octopus

surgeon a doctor who carries out operations

taper a thin candle or paper strip

vessel a boat or ship

vitamin a substance essential to the body and found in food

weevil a type of beetle

Further information

Books

The Usborne Official Pirate's Handbook by Sam Taplin (Usborne Publishing, 2006)
A handy guide to help you make your way as a would-be pirate in the days of sailing ships.

Horribly Famous Pirates by Michael Cox (Scholastic, 2007)
Real-life exploits of a selection of famous pirates, with lots of jokes and cartoons.

Eyewitness: Pirate by Richard Platt (Dorling Kindersley, 2007)
Detailed exploration of pirate life, with lots of fascinating photos.

Piratology by Dugald Steer (Templar Publishing, 2006)
Embark on a thrilling fantasy pirate adventure with interactive features, flaps and extras.

Websites

www.nationalgeographic.com/pirates/adventure.html
Take part in an interactive pirate adventure.

www.nationalgeographic.com/whydah/main.html
Meet Captain Sam Bellamy's crew, the pirates who captured the *Whydah*.

http://pirateshold.buccaneersoft.com/pirate_flags.html
See the scary flags that real-life pirates chose to fly on their ships.

http://jersey.uoregon.edu/vlab/Cannon/
Try entering different numbers to make a cannon fire at a target, just as pirates did.

Films

Pirates of the Caribbean: The Curse of the Black Pearl directed by Gore Verbinski (Disney, 2003)
In this action-packed movie, pirate Jack Sparrow helps to save the heroine Elizabeth from evil pirate captain Hector Barbossa and his haunted ship the Black Pearl. Follow more of Jack Sparrow's adventures in the sequels: **Pirates of the Caribbean: Dead Man's Chest** (2006) and **Pirates of the Caribbean: At World's End** (2007).

Peter Pan directed by P.J. Hogan (Universal, 2003)
A magical boy whisks three children away from their bedroom to a world of adventures, including a showdown with the evil pirate Captain Hook.

Index